PRAISE FOR
THE BALANCED BUSINESS

"Whether you're building a new business or restructuring a well-established one, *The Balanced Business* takes you through a step-by-step, human-centered approach to building both a commercially successful business and a winning culture. *The Balanced Business* is a comprehensive and pragmatic guide to improving your business one step at a time. From vision and purpose through to incentives, this book walks you through every lever you can pull to take your business from languishing to flourishing."

DANIELLE CHIRCOP, chief product officer, General Assembly

"*The Balanced Business* should be required reading in leadership courses and for every leader who wants to grow and flourish in their career."

DENISE PROBERT, CPA, CGMA, teaching assistant professor, University of Colorado-Boulder

"Many leadership gurus have claimed that they have cracked the code over the years, but have they really? This time, Andy has really done it! In *The Balanced Business*, he gives us not just what and why, but how. I have no doubt that this book will be an indispensable guide for anyone interested in creating a great organization."

KENNETH S. RHEE, PhD, dean, Girard School of Business, Merrimack College

"Many books on management teach us about what has been successful in the past. Andy instead focuses on what is needed for our future, with a focus on enhancing workflows to build organizational trust and account-ability. I recommend this book to anyone just starting their management career, as well as to those looking to take the next step up."

RAGHU KRISHNAIAH, chief operating officer, the University of Phoenix

"The Balanced Business is an impressive must-read for anyone starting up or running a business. The book is packed with a full career's worth of wisdom and insight."

IAN SCHNOOR, managing director, Financial Modeling Institute

"A must-read for managers and leaders to create a sustainable management operating system!"

MOHIT MALHOTRA, CFA, MIT Sloan Fellow and former managing director of Genesis Institute

"Not only will the tools in this book help realign your organization; they will also help realign the way you think about business and life."

DON VANPOOL, CEO and founder, OptaProfit LLC, and former GE executive

"In his latest book, Andy shares how the principles of continuous improvement and organizational health can be combined to create a highly effective business operating system. Having worked closely with Andy to implement a version of this system at Kaplan Professional, I can confirm its power to drive organizational alignment and clarity, while simultaneously fostering a culture of engagement."

TIM EIMERMANN, market insights leader, Thermo King

"Most managers become managers because they are good at their job, not good at managing. It's a big and growing problem in business. In *The Balanced Business*, Dr. Temte provides a management framework that can truly transition managers into leaders who seek to cultivate sustainable growth."

ANTHONY FASANO, PE, founder and CEO, Engineering Management Institute

"The Balanced Business distinguishes itself by integrating behavioral and technical principles of leadership, strategy, and operations in a meaningful way alongside pragmatic continuous improvement tools the reader can readily implement. It's far more comprehensive than I expected or have seen in other business books."

MATTHEW FLYNN, VP, learning operations, Kaplan North America

"Like farmers relying on an almanac to guide them through the seasons, business leaders and entrepreneurs should treat *The Balanced Business* as their own personal guidebook. This book is not just a set of lessons-learned anecdotes but a comprehensive guide for navigating the unique challenges and opportunities of building a truly balanced business."

CHARLIE CICHETTI, LEED Fellow + WELL AP, CEO, Green Building Education Services

"*The Balanced Business* is rich with solutions to nearly every 'how' business leaders might ask themselves as their business continues to grow and evolve."

DAN FLYNN, chief revenue officer, Barnum Financial Group

"With his decades of business experience, Andy expertly advises readers how to make sure your business is not behind the curve. He lays out a management ecosystem that will improve engagement through a unique combination of organizational health and continuous improvement tools to help your business drive sustained growth."

OLIVER DOWNER, transformational technology leader

"Andy's direct messages to leaders are much needed in today's ever-changing and chaotic world. If leaders and organizations would spend time discussing, crafting, and living the statements, philosophy, and management system Andy clearly lays out in this book, more organizations would be successful in retaining their talent, optimizing business practices, and delighting their customers."

KACIE WALTERS, talent management leader and author of *Succeed from the Middle*

an imprint of Amplify Publishing Group

www.amplifypublishinggroup.com

The Balanced Business: Building Organizational Trust and Accountability through Smooth Workflows

For more information, please contact:
Amplify Publishing, an imprint of Amplify Publishing Group
620 Herndon Parkway, Suite 220
Herndon, VA 20170
info@amplifypublishing.com

Library of Congress Control Number: 2023905199

CPSIA Code: PRV0623A

ISBN-13: 978-1-63755-750-1

Printed in the United States

Dedication

To my late mother-in-law, Karen Humm, who calmly handed me a copy of Spencer Johnson's *Who Moved My Cheese* in the midst of a very difficult episode in my life. At the time, she could not have known that this small act of kindness would help spark the journey of personal and professional transformation and growth that continues within me to this day.

I will be forever grateful for your grace and compassion, Karen.

To my readers—you never know when a small act of kindness will create a spark of transformation in others. Pass it on . . . kindness matters.

Teach. Coach. Mentor. Inspire.

THE BALANCED BUSINESS

BUILDING ORGANIZATIONAL TRUST AND ACCOUNTABILITY THROUGH SMOOTH WORKFLOWS

DR. ANDREW TEMTE, CFA

amplify

an imprint of Amplify Publishing Group

Contents

The Management
Operating System

With over thirty years of business management and leadership experience, I can attest that there are no silver bullets to management success. No quick fixes. Remember the Staples Easy Button? There are no easy buttons. Santa might have one, but they seem to be out of stock everywhere else.

In my global travels, however, I've seen prospective and current leaders continue their search for silver bullets. I've personally searched in vain for the easy button. I've screamed alone into the wind, "Running a business can't be this hard, can it?"

With the benefit of experience and hindsight, I now cringe when I see a new book or system that promises instant results. *The Seven Tips for X. The Five Secrets of Y.* These titles make for sexy book covers, but will they help or hinder in the long run?

Yes, you can get small nuggets from flavor-of-the-day management books, but does each nugget fit together into a holistic approach to business leadership, or is the theme just another shiny ball that distracts from your core purpose, vision, and North Star?

There are real costs to pursuing the shiny balls of management philosophy and practice. In the face of rapid change and fierce external competitive pressures, your team needs to know you'll lead with consistency and persistence. That your approach is repeatable, reliable, and strikes the right balance between agility and standardization. If your approach to management is constantly shifting, then the true foundations of business—*trust* and *accountability*—are incredibly difficult to establish and maintain.

Trust versus Accountability

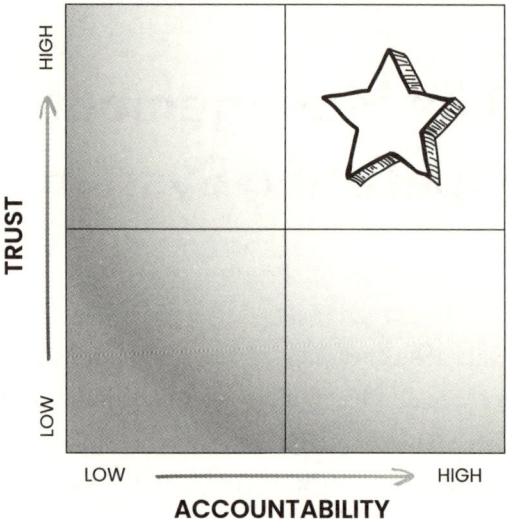

One of my main goals in this book is to help move the culture of your organization into the upper-right quadrant of a plot of organizational trust versus team and individual accountability, as illustrated by the star in the image above.

Leaders help organizations navigate myriad balancing acts, but in my assessment, striving for balance between trust and accountability ranks at the top of the list. It is essential that our people—a business's most valuable asset—work in a state of relative harmony, supported by a culture that promotes clarity, transparency, well-being, and psychological safety, with the aim of building trust between individuals and teams. Yes, conflict and tension cannot be avoided, but when harnessed with constructive intent, internal conflict can be channeled toward innovation and creativity, allowing the organization to return to a state of consensus, collaboration, and productivity more readily.

At exactly the same time, the *work needs to get done*, and a business must have proper accountability frameworks in place to ensure the business is delivering what the customer wants—on time and on budget. Well-being and psychological safety are not possible in an environment in which roles and responsibilities are not well defined, work processes are ad hoc, and team members are constantly looking for someone else to blame for break-downs in product quality and customer service. As I will make plain later in this book, working within the mud of obfuscation and passive-aggressive behaviors is soul crushing, even for the most resilient among us.

The tool we will employ to facilitate this all-important balancing act between trust and accountability is that of *flow*, or *workflow*. Smooth hand-offs of work product and information between teams and team members are essential to a high-functioning work environment, irrespective of the industry classification of your business. If we take the mystery out of how value is created at each step along the value stream that exists for every product or service—from idea to customer delivery—then accountability can be established and trust can grow. To be clear, flow enables account-ability, and accountability is necessary for trust to flourish.

The Search for Root Cause

If you've been following my work, you'll know that my management philos-ophy is based on the principles of organizational health, coupled with the tenets of continuous improvement. Defined in broad terms, a healthy orga-nization is one that nurtures clarity of purpose and objectives, embraces transparency, and fosters clear and routine communication. Continuous improvement is best described as the combination of (a) identifying and minimizing of waste, (b) showing respect for people—both customers and employees—and (c) possessing a laser focus on the customer's needs. These concepts will be discussed and illustrated throughout this book.

Hence, one of the most important lessons I can get across is this: before we jump to solutioning—which is standard practice for "busy," or strictly results-oriented management—we pause, ask **why**, and search for the root cause of the challenges we're facing. In the pages to follow, I hope to provide a road map for a management style that puts an organization's well-defined purpose, vision, culture, customers, and point of product differentiation at the heart of everything they do. Throughout this process, we'll explore how to reduce waste by moving away from a stop-and-start style of management toward one that embeds the organization's long-term goals and strategies into the flow of everyday business.

As I sit and think about the root cause for the proliferation of—and outsized demand for—marginally helpful quick-fix management training solutions, a "five whys" exercise, which I will outline in more detail in chapter 15, keeps leading me to the *accidental manager effect*.

I'm an accidental manager. You may be one too. There are *millions* of us. To illustrate, let's look at my path to becoming an accidental manager. You can play along by tracing your journey too.

My training for the workforce was a winding path. I started as a high school dropout rock 'n' roll road warrior, then transitioned to piano mover and bookkeeper during my economics undergraduate education, then on to teaching assistant and researcher during six years of graduate school in finance. I found my *purpose* as an undergraduate: I knew I was going to spend my life as a teacher and a coach. I also thought I knew where the path to becoming a teacher would take me—to a cloistered academic environment filled with pipes, argyle socks, and woolen sweater vests.

> **Note:** We'll be talking a lot about purpose moving forward, so I suggest you contemplate your own purpose as part of our Personal Planning A3 exercise, which can be found as a free resource on my website at andrewtemte.com/guidebook.

During my collegiate years, I *thought* the endgame was the role of college professor. The plan was to teach and perform research at the collegiate level for the remainder of my career. Done and dusted. All sorted, right? Wrong.

After earning a PhD, instead of searching for a teaching and research-focused professorship, we—my dear wife, Linda, and I—put all our eggs into the basket of the entrepreneurial venture Carl Schweser and I had started as a side hustle during graduate school. Our little venture was designed to help prospective financial analysts pass the rigorous CFA® exams.

All of a sudden, *bang*! I'm an accidental manager. Yes, I'd led classrooms of students as a teacher and was typically "that guy" in academic group projects who volunteered to lead the effort, but I had no formal managerial training. A combination of my own hubris and an urgent need to get things done led me to believe that my previous wins and experiences would translate into Andy Temte becoming an effective organizational manager. Hmmm, what could go wrong?

The Accidental Manager

I define the *accidental manager* as an individual contributor who entered the workforce with vigor and promise. The label "high potential," or HIPO, would likely have been placed on this individual early in their career.

The accidental manager knocked the cover off the ball as a new hire, demonstrating outstanding skill and delivering reliable, high-quality results to the business. The accidental manager typically holds a degree or skill portfolio in a field other than management—for example, nursing, marketing, biology, or in my case, finance—and has no formal training in leading teams of other humans. The accidental manager is placed into a managerial role as a "reward" for their exceptional performance, often with little or no training regimen to accompany the promotion, leaving the newly minted manager to fend for themselves and look after their own learning and development journey.

According to a 2021 Gallup study, 70 percent of the variance in team engagement is explained by the quality of the manager or team leader.[1] This statistic shines a bright light on the importance of management excellence to engagement and organizational health. Making the assumption that good individual job performance will correlate with management excellence is erroneous at best.

The tortured logic that's applied to decisions around promoting an individual contributor to a management position with no experience typically goes something like this: "Yvonne is awesome at her job and gets along with everyone on the team. She'll make a great manager," or "We don't have time to lead a full search for a new manager for department x, so let's tap Trevor for the role. He'll do just fine."

But more often than not, Trevor is not "just fine," and his transition from individual contributor to manager is fraught with challenges. Yes, he may have been well liked by his colleagues when he was part of the team, but the bloom comes off the rose very quickly once Trevor needs to make difficult choices that aren't congruent with his former peers' desires. Trevor likely suffers from impostor syndrome—the self-inflicted stress of feeling inadequate and unprepared for the role. To make matters even more difficult, he likely has not been provided clear guidance around the organization's purpose, vision, and culture. Instead, he is left to determine independently what kinds of behaviors are expected, typically by observing how other managers navigate the organization. If Trevor is not skilled in self-reflection, has not invested in grooming his emotional quotient (EQ), has not committed to a life of learning, or has a weak ego, all manner of unproductive and unhealthy behaviors are likely to manifest themselves as he attempts to build rapport with his new team members.

Yvonne may have performed well as an individual contributor, but was that because she was an awesome firefighter? You know, the go-to person on the team who knew how to fix problems quickly or could shoulder the weight of the team during times of crisis. Good firefighting and crisis management do not necessarily translate into sustained management excellence. Without intervention in the form of a clearly defined organizational strategy that includes goals, priorities and expectations, and a plan for professional growth as a manager, Yvonne will likely spend her career stuck, flitting from fire to fire, as a line manager. Worse yet, her team members will believe fighting fires is the norm. Rather than focusing their efforts on improving trust, accountability, and embedding the organization's vision, culture, values, and goals into the flow of everyday business, they will actively resist the difficult work needed to clearly identify roles and responsibilities.

Both Yvonne and Trevor will likely end up as members of the organizational permafrost (a.k.a. the clay layer) who adopt a fixed mindset and consciously or subconsciously work to avoid meaningful change. Yvonne and Trevor unwittingly slip into active supporters of "we've always done it this way."

As mentioned above, another key trait of the accidental manager is that they are not provided rigorous *experiential* training and development opportunities to fill the skill gaps that the hiring manager either knew or should have known existed upon the installation of the accidental manager. Consistent with the themes that led to the decision to promote based on performance as an individual contributor, hiring managers make the logical leap that either (a) "I was an accidental manager, and I turned out just fine, so therefore Trevor will be just fine," or (b) "Trevor is sharp and can figure out what he needs to be successful on his own." The lack of a clear organizational direction, reinforced through learning and development, can lead to the adoption of a fixed mindset and/or the shiny ball approach to management philosophy and practice.

Therefore, what we end up with are good-intentioned managers who, over time, develop a calcified mindset or are great firefighters but not prepared to lead teams of people. Moving toward a more productive organizational structure built on trust and accountability becomes an impossible task for an individual manager, especially a newly minted one, as colleagues prefer "the way it's always been done," despite their standard operating procedure's waste and inefficiency. Firefighting, crisis management, and resistance to change become the norm, and team members are routinely blindsided by an ever-shifting management landscape. Trust and accountability are impossible to sustain, as there is no reliable framework on which to hang those critical business characteristics.

The Management Operating System Defined

If there are no silver bullets to management success, and flawed managerial hiring practices perpetuate the adoption of quick-fix, flavor-of-the-day management philosophies and Whac-A-Mole business operations practices, what's the answer?

It's time to introduce the management operating system.

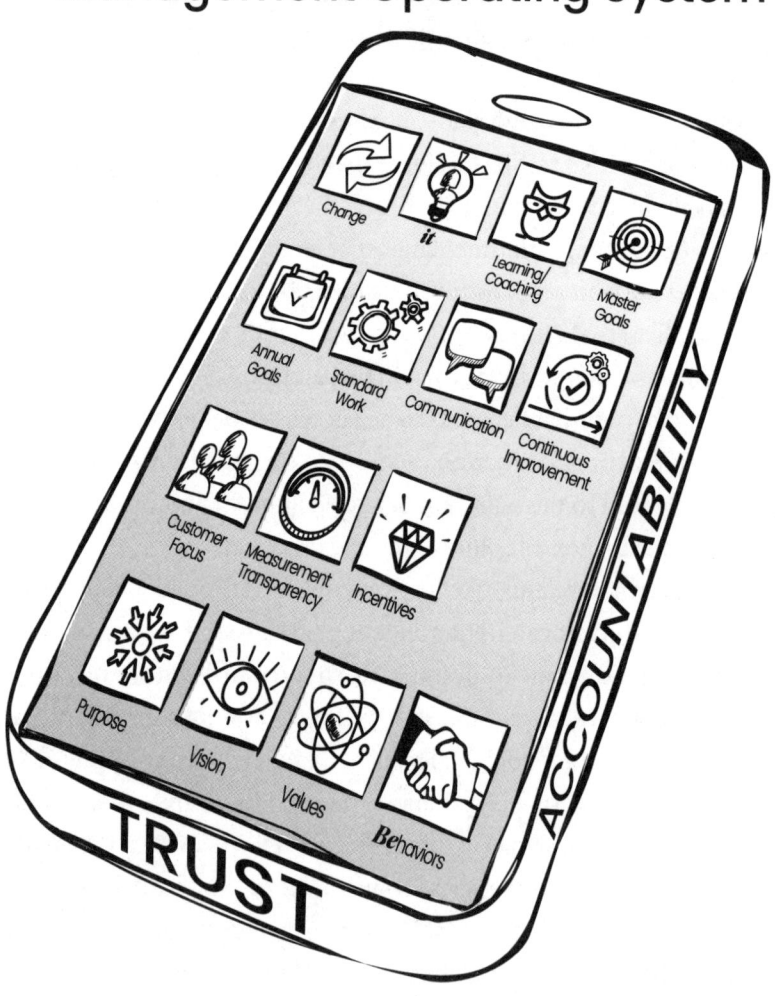

> *Merriam-Webster* defines an operating system as: "Software that controls the operation of a computer and directs the processing of programs (as by assigning storage space in memory and controlling input and output functions)."

Operating systems are all around us. They control our computers, phones, televisions, and even our automobiles. The function of an operating system is to provide a playground of sorts for independent applications to perform a wide variety of functions—everything from a simple calculator to wildly complex graphic design and video processing tools.

As with any playground, an operating system also provides guardrails and sets rules each application must abide by to ensure the entire system runs smoothly and doesn't come crashing down. Those of us who are a part of "computing generation number one" are acutely aware of what can happen when an operating system is poorly designed. When I was writing technical and test prep manuals in the 1990s and early 2000s, I pressed the "save" button after every few sentences due to the anxiety I had developed over losing one too many files to a system crash. In 2023 I'm *still leery* of losing my work!

Interestingly, many businesses, especially small and midsize businesses, take an ad hoc approach to their management philosophies and systems. At the time of business start-up, there was likely a unified approach driven by a single charismatic leader. But hubris, the addition of more disparate human voices, and the necessity to quickly reach financial sustainability put limits on the senior leadership team's ability to spend the requisite amount of time contemplating how the business will function as it grows. Accidental managers abound within the business because either (a) they were there from the beginning and got promoted out of loyalty or convenience, or (b) hiring for managerial talent took a back seat to hiring for technical expertise. "Who needs a management operating system? We need to get things done!"

Unfortunately, assuming the business is still functioning, entropy sets in, and the business winds up operating on a foundation of ad hoc rules and unspoken handoffs that no one questions, because "that's the way we've always done it."

Introducing Value Stream Mapping

To illustrate this point more clearly, let's wind the clock back to the early 2010s. The business unit I used to lead, Kaplan Professional, was just starting to recover from the devastating impact of the Great Recession. It was during this critical period that we adopted the tenets of organizational health and continuous improvement as the Kaplan Professional management operating system. After executing a necessary but dramatic and gut-wrenching reduction in force, it became obvious people were our most valuable asset and that we needed to identify and minimize waste and turn our attention outward, toward the needs of our customers.

During this time of significant change, we analyzed each product line and offering for market fit, portfolio fit, and profitability. The CFA training business Carl Schweser and I sold to Kaplan back in 1999 was humming along nicely, even during the depths of the Great Recession, and was the primary source of operating income that supported the rest of the Kaplan Professional portfolio. As a result, some in the business advocated to make an exception for the CFA product line and not put it on the table for review. After all, "if it ain't broke, don't fix it," right? Wrong.

Fortunately, the senior leadership team and I decided there would be no exceptions or protected asset classes. Nothing was off-limits. Instead, we took a no-stone-unturned approach and analyzed the golden goose *first*.

We knew from anecdotal evidence that *flow* was not maximized in the annual production cycle of all our product lines. Moreover, since CFA was the largest operating profit contributor, its production needs were prioritized throughout the year. CFA had priority to the point where "blackout periods" had been established, within which all production resources were dedicated to ensuring the next generation of CFA-related products made it to market in time, often to the detriment of other product lines and offerings.

Our first step in tearing apart CFA into its component parts was to engage in a multiday *value stream mapping* event. Experts and stakeholders from all departments that touched CFA, from the inception of a revision cycle to delivery of the finished product, gathered to map the work, actions, handoffs, wait times, and processing times along a simple flow diagram.

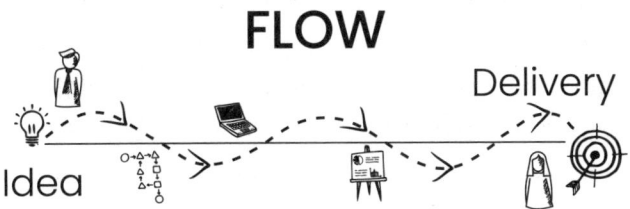

At the end of day two, I stepped into the room for a debrief on the team's progress. The smell of anxiety, coffee breath, and spent brain cells permeated the room. The fancy new dry-erase walls in the conference room were filled with scribblings and arrows that pointed in myriad directions. There was no simple flow diagram to be found.

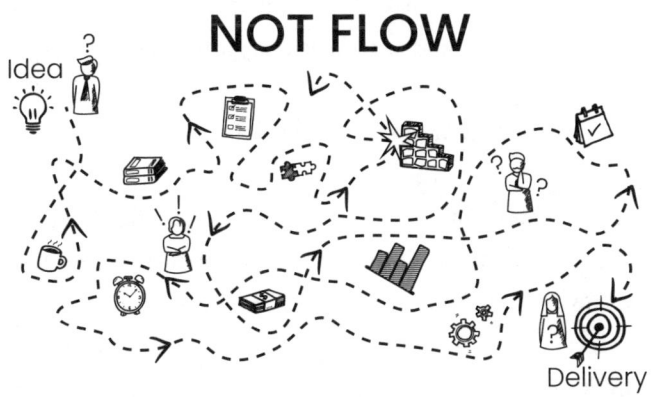

After two days of effort, a process map remained undefined because there were so many instances in which handoffs, work, and wait times were unknown. Everyone in the room was beside themselves because although the CFA revision cycle started and stopped year in, year out, no one knew or could codify how that work actually got done.

This was a wake-up call. If our most successful product line in terms of market reputation, revenue, and operating profit couldn't be defined on a sheet of paper, what efficiency gains were we missing in our other product offerings? Trust was at a low point because the CFA product line always received preferential treatment, and obfuscation and protectionism ran rampant to ensure the status quo was maintained. Accountability was also at a low point because, well, no one really knew *how* work was getting done, and roles, responsibilities, goals, and incentives were misaligned. In addition, if the process map for CFA looked like spaghetti code, was the customer *really* getting our best effort? Probably not.

After the value stream mapping event for CFA concluded, and the senior management team received the final readout, we knew we had a lot of work ahead of us to move the business toward the high-trust, high-accountability quadrant of a trust versus accountability cultural four-box.

If we had any hope of building a sustainable business model that would withstand the ups and downs of the business cycle, we had to stop operating as a portfolio of small businesses—each with competing business models and a feudal approach to leadership—and start thinking about Kaplan Professional as a platform for growth in the broader market for licensures, designations, and certifications globally.

We needed a management operating system.

The concept of a management operating system has been around for years but has encountered limitations on adoption, as existing models focus primarily on structures, processes, and systems that work together. My approach is different. I'm purposefully recognizing the impact of *philosophy*, the *human element* of business, and specifically engineering the operating system to promote the movement of organizational culture toward high trust *and* high accountability. Those that fail to account for human nature in the implementation of a new management operating system are likely to encounter resistance, delays, and in all likelihood failure in its implementation. That is why a keen understanding of basic human psychology is necessary, especially when it comes to subjects like change management, communication practices, competition, and emotional waste.

Hence, our definition of the *management operating system* is this: "The set of philosophical principles, business planning structures, and operational measurement tools that foster an environment of agility and flow while simultaneously promoting balance between trust and accountability within an organization."

Using the Management Operating System to Break Away from "Seasonal" Thinking

One of the key benefits of the management operating system that balances trust and accountability in the pursuit of flow—and one of the reasons why I'm writing this book—is to help organizations break away from the seasonal approach to business management and move toward something more cohesive and sustainable. My goal with this book—one of them, at least—is to help companies reduce the length of those seasons so they can do more *doing* and less *planning*. While it might seem counterintuitive, more planning up front should lead to less time managing each season.

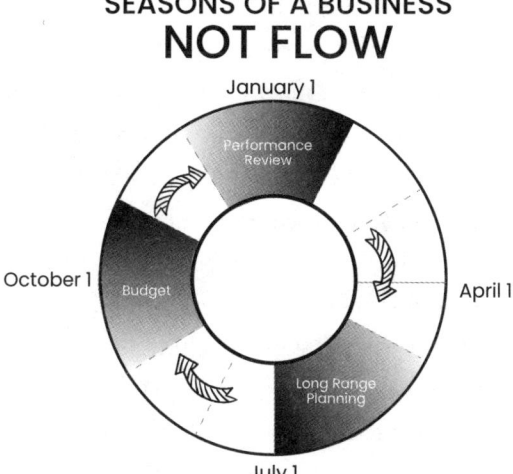

SEASONS OF A BUSINESS
NOT FLOW

Here are a few examples of seasonal thinking that should sound familiar. The average organization typically has long, drawn-out long-range planning, budgeting, and human capital performance review seasons, to name a few.

Each of these seasons brings about a certain degree of anxiety and creates a significant burden on everyone involved. If we can translate this seasonal thinking into a management operating system, these workflows become part of the organization's DNA; require far less time and resources; and for those involved in these processes, won't really feel like extra work. In short, your people won't be challenged to reinvent the wheel with every changing season.

For example, the annual long-range planning season typically starts in late spring with a deep dive into last year's strategy decisions, followed by high-level goal setting for the year ahead. Long-range planning season then concludes with a report to the board of directors and an organizational communications cascade. Time passes, everyone returns to business as usual, and the forgetting curve kicks into high gear.

In September, the CFO and other members of the finance team send out a flurry of emails alerting functional leaders that it's budget season! Not only does everyone have to dust off the results of the long-range planning exercise; they also need to be retrained on the mechanics of surviving budget season. The financial forecast for the next fiscal year that was included as part of the long-range plan becomes the benchmark for the budget, *and* the CFO is typically highly resistant to any downward adjustments to this benchmark. Early in the budget process, however, the high-level goals that were proposed during long-range planning must be refined and codified at the organizational, functional, and departmental levels of the business. As goals are refined, the reality of accomplishing them sets in, and cost estimates typically increase, leading to downward adjustments to the benchmark set during long-range planning. A series of tense interactions between finance and functional leaders ensues, with loop-backs and loads of rework along the way. All these machinations lead to unnecessary angst and are incredibly wasteful, to say the least.

But wait—we're not done, because in December we enter the annual performance review cycle, where individual goals are set, performance evaluations are completed, and pay improvement recommendations are formulated. This time it's human resources that sends out a flurry of emails with instructions on how to complete all the aforementioned tasks, many of which we have forgotten how to do and need to be retrained on. As it relates to goal setting, the budget was finalized back in late October or early November, resulting in another period of "business as usual" in which the forgetting curve gets the best of us. Hence, as we enter the new year, we're *finally* getting around to connecting the dots and explaining to individual contributors how their efforts tie into the operational and strategic priorities that were set months prior. Can you imagine how the average employee feels when they see the business changing around them months before knowing how they're going to contribute, or if their role, project, or department even fits into the company's vision that was set or reconfirmed months and months ago?

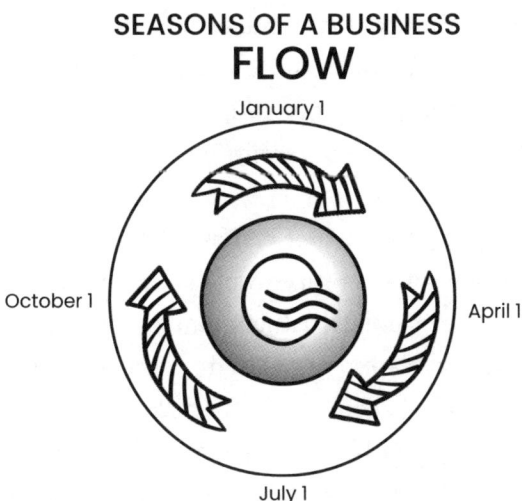

SEASONS OF A BUSINESS
FLOW

January 1

October 1

April 1

July 1

Here's a quick example of flow disruption due to "seasonality." Those who have had to manage business expenses know there are two different approaches to logging and filing receipts. There are those who stuff them into a shoebox and spend hours, even days, sorting, tracking, and logging expenses at the end of the year and those who file their expenses as they occur. Here's where I have to admit that I am in the former category, which is embarrassing to say as an accounting professional. Those who use the shoebox strategy know how much extra time and effort is needed to track down expenses. You begin to pull items out of the shoebox that aren't quite familiar. *Why did I include this expense again?* It's been months, and it will take some time and effort just to remember something you knew at the moment you put that little slip of paper into the shoebox. Not only are you leaving all this work for the last possible minute and tackling it all at once rather than in more manageable chunks along the way but the work itself is more difficult, time-consuming, and labor intensive than it would have been otherwise.

The management operating system is a way to reduce waste by embedding processes like budgeting, strategy, and employee reviews into day-to-day operations rather than stuffing those conversations into a shoebox and waiting for its designated season. Doing so not only improves these processes but it creates a type of flow that allows the business to operate without being at the whims of the stop-and-start seasonal structure many of us have adopted. Yes, it takes more work at the outset to build and implement these systems, but once adopted they allow the business to operate more smoothly, more cohesively, and with less waste.

> **A side note on performance reviews:** While we're on the subject, those who are familiar with my work know I'm no fan of the annual review. Managers don't like them, employees don't like them, and leadership often approaches them as more of a check-the-box human resources compliance activity. When performance reviews are done infrequently, neither party gets much value from them. The manager essentially has to relearn performance review best practices each year, and the employee is so nervous that any hope of a meaningful, two-way conversation is lost. Most of us can think back on a performance review in which what we heard was white noise and "blah, blah, blah."
>
> Instead, performance conversations should be ongoing throughout the year. If we weave reviews into our everyday workflows, it becomes more natural for both managers and employees to engage in *two-way* feedback conversations that add value to both parties. As a result, trust and accountability improve, and waste is minimized—specifically, the waste of emotion, which we will discuss further in chapter 14.

The Road Ahead

My goal is to help leaders and managers think about the foundation of the business as an operating system and install a set of universal guardrails and rules to allow myriad and disparate functional areas of the business to thrive within the management operating system.

If successful, this book will help you break away from seasonal thinking and embrace a radically different approach; one that can improve operational effectiveness, organizational accountability, and cultivate an environment of trust, collaboration, and belonging, all with a maniacal focus on the customer. In my opinion, this approach is needed now more than ever, and I'm not alone.

After struggling under the weight of the COVID-19 pandemic for several years, we as a society have reframed our relationship with work. According to Microsoft's annual Work Trend Index for 2022, which incorporates surveys from more than thirty thousand workers across thirty-one countries, 53 percent now put their health and well-being ahead of their work. Furthermore, of the 18 percent of respondents who quit their jobs in the previous year, the top three motivators they cited for their departure were well-being, work-life balance, and flexibility. In fact, compensation only ranked seventh.[2] That is not to say that workers don't care about compensation, but it is becoming abundantly clear we now operate in a world where people have clearer priorities and greater demands regarding their relationship with work. Organizations that fail to live up to these demands to facilitate a working environment built on trust, teamwork, collaboration, purpose, and belonging are ultimately going to struggle to hire and retain talent.

Prior to the pandemic, many put their work at the center of their lives. I have certainly been guilty of this at many points in my career, often with devastating consequences. But after living through the fear and uncertainty of the pandemic, where something can simply float along in the air and kill millions, few are willing to slave away at a job they don't care about or put their own health and well-being behind their professional ambitions.

Organizations that are still waiting to go back to the way things were, or are forcing their organization to do so, are ultimately going to struggle as they try to apply traditional thinking to a workforce that has adopted a completely different worldview with respect to their work. This book aims to offer a different way forward, using a combination of practical exercises as well as some of the latest research and data in the field. I will also share a few stories along the way from my own personal and professional experiences to help illustrate the points I'm trying to make, each with a specific purpose, to illustrate practical lessons and actionable takeaways.

This book is broken up into two distinct parts. In the first half, we will be doing deep dives into an organization's annual seasons and will explore how each ties into long-range planning events that occur within any mid- to large-size business. Specifically, we're going to start by introducing four distinct but corelated concepts that will serve to provide a deeper understanding of what your business is all about—purpose, vision, values, and behaviors. Each of these discussions will challenge your leadership team to do some deep philosophical thinking that will serve as the foundation for everything that follows.

Once we've established this conceptual foundation, we'll dig into the challenges and opportunities that come with instituting change, followed by two more chapters that will focus on what sets your organization apart. Next, we'll discuss the long-range planning cycle and master goal setting before finishing this first chapter of the book on a concept that is near and dear to me: learning and coaching. More specifically, we'll discuss how to weave learning and coaching into your business's day-to-day operations and how to make it more effective.

The second half of the book is filled with practical tools that are designed to help maximize flow within your business. You can think of it this way: the first half is intended to be more strategic, and the second half will be more tactical. It is in the second half of the book where we'll drill down on the specific continuous improvement and organizational health practices you can implement to improve trust, accountability, and flow.

BOOK ROAD MAP

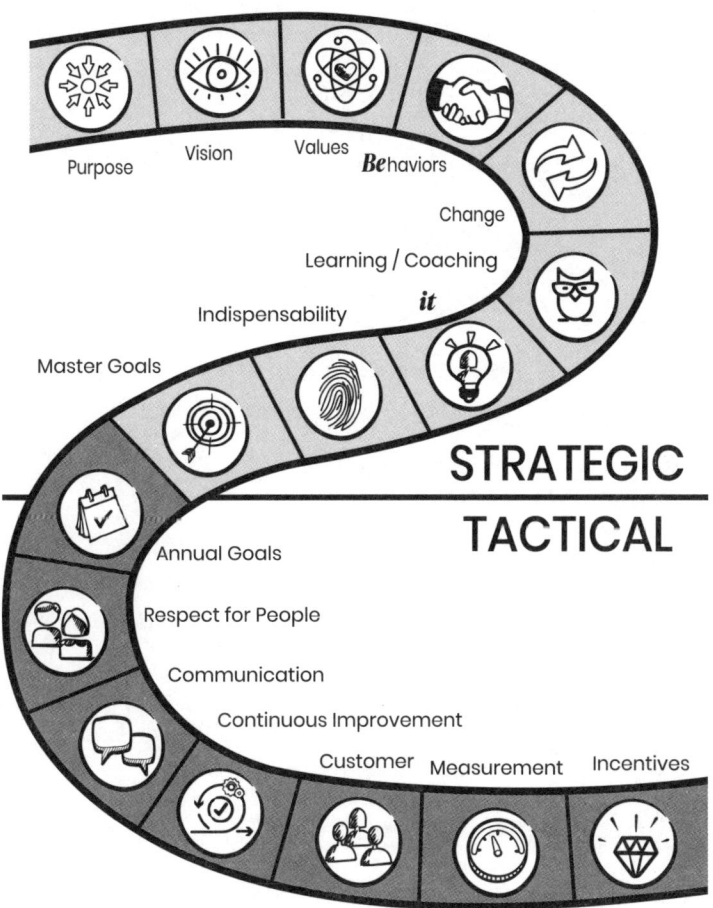

Purpose
Vision
Values
*Be*haviors
Change
Learning / Coaching
Indispensability *it*
Master Goals

STRATEGIC
TACTICAL

Annual Goals
Respect for People
Communication
Continuous Improvement
Customer   Measurement   Incentives

Purpose

It all begins with purpose.

As mentioned at the end of chapter 1, purpose is the first of four big philosophical conversations that will kick-start your journey of continuous improvement and creating a culture built on trust and accountability. Purpose is one of four foundational elements that should serve as grounding points for your business. It, along with vision, values, and behaviors, comprise what I refer to as strategy statements.

As I think back on my nearly forty years as a contributing member of the workforce, purpose was never really top of mind. It's only been during the last decade that the concept of purpose has made its way into my working memory. Recently, I've made time to quietly self-reflect on the "why" behind my historical lack of focus on purpose, and it's now obvious that my purpose was cultivated at a very early age and became woven into my subconscious mind.

During my formative years, my parents were both educators and performers. What amazes me today is that on the surface, education and the performing arts may *seem* like wildly different things, but at their core, education and performance art are integrally linked. To stand in front of a classroom and impart information in an engaging manner is very similar to building up the courage to stand in front of an audience and share your gifts. In both cases, painstaking preparation is needed to acquire the necessary technical competence for a successful outcome. Also, the human skills needed to build confidence and competence are remarkably similar—communication, persistence, resilience, and mental agility immediately come to mind.

As a result of my upbringing and the natural talents my parents passed on to me, my purpose was set by the time I entered junior high school. I would spend the rest of my life learning, developing expertise in technical trades that piqued my interest, and passing that knowledge on to others through teaching, coaching, and mentoring. The conduit through which I would apply my purpose shifted through the years and took the form of bookkeeper, college instructor, entrepreneur, product manager, and business leader, but my foundation, my *purpose*, never shifted—teach, coach, mentor, and hopefully spark a bit of inspiration in those around me.

Corporate Purpose

In late 1999, when I joined Kaplan, which would be my work home for the next twenty-two-plus years, I also didn't need to spend time contemplating the fit between my personal purpose and the organization's purpose. It never occurred to me. The fit was natural.

Back then, corporate purpose statements weren't yet a thing, but mission statements were everywhere. For the majority of my tenure, Kaplan's mission statement was the following: "Kaplan helps individuals achieve their educational and career goals, one success story at a time."

This mission statement has morphed and changed a few times over the years, yet the company's *purpose* has remained consistent since the day Stanley Kaplan started making test prep materials in his mother's basement. That purpose is "making the world a better place through education."

I had the luxury and privilege to be able to drive to the office every day, secure in the knowledge that we were making a difference in the lives of thousands of people around the world. I got to do that *every day* as CEO of Kaplan Professional. It didn't matter if there was a big budget meeting, business review, or some other form of corporate torture in store for me, because on any given day I got to fall back on the knowledge that *today* we were going to help individuals achieve some type of educational "yahoo" moment. Even the worst days were softened by the comfort of knowing my personal purpose and the purpose of the organization were aligned.

In retrospect, codifying Kaplan's purpose statement would have been healthy for the organization. Why? Of all the corporate framing mechanisms we will discuss in this book—purpose, vision, values, and behaviors—corporate purpose should change the least. In other words, purpose should be *durable* through time.

In contrast, the corporate *mission* can change over time based on changes in market-consumer dynamics, the scale and scope of product offerings, mergers and acquisitions, and the insidious effects of entropy. While the mission of an organization will shift more slowly than an annual planning cycle, it *will* shift as the business changes and grows. The foundation the business stands on is its purpose, and stakeholders, especially employees, should know what that foundation is.

Again, Kaplan is a wonderful example of this shift. Today Kaplan's mission is as follows: "Empower students, professionals, universities, and businesses to keep advancing in an ever-changing world."

Why the change? In the early 2000s, Kaplan was primarily focused on consumer-based exam preparation for myriad entrance exams and professional licensures, designations, and certifications. Today the company's reach is global and spans individuals, institutions, and corporations; however, if you peruse their website, the organization's *purpose* has not changed.

The company's culture page shows that the firm's purpose is still grounded in helping to make the world a better place through education. To the best of my knowledge, Kaplan does not have a formal purpose statement, but it's wonderful to see that from my new chair as an outsider, their purpose has remained remarkably consistent.

The Role of Personal Purpose

Everything begins with purpose, and that extends to both your professional life and your personal life. I recommend that you make time to contemplate and define your individual purpose by completing my Personal Planning Guidebook, which is a free resource available on my website. First, however, I want to emphasize the value of understanding your personal purpose, as it's something many of us take for granted or don't consider at all.

Why invest time in defining your personal purpose? First, true personal agency and freedom is derived from knowing one's own purpose. Not investing in the necessary self-reflection and educational journey that's required to determine and understand personal purpose can lead to a fixed mindset and the unwitting adoption of someone else's purpose as your own. Purpose must be genuine and authentic.

Second, unless you've been blessed like I have with an upbringing that led to an organically defined purpose, understanding one's personal purpose is essential for the alignment of one's self to work, play, giving, and community support. In my previous book, *Balancing Act*, I discuss the benefits of bringing one's "whole self" to work. It's impossible to bring your whole self into work, philanthropy, or to your seat on the local school board without having a keen understanding of purpose.

The global COVID-19 pandemic has put a sharp focus on purpose for many people. Prior to the pandemic, many in the employment economy were punching the clock in jobs where their personal purpose did not align with the purpose of the companies they worked for. The Great Resignation, in part, has been fueled by an awakening to purpose and the recognition that life's too short to be stuck in a job that doesn't support or elevate a sense of personal purpose. My prediction is that purpose will remain an important indicator of both personal and job satisfaction.

Purpose Defined

True to form, let's start with the dictionary definition of *purpose*. From Oxford Languages, purpose is: "The reason for which something is done or created or for which something exists."

As a derivative of the dictionary definition, the questions that must be answered to define both personal and corporate purpose are: Why do I exist? Why am I here? How will I make an ongoing positive impact on society? And why does this company exist? How will our company contribute to a better tomorrow for its stakeholders and society at large?

In our continual search for root cause, purpose is the ultimate root cause statement. On a personal level, determining and putting words to your purpose is a very deep exercise that requires the human skills of self-love, self-reflection, curiosity, courage, and compassion. In the boardroom, determining corporate purpose is a team sport that is driven from the office of the CEO, with input from the senior executive team. Like its personal counterpart, a high level of human skill is required for the best results. Quiet egos; open ears; curious, agile minds; and courageous yet compassionate voices are necessary conditions for success.

The Nine Elements of Purpose

Purpose statements are:

- *Transparent.* Purpose statements should not be shuttled away to an obscure corner of the website or stuffed in a drawer, never to be seen again. Purpose should be clearly visible to clients, customers, employees, prospective hires, and all other stakeholders in the organization.
- *Authentic.* This is why purpose statements should be driven from the CEO and not delegated to HR, marketing, or a third-party consultant. Put simply, if the CEO doesn't believe in and live the organization's purpose, how on earth is Naomi in accounting going to understand the company's purpose and make decisions about how her personal purpose aligns with her work? Customers should also be able to authentically connect to a company's purpose statement and perhaps feel inspired by it.

- *Durable*. Optimally, a company's purpose statement endures through time. While it's unlikely that the purpose statement will *never* change, it should be the foundation upon which the company's activities stand. As we get into the practical application of this book, I recommend that the purpose statement be the first thing discussed at the beginning of the annual planning cycle; but after it's set, this discussion should be confirmatory and not controversial or drawn out. If you find that annual discussions regarding purpose *are* contentious, then it's time for a deep-dive search for the root cause.

- *Simple*. Avoid flowery or confusing language that leaves the purpose statement open for interpretation. Purpose statements should be inspirational but also practical. Keep in mind that your investors, customers, and employees will be connecting and aligning their own purpose to your company's. If stakeholders have to spend more than ten seconds trying to divine its meaning, it's time to go back to the drawing board.

- *Conduit for alignment*. When Max applies for employment at the firm, he will be looking to align his personal purpose with that of the business. Purpose matters to your most valuable asset—your people resources. Your company's purpose statement is a beacon to attract individuals who have dedicated their lives to the advancement of your cause.

- *Equitable, inclusive, and diverse*. Purpose statements should not be exclusionary. They should be welcoming and inviting to a broad range of audiences. One of your goals as a modern leader is to gather a diverse set of voices that challenge your thinking, drive innovation, exhibit resilience in the face of continual change, and row in unison once goals are established and execution begins. Although it may seem counterintuitive, it is not incongruent to hire for diversity of thought, gender, race, et al., *and* build teams that share and rally around a common purpose. We'll discuss this point further in chapters 4 and 12.

- *Connected to societal well-being*. The reader of your purpose statement should be able to draw a direct line between your company's purpose and how your business will act as a force for good to benefit society in the long run.

- *Not marketing slogans*. Purpose must not be a manufactured statement but instead must genuinely reflect the "why" behind the company's existence and the "how" the organization will engage to aid and develop societal fabric. If marketing and/or legal wants you to attach a registered trademark symbol to your purpose statement, that should be the first sign that you've created a marketing catchphrase and not a purpose statement.

- *Specific*. The best purpose statements provide some indication, even subtly, about what it is the company actually does. Just about every company can say they strive to "make the world a better place," but Tesla's solution will probably look quite different than what Disney has in mind. Products and services and business models change over time, but the value the company offers—which we'll get into in greater detail in chapter 7, when we talk about the *it*—should be relatively consistent and easily identifiable within the purpose statement. In other words, if you hear "to be one of the world's leading producers and providers of entertainment and information," and "to create the most compelling car company of the twenty-first century by driving the world's transition to electric vehicles," you know which one is Mickey and which one is Musk.

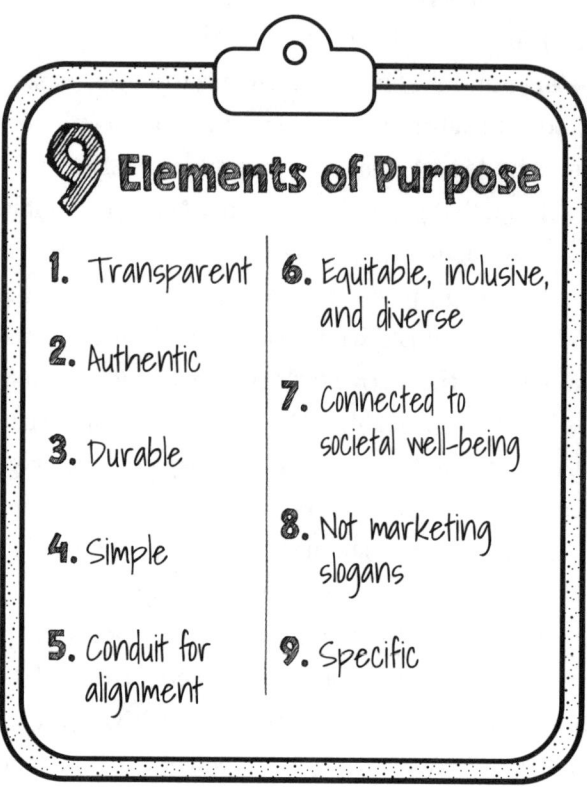

9 Elements of Purpose

1. Transparent
2. Authentic
3. Durable
4. Simple
5. Conduit for alignment
6. Equitable, inclusive, and diverse
7. Connected to societal well-being
8. Not marketing slogans
9. Specific

Purpose versus Mission

You may be wondering, "What about the mission statement? Does mission still have a role?"

Definitions of the *mission statement* abound and are wildly inconsistent. They range from a simplistic overlap of purpose, such as "a brief description of why the organization exists," to multipart statements that touch on purpose, values, goals, capabilities, and even legacy—far too much content to pack into one or two pithy sentences. Mission statements do too much heavy lifting, and the resulting product can be confusing at best.

Therefore, my recommendation is that your firm *dump the concept of a mission statement* and instead invest time in establishing a purpose statement and combining it with the company's vision, values, and behaviors statements (discussion on these strategy statements follows in chapters 3 and 4). Yes, you may need to maintain a mission statement for compliance, governance, or regulatory purposes, but it can simply be a derivative or combination of the aforementioned statements.

Should your executive team just slap the name "purpose statement" on its old mission statement? The answer is an emphatic *no*. The exercise of starting from the ground floor with fresh thinking is invaluable. Don't take the easy way out.

The goal of corporate strategy statements like purpose, vision, values, and behaviors is to create and reinforce clarity. Strategy statements should *flow* and *connect* to one another. Unnecessary complexity should be avoided at all costs.

Purpose Statement Examples

Here are some examples of purpose statements from a few prominent organizations:

The Coca-Cola Company: "Refresh the world. Make a difference."

This purpose statement ticks all the boxes noted above, offering insight into both what they do as a company and a nod to the "greater good" in six words total. That degree of clarity is itself refreshing. Anyone else suddenly feel thirsty?

> **CVS Health:** "We help people with their health wherever and whenever they need us. And we do it with heart. Because our passion is our purpose: Bringing our heart to every moment of your health™."

This statement is as long as a CVS receipt for a single bottle of water; it stretches well beyond what's necessary and then keeps going. It's so long it has no chance of being memorable or meaningful to the company's stakeholders. You just read it: Can you remember any part of it without looking at it again? Probably not, and the reason behind this mess is stated clearly at the very end. The trademark symbol tells us everything we need to know about how this statement was devised—not the result of hours of reflection and deliberation by company leaders but by a marketing team or consultant who was trying to cram all the company's keywords together. Eventually, someone realized they could trim a lot of the fat and recently updated it to just include the last statement—"Bringing our heart to every moment of your health"—and dropped the trademark. It still sounds a bit too much like a marketing statement, but at least now it's clearly connected to societal well-being, gives some indication of what it is the company does, feels a bit more authentic, and is a bit simpler, so we can give CVS a few bonus points for that effort. Maybe next they'll shorten those receipts.

> **Kroger:** "Our Purpose is to Feed the Human Spirit™."

The Kroger statement is exceedingly vague, to the point where I had to search for an explanation, which I found in a pandemic-related letter from the CEO to stakeholders. That clarification read: "Which means we are driven to do more and help make the lives of those around us better…" So with the clarification, I get it, but the use of the word *spirit* can be interpreted in numerous ways, and if interpreted through the lens of religion, it could be viewed as exclusionary. It's also hard to ignore the red flag that comes at the end of the statement in the form of a trademark. Going back to our list of purpose statement elements, giving Kroger points for transparency, durability, specificity, simplicity, conduits, or for not feeling like a manufactured marketing slogan is hard. That said, the elaborated explanation from the CEO allows them to make up for it with some points for authenticity, equity, and societal well-being. Overall, not great, but it won't be the worst example on this list.

> **Ford Motor Company:** "To help build a better world, where every person is free to move and pursue their dreams."

This is an excellent example of a well-crafted purpose statement. It checks every single box on the list and could have come straight from Henry Ford's mouth. In fact, Ford invented the very first assembly line in 1913 with the express goal of making mobility affordable and accessible to every one of his factory workers.[1] The company's purpose has remained consistent ever since, and its purpose statement is a reminder of that history, tradition, and world-changing innovation. Bravo.

> **PwC:** "To build trust in society and solve important problems. By doing this, we aim to make a meaningful difference in the world."

Since starting the process of writing this book, PwC has made significant strides in their purpose statement, going so far as to align their business operations with its two primary tenets: trust solutions (audit, tax, and governance) and "solving important problems" (business and process consulting). From an outsider's vantage point, it appears they've dumped their mission statement and are focused on purpose to the point of hiring a chief purpose and inclusion officer. I'm not a fan of the generic "we aim to make a difference in the world," but overall, well done, PwC!

> **Walgreens Boots Alliance:** "More joyful lives through better health."

Wonderful! CVS could learn a thing or two from their biggest competitor, at least when it comes to defining purpose. It's simple, elegant, transparent, indicates what the company does, and doesn't sound like a marketing slogan. It also suggests the company has higher aspirations than financial performance and makes two different nods to societal well-being within six words. Again, bravo.

Make Time to Define Purpose

I am fortunate to have spent the vast majority of my working life living my purpose. I'm grateful for the work early Kaplan leaders invested in cultivating a purpose-driven culture, even though the formal concept of corporate purpose was not yet well established. Looking back, I can now connect the dots in jobs I've had where my personal purpose and corporate purpose were *not* aligned. In those jobs, I felt like just another cog in a big wheel, punching the clock for a paycheck to make rent.

We all deserve rewarding work. A former colleague of mine made this clear through the illustration of the following virtuous cycle: rewarding work leads to individual fulfillment, which can unlock additional discretionary effort. As a result, my advice to individuals reading this is to make the time to contemplate and define your purpose. My advice to corporate leaders is to make the time to clearly define your company's purpose and share that gift with stakeholders to improve organizational alignment and outcomes.

> **A disclaimer on individual company examples:** The strategy statements from individual companies (e.g. Ford Motor Company) used throughout this book are "snapshots in time" and it is likely that by the time you're reading this, some purpose, vision, values, and behavior statements may have changed.

3

Vision

Now that you've spent some time working on your purpose statement, it's time to translate that high-level answer to a more practical question: "Where do we go from here?" As mentioned above, vision is the second of four strategy statements that will set the stage for your business's continuous improvement journey.

In the early days of your organization, seeing a distinction between purpose and vision might be difficult because they often begin as one in the same. Your vision might also pivot quite frequently and dramatically as new products and markets are tested. Over time, however, as your company's purpose rubs up against reality, vision can get a little clouded. While purpose typically stays constant, aside from a few minor tweaks from time to time, your vision statement should be considered and updated on at least an annual basis. That is because seeing deep into the future is simply not possible, no matter how big or influential your business is. If your purpose explains why you exist, your vision informs the steps you intend to take in service of that purpose.

This is a particularly important concept for your employees to rally around, especially in a post–COVID-19 context. Ideally, you employ a staff who already buys into your company's overall purpose, but they should also have a strong understanding of the organization's vision for fulfilling that purpose and, most importantly, how their individual contribution fits into the bigger picture.

According to Microsoft's 2022 Work Trend Index, 40 percent of workers say that having "a sense of purpose or meaning" at work is "very important," which ranked third behind a positive culture (46 percent) and mental health and well-being benefits (42 percent).[1] Also worth noting is that a sense of purpose and meaning at work was prioritized above flexible work hours (38 percent) and more vacation time (36 percent). That's pretty incredible, if you think about it—staff would prefer having a clear purpose over more vacation time and workplace flexibility, and it's hard to blame them. Nobody wants to be the person grinding away in some back office without knowing how their outputs fit into the bigger puzzle. From an employee perspective, having a clear purpose can help improve employee sentiment and engagement, which is especially important in today's more competitive talent marketplace.

Mission Statements

As you're reading this, you might be thinking to yourself, "I've already ticked the vision box." Some time ago you probably sat down with your leadership team, put some time and effort into figuring out where you want the business to go from here, and created a mission statement. Before you skip ahead to the next chapter, however, I want you to really think about how much of an impact that mission statement has on how you run your business day-to-day.

Mission statements have been around for a long time, but they're usually developed as part of an organization's governance and compliance process and then stuffed in a drawer for the next twenty or thirty years. In an ideal world, a mission statement is a tool that helps guide decision-making, gets dusted off and updated from time to time to remain relevant, and is something each employee can recite by heart. I would suspect this isn't the case unless the company is relatively new, or you had a direct hand in writing it yourself. This is why I advocated for organizations to dump their mission statements in the previous chapter of this book.

Thanks to the rapid advancement of technology, businesses now operate at such breakneck speeds that most mission statements just can't keep up. When retrieved from the drawer it was stuffed in, it sounds like a relic of a bygone era, far removed from the realities of the business today.

Operating without a vision, however, is like trying to navigate a foreign city without a map or GPS. Sure, you might make it to your destination, but without some idea of where you're going you'll probably get there later than necessary, stop for directions a few times, and probably travel along a less-than-optimal route. Having a clear vision is like having a North Star shining up in the sky, lighting the path forward. Anytime you feel less than confident in your navigation, you can look up and see whether you're on the right path and adjust accordingly.

Enter the A3

So how do you determine your organization's vision? How do you create a picture of the future that you and your team can rally around and work toward? By drawing one. Literally.

The concept of the A3 as a planning and process management tool got its start at Toyota in the 1940s, and its use was widely expanded in the latter half of the twentieth century.[2] According to John Shook in his 2008 book *Managing to Learn*, A3 thinking was adopted as a solution for "clarifying our own thinking, learning from others, informing and teaching others, capturing lessons learned, hammering down decisions, and reflecting on what was going on." Shook was Toyota's first American manager working in Japan and is senior advisor at Lean Enterprise Institute.[3]

The solution was dubbed A3 thinking, a problem-solving and discovery tool named for the single sheet of ISO A3-size paper the exercise was conducted on—paper that's slightly fatter and shorter than what we in North America refer to as "tabloid-size" paper. Right now you're thinking, "Of course we've got different paper sizes than the rest of the world!" For the purposes of this exercise, you're essentially working with a piece of paper that's eleven inches by seventeen inches.

Another question you might be asking yourself, in a Jim Gaffigan–style whisper, "Why on earth is he talking about paper sizes?" The answer is straightforward. The A3 planning process is meant to be *tactile*, not digital. Creating an A3 is an experience that relies on hand-to-brain communication to spark creative juices, which don't flow as easily in more passive educational settings, like reading or watching a video.[4]

In addition, building an A3 is an iterative process. The first go-round is likely to be a mess, but that mess is an important part of the process. Having several blank templates printed out and at your disposal is a prerequisite for a strong finished product.

This single piece of paper can be organized and divided in a number of different ways, but what's important is that the problem you are trying to solve gets written clearly at the top. Simply spending the time and energy coming up with a problem statement is itself a strong practice that can help determine solutions, but that's just the beginning.

Below the problem statement comes a description of the problem. While some prefer to describe the current state of the situation in point-form notes, I strongly encourage you to draw it. I'm a visual person, and the practice of drawing the problem helps me visualize my perception of the challenge as clearly as possible.

Next to or beneath that drawing you describe (or draw) the future desired state, visualizing a world in which this problem has been solved. The rest of the page is dedicated to different ways of going from the current state to the desired future state, such as a breakdown of root causes, identifying potential roadblocks, analyzing potential solutions, outlining a plan for implementation, and a structure for ensuring ongoing iteration. We'll discuss each of these steps in more detail below.

> **Side note:** The A3 process outlined below to determine the vision of your organization is a derivative of A3 thinking as applied at Toyota and many other manufacturing firms around the world. Put simply, my proposed version of an A3 for both corporate visioning and personal planning is customized for these applications and does not strictly adhere to Toyota's model.

The Master A3 and Vision

While the system was refined by Shook and his colleagues at Toyota to solve specific problems between employees and managers, they soon realized that A3 thinking could be applied to a range of business problems, from the day-to-day to more foundational challenges. This is where the A3 solution begins to intersect with the broader concept of vision.

"The widespread adoption of the A3 process standardizes a methodology for innovating, planning, problem-solving, and building foundational structures for sharing a broader and deeper form of thinking," wrote Shook. "This produces organizational learning that is deeply rooted in the world itself–operational learning."[5]

Unlike the everyday solutions that the A3 was initially intended to help solve, we refer to those that answer more foundational questions, such as the company's overall vision, as a Master A3. I've included a sample Master A3 in figure 3.1 below.

Figure 3.1: The Master A3

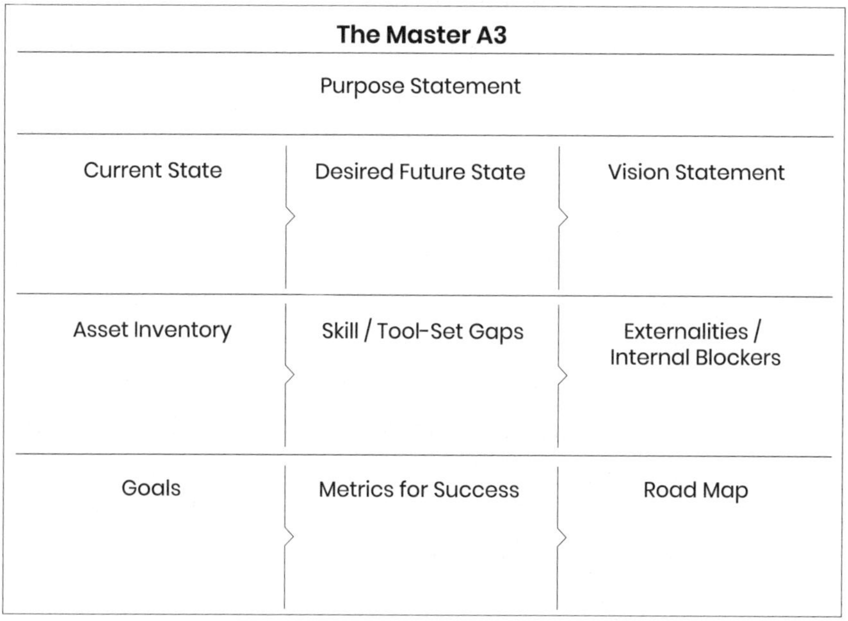

The Master A3		
Purpose Statement		
Current State	Desired Future State	Vision Statement
Asset Inventory	Skill / Tool-Set Gaps	Externalities / Internal Blockers
Goals	Metrics for Success	Road Map

When considering your organization's vision, simply take out a sheet of A3 or tabloid-size paper and put your company's purpose at the top. Then draw a picture of the problem your organization is attempting to solve, accompanied by a picture of the desired future state. Then you can use the rest of the page to go through the steps that will help provide a road map for going from the current state to the desired future state. Tucked away in the middle of this page is a vision statement—a clear and concise explanation of what you want to achieve in the desired future state. It provides that North Star that can help guide your organization whenever it is traversing foreign lands or could benefit from a course correction.

Instructions for Completing the Master A3

Step 1: Gather your senior leadership team at an off-site location. It is essential that the time allotted for building and/or revising the company's Master A3 is sufficient and focused. I strongly recommend the use of a third-party facilitator to ensure participation is maximized and unconscious bias is minimized. Be wary of taking a do-it-yourself approach, as unhealthy team dynamics and favoritism can unintentionally poison the exercise. A good facilitator knows how to pick up on unspoken cues and is not afraid to call executives on their crap. Phones and other digital distractions should be banned from the room. Dress should be casual and comfortable—put all the usual airs aside and show up with your whole self. Leave the emotional suit of armor at home and let creativity, curiosity, and vulnerability out to play.

Step 2: Use a whiteboard, flip chart, or other tactile means to create the first draft. Avoid the use of fancy technology; there will be plenty of time to codify the results of this exercise digitally. The mess of dry-erase markers, incoherent scribbles that need clarification, and the smell of hours-old coffee aids in the innovation process, in my experience. I'm definitely showing my age here, but I used to love doing this kind of work with an old-school chalkboard. There's something uniquely satisfying about ending the day with chalk dust or dry-erase marker smudges on your hands, face, and pants.

The bullets that follow are purposefully brief descriptions of what each box in figure 3.1 means. I'm not going to be providing concrete examples of completed A3s, because I don't want to influence your decisions and choices or provide shortcuts that unintentionally color your thinking.

- *Purpose.* It all starts with purpose. The purpose statement that you created in chapter 2 of this book is placed prominently across the top of the A3.
- *Current state.* This is the depiction of how your business operates today. Do your best to use pictures and symbols to describe your current state. I recommend that everyone in attendance draws their own diagram that illustrates the current state of the business. Next, have each senior leader present their version of the current state to the rest of the team. You'll be *amazed* at how much comes out of the woodwork and how variable the descriptions of the current state are during this process.
- *Desired future state.* Same thing—draw a picture of where you want the business to be at the end of some predetermined time period. I personally have found that trying to look forward more than five years is a futile exercise, but the time horizon of the future state drawing is completely up to you and will be driven in part by the idiosyncrasies of your business and/or industry sector.
- *Vision statement.* These are the words that describe your desired future state. In terms of length, it's longer than your purpose statement but is still punchy and direct.

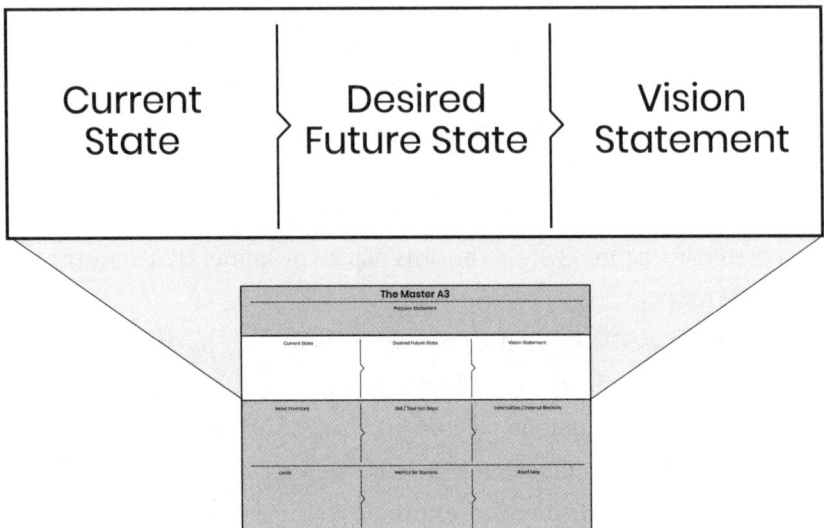

- *Asset inventory*. These are the skills of your teams, physical assets, capital or lending capacity, and intangible assets like brand and reputation that you have at your disposal to achieve your vision.
- *Externalities*. These are the external challenges that influence your current state and are out of your immediate control. As we learned in economics 101, everything is variable in the long run, but these are the short-run environmental and physical factors that constrain your business.
- *Skill and tool-set gaps*. This is a critical step in the process and represents the difference between the skills and tools you'll need to make progress toward the desired future state and your current asset inventory (see above).
- *Goals*. We're going to talk in detail about master goal setting in chapter 9, but this is your team's first go at defining what we will be calling vision-specific goals. Word of caution: the primary objective of the Master A3 is to determine the vision statement. Don't get mired in master goal setting at this stage of the process. The goals you and your team determine here will give you a head start on master goal setting, but finalizing them should not be the objective at this moment.

- *Metrics for success.* How will you know you've made progress? How will you measure goal attainment? In chapter 17, we're going to spend considerable time discussing key performance indicators (KPIs). Similar to our discussion on goal setting, don't get mired in deep discussions about your company's master KPI structure. Instead, develop a list of candidates that align with your preliminary vision-specific goals, and use this list as a head start to the formal identification process that will follow.
- *Road map.* As the name suggests, this is literally a picture of a road map that illustrates the significant milestones on the journey from current state toward the desired future state. Put symbolic curves in your road map in recognition of the fact that life is filled with curves, roadblocks, and loopbacks.

Step 3: Let it sit—preferably overnight. The executive off-site should be multiday for a reason: you need time to let your Master A3 sit and the ideas to coalesce. Rushing the process will result in unnecessary waste. Take breaks to attend to other business and then revisit the initial set of responses. Most importantly, push each other. Engage in constructive conflict. Complacency and a desire to "move on" will yield poor results that need to be corrected down the road.

Step 4: Collect opinions from the extended leadership team. After the off-site concludes, the process of defining the Master A3 is not finished. We're going to talk about playing catchball at several points throughout this book, but for now, take the Master A3 from the off-site and "toss" that work product to the members of your extended leadership team for review and feedback. This is a great opportunity for each member of the executive team to take the preliminary Master A3 back to their direct reports for a robust discussion about the future direction of the business. After these crucial conversations have occurred, the senior leadership team reconvenes for a shorter but no less important session to finalize the Master A3 by incorporating the input and opinions of the extended leadership team. This is an essential part of the process!

Step 5: Move to master goal setting. In chapter 9, we'll engage in a more detailed discussion about master goal setting. As mentioned above, master goal setting should be a separate long-range planning off-site or series of meetings, and I strongly recommend the use of a third-party facilitator here too.

Step 6: Monitor and adjust. Your company's Master A3 is a living document. As mentioned above, change is messy. The road map you drew in your A3 is purposefully curvy in recognition of the fact that life is not linear. Throughout this book, I'm advocating for weaving goal setting and the development and maintenance of your organization's strategy statements into the *flow* of business. They should not hide in desk drawers, only to be revisited occasionally. Revisit your A3 and progress against goals, relying on the metrics for success you chose, at least once every year, preferably every six months.

The Six Elements of Vision

1. *Forward-looking.* A primary goal of your vision statement is to set the bar for the desired future state. As a result, vision statements are, by definition, forward-looking and aspirational. As you approach completion of the goals that support your vision statement, it's time to draft a new one.
2. *Realistic.* At the same time, realism is also important. Your vision should be aspirational such that your employees will look at it and see a challenge that excites rather than intimidates. Similarly, sticking with aspirations that can be accomplished within a reasonable time horizon is important. You want to give your team a goal that doesn't make them think it won't come to fruition until after they've moved on from the company. Keeping your vision aspirational while remaining within reason can give your team members a reason to stick around and see that vision through to the end.
3. *Clear.* As with purpose statements, everyone within your organization should be able to identify with your vision statement. That means no

flowery language or words that necessitate an online search for a definition. Unlike purpose statements, however, your vision statement can be a little bit more jargony, as it is primarily for internal purposes. So long as those in your organization, industry, or customer base can easily understand the language you're using, it doesn't really matter if the rest of the world can too.

4. *Universal.* While your vision is set at the top, it shouldn't just speak to high-level goals. In an ideal scenario, it is something that everyone in your organization, from the intern to the CEO, can work toward—a direction that lets everyone move in unison. If your vision statement is about sales figures, for example, that probably won't rally the enthusiasm of your IT department. Instead, ensure that it speaks to everyone within your organization equally.

5. *Specific.* While making your vision statement broad enough to apply to your entire organization, it should also be something that speaks to what makes your organization unique. As with purpose, your vision should allude to the thing the business actually does, or at least aspires to do, and be specific enough that it can't be easily cut and pasted onto a different company's website without anyone noticing. As mentioned in the previous chapter, every business wants to change the world, so be specific and give us an idea of how you're going to do that.

6. *Concise.* As with purpose statements, brevity is key—not just for simplicity but for more practical reasons as well. If this statement is going to be repeated by employees, printed on banners, used in email signatures, etc., it shouldn't require a whole paragraph. The shorter it is, the more effective it will be.

Vision Statement Examples

Here are several examples of vision statements from major brands around the world.

IKEA: "Our vision is to create a better everyday life for many people."

Unfortunately, IKEA has ignored element number 5 on our list, but this vision statement serves as a strong reminder of the importance of specificity. As mentioned, every company wants to make the world a better place, but this vision statement doesn't give any insight into how they intend to accomplish this goal. While forward-looking and aspirational, it is not well grounded in reality and doesn't give the organization's employees a reasonable goal or cause to rally around. It could also be applied to just about every company on earth. Perhaps there are just a few pieces missing from IKEA's vision statement, and some additional assembly is required.

> **Nike:** "Bring inspiration and innovation to every athlete* in the world. (*If you have a body, you are an athlete.)"

While the added clarification does add a little bit of bulk to the statement, anyone who knows the brand well knows they already view every human as an athlete, so the parentheses are really for the benefit of non-Nike employees. With that in mind, this is a great example of a strong vision statement. It's forward-looking, realistic, specific, and can be applied to anyone from the front office to the in-store clerk. In other words, it checks every box with an emphatic swoosh.

> **McDonald's:** "To be the best quick service restaurant experience. Being the best means providing outstanding quality, service, cleanliness, and value, so that we make every customer in every restaurant smile."

For the brand that invented fast food, this vision statement is a little slow. As with some of the purpose statements we explored in the previous section, it feels more like a marketing exercise that is striving to incorporate a series of keywords than a rallying cry to its hundreds of thousands of employees worldwide.[6] It also isn't very forward-looking or aspirational. If I were a McDonald's executive, I'd hope my restaurants are already providing quality, service, and value. Isn't cleanliness table stakes?

> **Amazon:** "We strive to offer our customers the lowest possible prices, the best available selection, and the utmost convenience."

While this vision statement does border on the generic, Amazon's customers would probably recognize these efforts in their interactions with the brand. That said, these same words could be applied to numerous competitors as well. It is, however, a realistic vision; it can be applied across the brand's many domains universally, and it's fairly concise. We can't give this one a "prime" score, but it's just good enough for a passing grade.

> **Walmart:** "Be the destination for customers to save money, no matter how they want to shop."

This one is executed with near perfection. It speaks to the brand's primary value proposition, which is saving customers money, while also being aspirational by committing to becoming a leader, presumptively within and beyond the in-person retail space. It is also universally applicable, from in-store greeters to the C-suite. Well done, Walmart.

> **Google:** "To provide access to the world's information in one click."

This is another great example of a brand that has clearly put some time and effort into their vision statement. Those who have heard executives speak about the company know their broad range of software and hardware products all come back to the concept of providing access to the world's information. The additional goal of providing that information in "one click" also adds a little bit of aspiration while remaining realistic. I don't think you could apply this vision statement to any other company in the world, and yet it is concise, specific, and applicable to anyone who works for the Silicon Valley behemoth.

> **Microsoft:** "To help people and businesses throughout the world realize their full potential."

Here Microsoft has done a great job balancing the aspirational with the realistic while maintaining clarity and brevity. It is specific while also being broad enough to be applicable to employees working on a wide range of products and services. It also demonstrates the customer-centric approach the business espouses in many of its internal and external communications and positions the company's products as enablers of their customers' success. Top marks for Microsoft. Clippy would be proud.

Starbucks: "Treat people like family, and they will be loyal and give their all."

Starbucks is known for a lot of things, but treating customers and staff like family probably isn't topping that list. Given the recent, often ugly public battles over unionization, believing that they're taking this vision seriously is also hard. This statement isn't very clear, realistic, forward-looking, or specific. In fact, it puts the onus on everyone else to give the brand their "all," which I doubt is a cause people will eagerly line up to support. I don't know about you, but my family has never had that much trouble spelling my name correctly on a cup.

Samsung: "Inspire the world with our innovative technologies, products, and design that enrich people's lives and contribute to social prosperity."

Samsung's vision statement could be a bit more concise, but it checks most other boxes, including brevity, specificity, universality, aspirationality, and realisticness. It would be more effective if it were just a little bit shorter and clearer, but it's certainly effective.

Patagonia: "We're in business to save our home planet."

You could criticize Patagonia for coming up with a vision statement that could be applied to just about any environmentally focused organization, but the fact that it's coming from a clothing brand—and the fact that it has a reputation for actually following through on this vision—makes it very powerful. What it lacks in specificity it makes up for in brevity, clarity, aspiration, and, to the brand's credit, reality. It's the kind of vision statement that could be put on eco-friendly bumper stickers and other promotional material. While most brands would get an eye roll for suggesting it's on a mission to save the planet, it's actually quite credible for Patagonia, given the brand's reputation.

Putting Your Vision Statement to Work

I know I said it earlier, but it bears repeating: your vision statement is not just a thought exercise for your executive team or a compliance box to be checked and then forgotten about. Your vision statement and Master A3 are living documents and should be prominently featured throughout the organization, including internal and external communications. It should make an appearance at quarterly meetings, employee check-ins, shareholder meetings, press releases, even in your email signature, if you so choose. It should offer a benchmark for your progress toward both short- and long-term strategic planning activities day in, day out.

The repetition of a crisp, clear, and concise vision statement can also help employees and managers take more ownership over their work. It allows them to make decisions more confidently, with fewer layers of approval, so long as those decisions remain in service of the organization's vision. This is what I mean by providing a North Star. Having a clear vision statement means everyone knows which direction the business is moving, and everyone is thus empowered to make decisions at every level that can help further that vision.

> **Side note:** When's the last time you sat down and created your own personal roadmap? Do you know what your personal purpose is? Have you determined what "success" means and how you'll measure it to know if you've strayed from your intended path? To learn more about how the A3 can be applied to create an actionable vision for your future, please visit my website at andrewtemte.com/guidebook to download your free copy of my Personal Planning Guidebook.

Culture

Culture starts at the top. Period.

I've seen many leaders scratch their heads when considering the culture that has organically sprouted around them. The culture they see, however, is a direct reflection of them: specifically, their actions and, equally as impactful, their inactions.

There's an old saying with unknown origins that suggests "what you permit, you promote," and this is especially true of weak leaders who, as much as possible, take the easy route and avoid confronting the problems that surround them. My personal version of this saying is "you are what you allow."

Failing to address tensions or issues or conflicts or problem behaviors is, in effect, a promotion of those actions. Letting someone get away with abusive behavior is sending a powerful signal regarding what is tolerated in the workplace. Over time, these problem behaviors become so ingrained that they morph into a prominent feature of the corporate culture.

That is the danger of allowing culture to take shape without some degree of forethought and intentionality. But sitting down with a notepad and coming up with a list of values is in itself of little consequence. Defining your values is the easy part; real courage is needed to reflect those values in your actions every day. No matter how much time, energy, and resources you or your HR team puts into crafting a compelling narrative about your workplace experience, the values and behaviors demonstrated by your leaders will have the greatest effect on your company culture.

Those are the final two pieces of the philosophical foundation I've alluded to above. Our values, whether as a company or an individual, are almost like a wish list for what we aspire to be, but they're only as good as the behaviors that demonstrate and enforce them. Here I need to give credit to author and team dynamics expert Patrick Lencioni, who has inspired much of my thinking on this topic.

In his 2012 book *The Advantage*, Lencioni is very specific about the fact that values and behaviors are different, and I want to really emphasize the importance of this distinction. The two are connected, but if you treat them as if they are the same thing, they often result in a long list of abstract concepts and specific actions that are overly complex and of little value. The common mistake organizations make when they fail to see this distinction is that the values do a lot of the heavy lifting, not unlike the mission statements that have gone the way of the dodo bird. If you can't see a distinction between codifying your values *and* how you want to behave in service of those values, neither exercise will be as effective.

I also need to confess that engaging in a conversation about values these days is a little more challenging because the term has been so heavily overused by corporations that fail to demonstrate them through their actions. That is because over time, values have evolved from a declaration of an organization's aspirations to a recruiting and marketing tactic. In recent years, and especially since the COVID-19 pandemic, there has been a clear shift in the way individuals approach their careers.

In previous generations, my own included, the primary goal when pursuing a career was to find something that you could excel in and, by extension, make lots of money doing. Sure, you wanted to find a job that inspired you, a team you enjoyed being around, and a role that was a strong match to your skills and interests, but most of these alignments were in the service of greater compensation. If you were inspired by your work, you would be more inclined to go the extra mile, more likely to get a promotion, and more likely to make more money. If you found a job that aligned to your natural talents and interests, you'd also probably get promoted faster and make more money.

That all changed in the mid-2010s, when the millennial generation started to enter the workforce in large numbers, bringing with them a different set of career priorities. If you go back into the news archives from about 2014 to 2018, you'll find headlines about work dominated by confusion over this new generation of workers who had, in statistically significant numbers, prioritized things like "purpose" and "meaning," and here's the big one, "values," over compensation. This conversation got so much attention because it so starkly contrasted with the priorities of previous generations. If you were an employer in the mid-2000s, reading headlines like "Millennials want purpose over paycheck," you might start thinking to yourself, "Hey, I could pay these kids a little less and have an easier time hiring them, as long as I offer them a sense of purpose."[1] And thus began the era of corporate values as a recruiting tool.

In the ensuing years, the trend took off like wildfire. First in Silicon Valley, home of the world's most competitive talent market at the time, where such workplace trends often begin, before popping up in other places that were competing for the same tech talent. Then it became popular in tech-adjacent industries, then in the labor economy more broadly. By the late 2010s, you couldn't apply for a minimum-wage job at a grocery store without finding their corporate values prominently displayed on its careers and recruiting page.

In the best-case scenarios, organizations and their leaders would put a lot of time and energy into constructing "values statements" and encourage everyone in the organization, themselves included, to consult them before making any consequential decisions. In most cases, however, they remained little more than a recruiting tool—a signal to job seekers that they could find meaningful work here because of how prominently we display our list of warm-and-fuzzy feeling altruistic values. Oh, and by the way, those values come at the cost of compensation. But hey, wouldn't you rather work somewhere that shares your values than somewhere that pays you more?

You could visit just about any corporate campus in Silicon Valley and find a list of corporate values hung prominently in the lobby, on the same day that the company's executives are hauled into congress to explain behaviors that clearly divert from those stated values. By my estimation, the most egregious example of this is the Elizabeth Holmes–led Theranos debacle that resulted in the company's demise in late 2018. Using the Wayback Machine to review archived websites, Theranos actively recruited employees with the promise that joining the firm would allow one to "do work that will change the world." Well, Theranos and Holmes didn't change the world, but instead duped investors, lied to employees and customers, and nurtured a culture of secrecy and division. Holmes has been ordered to report to prison in April 2023.[2,3]

For more scandalous fun, check out the travails of Travis Kalanick, founder of Uber, back in 2017. A quick internet search with the words *Kalanick*, *Uber*, and *scandal* will yield plenty of results.[4,5]

What many organizations are missing is a strong demonstration of the **be**haviors that speak to their values. More recently, however, people have begun to get more vocal about those organizations that don't take their own values seriously. The rise of anonymous employer review websites, like Glassdoor, has given current and former employees a forum for assessing and evaluating their experiences. These sites give a voice to those who see their organization demonstrate behaviors that don't align with their own values.

For much of the last decade, employers have been able to get away with having a list of values to help with their recruiting efforts, without demonstrating them through corresponding behaviors. Those days, however, are largely over. Good riddance.

Your Colleagues Are Not Your Family

One word that has been embedded into conversations about corporate culture is *family*, and, in my opinion, it's a terrible way to refer to team dynamics. It's become a common refrain from both employers and employees: "My team is a family," or "Come work for us. Our company has a real family atmosphere." While typically meant to convey a sense of warmth, belonging, and bonding, I believe the word *family* should exit our business vernacular.

Here are several reasons why:

1. *Family is precious.* Your family is one of a kind. Mine sure is—both sides. Since family is unique, it should be protected and nurtured. We shouldn't diminish or water down the concept of family by including people who will shift and change in both the short and long run. The idea of family has already become too disposable and transient. Getting divorced and pressing the reset button without engaging in the meaningful work needed to repair a marriage and keep a family together is far too easy. If we remove *family* from our business jargon, maybe we won't quit our families with the same indifference we sometimes use when we quit our jobs.

   Business relationships come and go. Family is precious and enduring. Period.

2. *Family is messy.* On a good day, a family is a messy organism. Communication within a family unit is extraordinarily difficult because our lenses are clouded by strong emotions and the intensity of the family bond. As a result, conflict is difficult to resolve and can fester for years, even decades. Factions and rifts develop as like-minded family members gravitate toward one another. Drama ensues.

   Referring to the business as a family gives implicit permission for these kinds of behaviors to take root. Whenever I hear someone describe their coworkers as "one big happy family," I also hear the undertones of dysfunction and chaos. Labeling your team as a family may unintentionally give team members permission to act badly. Yes, you may give nutty Uncle Billy a pass for his Far Right or Left political rant at Thanksgiving, but we shouldn't be handing out family passes at the office.

   Do we really want the messiness of family in our businesses? The answer is an emphatic *no*.

3. *Family is 24-7.* By definition, family is always on—a 24-7 endeavor. Thinking of the business as family risks bringing business home with you more often than you should. We should be married to our spouses, not the business. We should be able to "leave the office" and go home. During the COVID-19 pandemic, this separation became much more

difficult since, for many of us, the "office" was—and may still be—the spare bedroom down the hall, and the lines between work and home were more blurred than ever.

If you're like me and have previously made reference to the "office as a family" and want to leave that comparison in the past, but at the same time want to stress the importance of family, I recommend the adoption of a "family first" culture.

Family first is a very simple concept. If a team member has a family emergency or requires some flexibility to care for their family, respond with "family first." Repeating this tune with equity through time will send the signal that family is indeed precious, that you take family seriously, and that there is a clear separation between work and home.

Yes, there will be team members who may take advantage of this mindset in the short term. In the long run, however, retention and engagement should improve because your people will see clearly that you care about them and the balancing act they continually play between work and family.

Adopting this mindset will also shine a clear light on any lack of backup coverage or talent management redundancy issues the business may have.

Work is a wonderful place to build a professional network and forge meaningful friendships; however, work is not your family, and conflating the two can lead to serious disappointment when the stark reality that "it's just business" kicks in during tough economic times or the next restructuring.

Values and *Behaviors*

Rather than chalking your corporate culture up to being a "family-like" atmosphere, making the necessary time and putting in the work to define your values—what you stand for as an organization—is important, but that's only the first step. Your corporate values serve as your organization's cultural cornerstones. They cement a set of expectations that serve as the basis for how you expect everyone in the organization to behave, including and most importantly those at the very top.

As mentioned above, values without **be**haviors are of little consequence; you can't really have one without the other. Values without **be**haviors become hollow and meaningless, while **be**haviors have little grounding in reality without corresponding values. They are inextricably correlated, which is why it's difficult to talk about one without the other.

I think of it this way: values are like nouns and refer to an idea or object in a static state, while **be**haviors are like verbs, or action words, and you can't communicate clearly without both. That is also why I put the "be" in a special font—because they are actions. Be kind, be civil, be students of the business, be exceptional, be yourself, etc.

Demonstrating Values through *Behaviors*

At Kaplan Professional, every member of our team had a minimum of two items on their desks at all times. One was a big sign that listed our thematic goal, our standard operating objectives, and our defining objectives. The other was a mouse pad that showed our company's values and **be**haviors. Our team members literally spent their day with the company's values and **be**haviors just below their fingertips. Figure 4.1 below is a stylized version of that old Kaplan Professional mouse pad.

Figure 4.1: Bes and Values

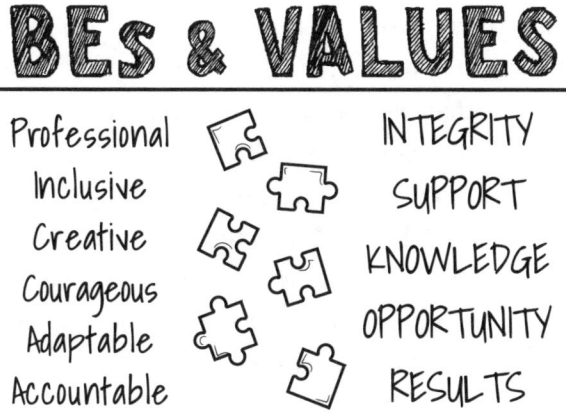

Sometimes leadership teams need some external resources when tackling hard questions, and our business was no exception. As we began a journey toward defining our values and *be*haviors, we employed the services of an external facilitator. Their job was to ask probing questions that would help the team define the organization's purpose, then its values, and finally its *be*haviors, in that order. As I've hopefully demonstrated thus far, each one builds on the other, and the ultimate goal of these exercises is to arrive at a short list—short enough to count on one hand—of crisp, clean, memorable, and easily understandable values and a similar list of corresponding *be*haviors.

Why should you keep it to less than five? I don't know about you, but that's about as many items I can go looking for at the grocery store without bringing a list, on a good day. We want values and *be*haviors to be top of mind, and if the list gets too long, most people won't be able to recall all of it.

During this mediated exercise, our leadership team put aside a sizable chunk of time, pulled out a whiteboard and dry-erase marker, and took turns putting values and *be*havior candidates up on the board. After the list was complete, we engaged in a conversation about each item and debated its inclusion, favoring those that were memorable, simple, authentic, and true to our organizational DNA.

Once we arrived at our shortlist of candidates, we had each senior leader take this list back to their team to discuss it (this is a form of catchball that we'll get into more deeply in chapter 7). Each department would then engage in a similar exercise, with their senior leader acting as the facilitator, discussing each of the candidates and making suggestions and refinements. Once that exercise was complete, team leaders assembled once again in the boardroom to share their results.

What's important to note is that we had agreed on the importance of ensuring that our *be*haviors were always aligned to our values, which is why the two were always displayed prominently together. Even if the emphasis was on *be*haviors, we felt demonstrating that connection was important—how these *be*haviors enabled us to exemplify the values we had all agreed to embrace when we joined the company. We were saying, "This is who we want to be," and "This is *how* we need to act."

By printing out our values and *be*haviors on mouse pads and other work-place paraphernalia, and displaying them prominently throughout the workplace, there really was nowhere to hide.

Equally important were the policies and procedures that reinforced them. For example, at Kaplan Professional, we made a habit of directly referencing our values and *be*haviors in employee reviews and actually scored performance based on how well employees exhibited them.

Then we went a step further and began offering awards to employees who had best demonstrated our values and *be*haviors. Someone who really exhibited exemplary accountability could get an award for doing so. At the same time, we also refrained from giving awards out to anyone who didn't check all five *be*havior boxes. Billy may have done an incredible job this year, clearly outperforming the rest of his team; but he didn't demonstrate accountability in a few critical moments, so we gave the award to someone else. In other words, nobody could receive an award without holistically demonstrating our values and *be*haviors.

In that way, we were able to ensure follow-through on the brand promise we made to prospective hires when we showed them our list of corporate values. Over time, our values and *be*haviors became so ingrained that we didn't need the visual reminders everywhere, though they remained prominently displayed. Eventually, they became second nature to everyone who worked on our team. In other words, they became woven into our culture.

Courage in Business

The top-ten lists of key human (a.k.a. soft) skills that abound in the popular business press frequently include the word *courage*.

In a business context, *courage* does not mean you're willing to run into a burning building or otherwise put your life on the line. Instead, we're talking about psychological courage, or what some would refer to as "fortitude."

Fortitude is an interesting word and is typically defined as "strength of mind that enables a person to encounter danger or bear pain or adversity with courage." While most of us don't have jobs where we encounter physical danger, we do routinely encounter adversity and situations that can lead to emotional anguish.

Ever been asked to do something at work that made you feel like you can't tell your mom about it? Ever had to hold a coworker or team accountable for substandard performance? Ever had to challenge a hierarchical superior in public or private? Ever had to admit an error and take responsibility for not holding up your end of the bargain? Many of us would rather go skydiving or engage in some other risky activity than engage in constructive conflict.

These are all situations in which real courage is needed to speak up and do the right thing for yourself, your peers, your customers, and the business. This is where the values and *be*haviors you've outlined face their ultimate test. You need courage to follow through on them, but failing to do so will have consequences that can reverberate throughout the organization. Remember: "You are what you allow."

For courage to flourish within the culture of your organization, leaders must create an environment of *psychological safety*. If new ideas or challenges to authority are met with a swift smackdown, then courage will not be fostered. In a smackdown culture, everyone will be looking to protect themselves, their jobs, and their immediate priorities.

Let's suppose you're a leader operating in a smackdown culture and are awakening to the benefits of changing tack toward trust, collaboration, diversity, inclusion, and constructive conflict. Moving the culture from smackdown toward "high trust and high accountability" may seem daunting.

The starting point for the journey to change your culture takes real courage and is an application of courage that doesn't get nearly enough airplay. In addition to my previously stated recommendation to install continuous improvement plus organizational health guardrails to improve transparency, collaboration, and results, I recommend you find the courage to hire people who have the potential to surpass you.

But simply hiring team members who can surpass you isn't enough; helping team members achieve their potential by continually investing in their development through coaching, mentoring, and formal and informal learning opportunities is also essential. This investment must be coupled with making the time and space for learning a business imperative—not just piling learning on top of everyone's day job. In chapter 6, we'll be taking a deep dive into learning and coaching.

In addition, the concept of equity should be applied to decisions regarding coaching and learning or development opportunities for your team members. Reserving development opportunities solely for those who fit in the upper right boxes of a nine box or those who have otherwise been labeled as high potentials (HIPOs) should be avoided.

Skill inventory alignment conversations should take place on an ongoing basis with all team members. The purpose of these conversations is to identify skill gaps and experiential learning opportunities to fill those gaps. Having skill alignment conversations with everyone will help avoid unintended discrimination and the inevitable (and unnecessary) team tension that will result between the "haves and have-nots" if learning is reserved for HIPOs.

Some leaders may bristle at my recommendations, especially the insinuation that many leaders consciously or subconsciously hire team members who they have a higher probability of controlling or molding into their own image versus those who will challenge them and the status quo.

If you take a step back and recognize that most of us are conflict avoiders and carry around a great deal of self-doubt and hidden insecurities, a bit of quiet self-reflection and personal vulnerability will likely uncover episodes and actions that align with management and hiring practices that have led to suboptimal results. From my own personal experience and self-reflection, I can attest to past hiring decisions that were less than courageous.

Real courage is needed to adopt a stewardship mindset to leadership and accept that the business and team are not about you but are instead about helping the business's most valuable asset—its people—thrive in the current and future world of work.

Six Tips for Crafting Your Organization's Value and *Behavior* Statements

1. *Start from the top.* As mentioned at the beginning of this chapter, culture starts at the top. As a result, you can't engage in an honest conversation about values and *be*haviors without the input of those in leadership positions. In drafting your values, assembling a small team of company executives, including the CEO and any remaining founders, as well as a few key employees, is usually best. If senior leaders believe in the values they author, and demonstrate them through their actions, the rest of the organization's culture will eventually follow suit.

2. *Keep it short.* As with vision and purpose statements, the more words you use, the less likely those words will be remembered. Notice how Kaplan's values and *be*haviors from figure 4.1 are a single word each? While you don't always need to be that concise, you should always try to keep it as short, and thus easy to remember, as possible. When in doubt, use the grandmother test. If it's not something your grandmother (or grandfather or mom or dad or uncle or aunt, etc.) could read and easily understand, it's probably too jargony or complicated for your average employee or prospective hire.

3. *Be authentic.* The most important feature of your values and *be*haviors is authenticity. People need to believe that *you believe* in order to believe themselves. Once you've codified your values, going back and removing any one of them is hard, and failing to live up to a single one gives the rest of the team permission to ignore the others. As a result, anything that isn't a natural fit could threaten the integrity of the entire exercise.

4. *Take your time.* Coming up with a list of values and *be*haviors can take time, and that's okay—it's supposed to. This is one of the few instances in which letting perfection win out over the "good enough" is okay. This shouldn't be a quick-and-easy process; it requires deep and authentic soul-searching. Don't try and skip to the end.

5. *Be specific.* Your values and *be*haviors should be broad enough to be applicable to a range of situations and decisions but shouldn't be so

broad that they lose their meaning. Your values and **be**haviors should be specific to your organization, without being too jargony for your staff to internalize.

6. *Weave them into everything you do.* This piece of advice is straight from Lencioni himself. From hiring and promotion to communications and performance reviews, everything comes back to values and **be**haviors. As demonstrated from my personal experience above, the more you weave them into day-to-day decisions and interactions, the more they become ingrained and gradually morph from a wish list to a lived experience, or what we call culture.

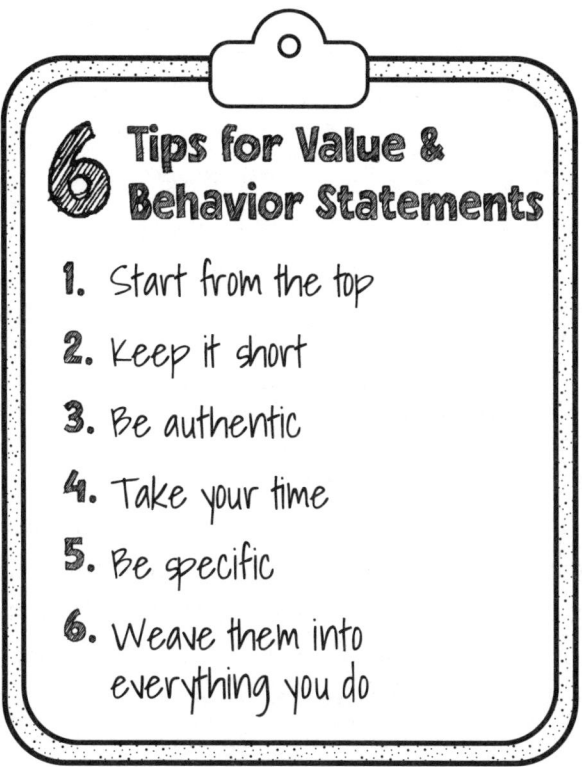

6 Tips for Value & Behavior Statements

1. Start from the top
2. Keep it short
3. Be authentic
4. Take your time
5. Be specific
6. Weave them into everything you do

Value and *Behavior* Statement Examples

Though a bit wordier, what makes this list of values and *be*haviors particularly meaningful is that they were part of early company lore, when it was
still just a modestly sized search engine. At that time the founders came
up with its list of "Ten Things We Know to Be True," which was later trans-
lated into a list of values and *be*haviors that would serve as the basis for its
culture through rapid growth.[6] While history might find that some of these
values were ill-informed—I don't know if we're as convinced democracy is
still working on the web, for instance—they come from an authentic place
and have served the company well through its meteoric rise.

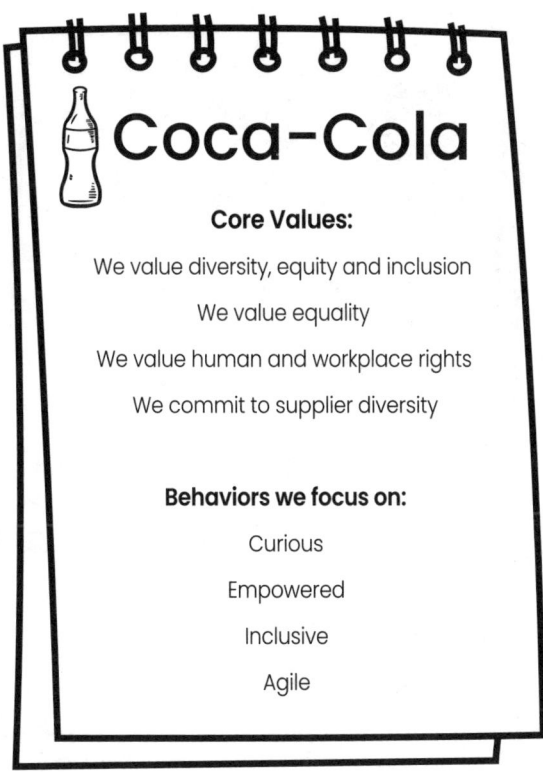

Coca-Cola is one of very few companies that actually splits their values and **be**haviors, which already puts them ahead in my books.[7] While their value statements could be shortened a bit, you can list them on one hand. Similarly, the **be**haviors are concise, memorable, and to the point.[8] The company also offers further explanation of each on its website, including their definitions of each value and **be**havior. This is one of the best examples I can offer of a company that understands the difference between values and **be**haviors and the importance of separating the two. As always, Coca-Cola is very refreshing!

The list of values Uber displays on its website each have a corresponding **be**havior or way of implementing that value, which is a step in the right direction. The list is also very specific to Uber, while being broad enough to apply to everyone from the front office to the food delivery bike. Though it's a bit wordy, and while its corporate culture has very publicly failed to demonstrate these values in the past, their values and **be**haviors offer a strong reinforcement of the culture the company hopes to achieve.

Amazon

- Customer Obsession
- Ownership
- Invent and Simplify
- Are Right, A Lot
- Learn and Be Curious
- Hire and Develop the Best
- Insist on the Highest Standards
- Think Big
- Bias for Action
- Frugality
- Earn Trust
- Dive Deep
- Have Backbone; Disagree and Commit
- Deliver Results
- Strive to be Earth's Best Employer
- Success and Scale Bring Broad Responsibility

Did you also give up halfway through reading this? For a company that invented quick delivery, this list of values is anything but efficient. Amazon's fourteen "leadership principles," as they call them, leave a lot to be desired. While some make a lot of sense and are really authentic to the brand, others are just BS. Sorry, Amazon, but "earning trust" and being "earth's best employer" isn't exactly your strong suit; just ask the warehouse workers who can't get fifteen minutes for a bathroom break. These statements are also all over the place in terms of clarity and brevity, with some offering just one word and others bordering on a full sentence. There are also a few I would have left off the list. For example, declaring that one of your values is that your leadership staff "are right, a lot" is a little bit contrived. On the company's website, they further explain, "Leaders are right a lot. They have strong judgment and good instincts. They seek diverse perspectives and work to disconfirm their beliefs." But I'm not buying it. Declaring that your leaders are often right makes it very difficult for staff to offer those diverse perspectives you claim to seek.

Short, simple, easy to understand and easy to internalize, Salesforce's list of "culture and values" looks like a footnote compared to Amazon's, and I mean that in a good way. While perhaps too broad to be entirely specific to Salesforce, the company does offer a lengthy description on its website about what each value means to them and what actions the company has taken to live those values. The only problem is that the company hasn't made the time to also offer an equally simple and easy to understand list of **be**haviors that accompany their values. Having lengthy blog posts with examples of how the company demonstrates these values is great, but not everyone is going to read and remember all that information. Ideally, there would be an equally simple list of one- or two-word **be**haviors to go with it.

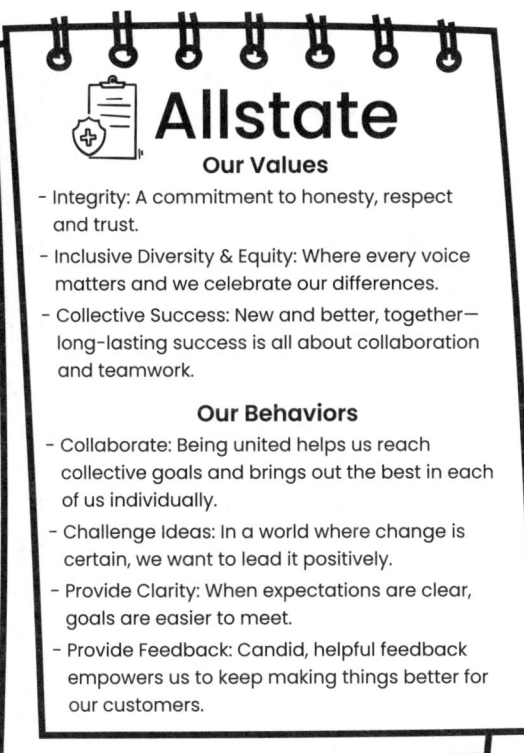

It might be difficult to fit all these **be**haviors and values on a mouse pad, but it's great to see another company that understands the importance of separating values and **be**haviors. Allstate could have gotten the point across in one or two words for each, which would have made these values and **be**haviors easier to memorize and ultimately live.[9] That said, the company has clearly outlined what they value and how they act in service of those values, and that's a great start.

Corporate Culture and Diversity

I can't conclude this conversation about culture without first acknowledging how, in some egregious circumstances, culture has been used to justify homogeny. During the period I alluded to earlier, when corporate culture was in vogue as a recruitment tactic, and before there were any real insights into whether or not organizations were living those values, we saw some pretty ugly examples of culture being used in the worst possible way: as an exclusionary tactic for those who weren't a "good fit."

Organizations were able to use this broad term to turn away candidates with no other justification, which often affected the most marginalized members of our society in a disproportionate way. Those who misinterpreted the whole point of the movement toward defining and celebrating workplace culture took it as license to only hire people from the same backgrounds, with the same education, the same upbringing—whatever euphemistic term you want to use for other straight white men who went to the same top-tier universities.

Stating the obvious, I'm a sixty-year-old white male from one of the least diverse places in the country. What do I know about diversity? Probably not enough to be your primary source on the matter, and I strongly encourage you to expand your horizons on this topic, but I'll share what I do know and what I can prove.

First and foremost, diverse teams outperform their competitors. For all the thinly veiled xenophobia out there claiming that organizations benefit from ensuring everyone "speaks the same language," what countless studies have shown is that organizations that promote a diversity of experiences, backgrounds, and perspective are more innovative and profitable than their competitors.[10]

Also important to note is that culture and "cultural fit" have absolutely nothing to do with your race, gender, ethnicity, societal and cultural background, education, etc. Instead, culture should be about values and **be**haviors. If a candidate I'm interviewing is a white man from a farming community in Wisconsin or a female immigrant from Kenya doesn't matter. What matters is that they believe in integrity, support, knowledge, opportunity, and results—that is, our core values. Values and **be**haviors are not a litmus test for homogeneity; they are a set of shared aspirations and operating procedures. If you believe in the things we outline as priorities in the form of our corporate values and **be**haviors, then you're already a "cultural fit."

A brighter, more enlightened future is one in which we all stand up for diversity, especially those of us who have the privilege of choice to speak up. And yes, I'm speaking directly to my fellow white males who were born into a position of privilege like I was.

If the previous paragraph made you recoil or get defensive (as it would have to an earlier version of me), I recommend that you not immediately react or lash out. Instead, find a quiet place to live with and process your reaction and ask why you feel that way. I'm not admonishing you or painting you into a corner. Rather, I feel strongly that you'll benefit from some self-reflection on where you are in your own personal journey with diversity, equity, and inclusion.

By listening to more viewpoints, we can do more, learn more, and create a geopolitical environment that fosters the kind creativity and innovation that will be necessary to ensure the future of our species.

So where do we start? We start by supporting the efforts of organizations like the Kaplan Educational Foundation. You see, education is the ticket to that brighter, enlightened future described above. For us to succeed, education cannot be reserved for the elite—we must improve access, affordability, and outcomes. Clearly, education is important to me personally, and to my former employer, Kaplan, as an organization. I encourage everyone to take some time, do some research, and find causes that similarly speak to them on both a personal and professional level.

Citing the old African proverb: "If you want to go fast, go alone. If you want to go far, go together." I'd like to go far and leave a robust, vibrant, sustainable pale blue dot to future generations. Let's choose "together."

5

Death, Taxes, and Change

As the old saying goes, there are two constants in this world: *death* and *taxes*. In my opinion, we need to update this adage with one more constant: *change*.

The funny thing about these constants (not in a "haha" sense) is that humans typically have challenging relationships with each one. We routinely avoid conversations about death, opting instead to imagine that we'll live forever. We often bury our heads in the sand to avoid thinking about our fragility and limited time on our pale blue dot until it's too late to do or say the truly important stuff. We don't write down our final wishes, avoid completing health-care advance directives, and leave our loved ones with a huge mess to clean up once we're gone because we didn't develop a legally binding will or trust.

To say we have a complicated relationship with taxes, too, would be an understatement. We love to hate the idea of taxation and work extraordinarily hard—to the point of contortion—to avoid or minimize our tax burdens. We rail against governmental inefficiency, argue endlessly about the appropriate balance between "big" and "small" government, and put our thumbs on the scales of the programs that have meaning to us at the expense of programs that help groups we don't care about or can't relate to. We want every one of our hard-earned dollars accounted for and are prone to outrage when, inevitably, some is spent in ways we can't or won't understand.

Alas, I could go on talking about death and taxes, but we're here to chat about the importance of developing a deeper understanding of the third constant—change.

Why Is Change So Important?

Change is everywhere. Change is necessary. On balance, change is good. Change for the sake of change is bad and represents a significant form of waste. As a part of our continuous improvement practice, we should keep a vigilant eye out for *unnecessary* change.

Speaking of complicated relationships, the important thing to note about change is that most humans *abhor* it. That's right—we avoid change like the plague. In fact, neuroscientists have found that our natural hatred of change is built into our brains.[1] Predictability and repetition bring comfort because they allow our brains to coast on autopilot. Throw a wrench into that machine in the form of change, however, and our brains go into hyperdrive, considering implications, ripple effects, and digging deep into our mental archives for clues on how to adapt. We're forced out of a steady state and into one of chaos and uncertainty, a process that is less than comfortable. The amygdala, located near the base of the brain, interprets this activity as an incoming threat and releases hormones that trigger our flight-or-fight response.[2] Feeling like those around you are actively fighting against change or actively running away from it, is not an illusion—it's evolution. We are literally wired to fight or run from change. In fact, research shows that monkeys do a better job at managing change than humans.[3]

Similar to death and taxes, we contort our lives and go to extraordinary lengths to keep things just the way they are. In the face of change we don't understand, we rally around messages and leaders who falsely promise a return to simpler times. So much of our modern culture wars goes back to this basic human neurological feature. Just about all our political discourse comes down to the threat of change versus the threat of stagnation. The world is constantly changing, and we must adapt to those changes. But change goes against our every natural instinct. No wonder it's hard to get individuals on board with even minor changes to the status quo. They're not intentionally being unreasonably stubborn; they're literally wired to resist it. As time marches inexorably on, the only things that can send us backward are a nuclear winter, a massive solar flare, or some other scorched-earth natural disaster—all things that most rational humans want to avoid. In the absence of a horrific natural disaster, the only way is *forward*.

Interestingly, death and change are connected to one another. How? In my book *Balancing Act: Teach, Coach, Mentor, Inspire*, I introduce the concept of entropy. Put simply, entropy, which is technically based on the second law of thermodynamics, states that over time, and in the absence of intervention, *everything falls apart*. Hence, if we do nothing or the bare minimum to maintain the current state, our bodies break down and eventually die. Over the course of our lives, we apply many interventions that are designed to promote change and growth that will (hopefully) delay our ultimate demise. Note that the same concept applies to the shiny new car or the cool new phone you just bought. With no intervention, they will fall apart and cease being useful tools. Even with strong intervention, those tools will eventually succumb to the ravages of time. In other words, change is inevitable, yet we are wired to resist it.

ENTROPY

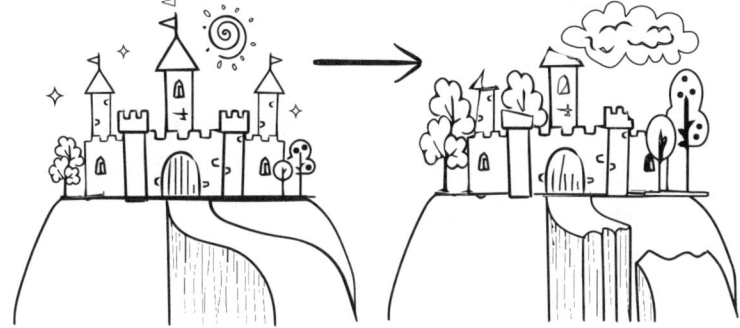

What makes business different is that a business is a *going concern*. What this means is that a business should—theoretically—last forever, at least on paper. But just like a human or your automobile, entropy is out to get your business. Without significant maintenance and substantive change through time, your business will fall apart and return to the stardust from whence it came. Therefore, change is a necessary condition for the success and survival of any business. Operating a business without a plan for how to deal with change—or imagining that change is not an important feature of success—is akin to having a death wish. Left unattended, the opposing forces of change and entropy will rip the organization apart.

The American journalist and novelist Hunter S. Thompson wasn't always known for clear thinking, but on occasion he offered his readers a few deeply profound words of wisdom. One of the *Fear and Loathing in Las Vegas* author's most famous quotes gets at the heart of this dichotomy. He wrote: "A man who procrastinates in his choosing will inevitably have his choice made for him by circumstance."[4] Think about it this way: if you are deciding between two different cars—or any other item you want to purchase—and you continually delay purchasing one out of fear of making the wrong choice, eventually the more popular one will run out of stock, and just like that the choice is no longer yours. Our natural tendency, built deep into the infrastructure of our brains, is to resist choosing, to avoid changing, as much as possible. But waiting until the last moment to accept the inevitability of change only leaves you with fewer options and less room to adapt.

Leaders and Change

Early in my career as an executive leader, I took the "Andy said" approach to management. I did very little to empower independent or collaborative decision-making. Instead, nearly every decision about the organization came across my desk—even decisions on what kinds of holiday gifts we should buy for employees and vendors! I'm not going to rehash the challenges with the "Andy said" approach here. What's important is its impact on how change is managed within the organization.

Directive managers with underdeveloped egos and emotional quotients (EQ) will tend to make a decision to "take the next competitive hill," wave their arm, point in a forward direction, and call back to their people with a strong voice, "Follow me!" Directive leaders then start running toward the execution of the plan, get ahead of the team, turn around and scratch their heads, bewildered that no one is behind them.

The directive leader with a low EQ has already processed the upcoming change and is mentally prepared for myriad potential outcomes. In contrast, the rest of the team—having learned of the plan and upcoming change much later than the leader—are milling about, stuck wondering what the plan, and the change that accompanies it, means for them personally and their immediate team. I've found myself in this position many times—naked and standing alone out front—wondering why in the heck it's taking everyone so long to get on board. I would mutter under my breath, "What on earth is the matter with everyone?" It turned out that the problem was my lack of focus on change management.

During my career, I've analyzed scores of businesses for potential acquisition, written nearly as many acquisition memos, and have led the purchase of more companies than I can count on the digits that populate my hands. I won't name names, but on one occasion I drove an acquisition to completion but did not properly gauge the impact the acquisition would have on morale and team psyche. I checked all the boxes of organizational fit, profitability, consumer need, etc., but I totally ignored the massive change impact that integration would have. This lack of focus on change ultimately led to the destruction of the value the acquisition promised.

In *my* head, the transaction was a great deal and was going to be a phenomenal addition to the portfolio. I had already fully rationalized the change in my mind and was ready and raring to go. Senior management was with me, our investors were with me, but the rest of the team was not. They were still stuck on questions like: "What about me?" "Tell me again what this business does and why we're buying it?" "Why are we doing this now?" and, "How will this impact existing workflows and customers?"

When the deal was done, and it became time for integration, it failed miserably because individuals and teams were working at cross-purposes.

In fact, some were *actively* working to ensure the integration failed. My lack of willingness or ability to properly gauge how the deal would be processed from a change management perspective destroyed value on a number of levels.

Modeling Change

It turns out that what ailed the team was that *everyone*—and that's not an exaggeration—had a change curve that was unique to them. Like fingerprints or the nooks and crannies of the outer ear, the human change curve is distinct, and no two are the same. Moreover, each individual will have multiple change curves that apply to different change events. We make the fatal error to stereotype and assume that certain groups of humans process change in a particular way. Sure, stereotypical groupings can help explain human behavior at a high level, but when you're managing a team and dealing with change, it's best to assume *everyone* will approach change differently.

Therefore, understanding the concept of the human change curve can be very useful to help us frame how our people will respond to change. It helps us understand how, as organizational leaders, we can manage change to ensure we're driving optimal results and not generating unnecessary emotional and physical waste within our business.

Change management modeling and consulting is a thriving cottage industry. From small to midsize companies, like Prosci, Kotter, and Conner Partners, to large consulting firms, like BCG, Bain, and McKinsey, there is no shortage of third parties who are ready and willing to jump in and help manage change and transformation within your organization. In this chapter, we're not going to reinvent the wheel but simply discuss the importance of organizational change and outline the components of a generic change management curve.

In figure 5.1, we've drawn two change management curves that belong to two different people—individual one and individual two. Curve C_2 shows that individual two processes change more efficiently, whereas curve C_1 shows that individual one processes change less efficiently. Note that each person goes through roughly the same process of grappling with change.

If we look at curve C_1, we can see that upon the announcement of Event A, morale and/or confidence grows. This period is short-lived and is primarily attributed to a combination of unjustified initial excitement and shock. This initial excitement and shock quickly transitions to a state of denial, denoted by the initial peak of curve C_1 at point D_1. Frustration sets in with the decision, which is typically exacerbated by a lack of communication or clarity regarding the "why" behind the change that's driven by Event A. Point D_2 represents a period of depression, anger, or what some change experts refer to as the "valley of despair." The individual represented by curve C_1 then spends time wallowing in the valley of despair before beginning the process of experimentation with the change wrought by Event A. This experimentation ultimately leads to a decision to accept the change, integrate it into workflow, and ultimately reach a new steady state of morale, confidence, and competence represented by point B_1.

Figure 5.1: Stylized Change Curves

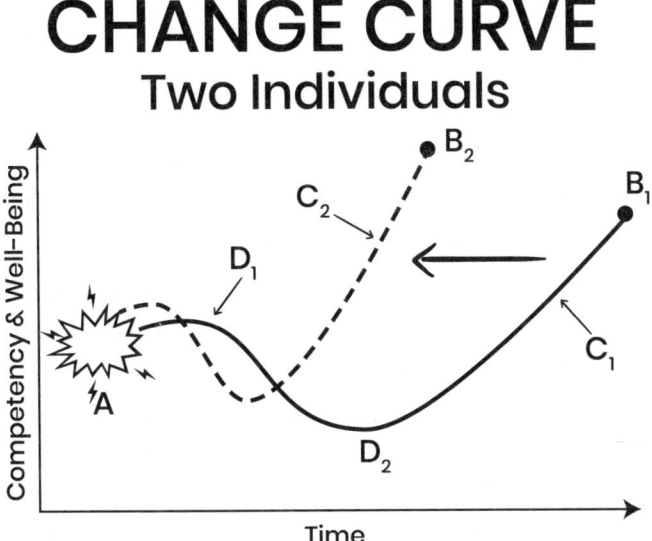

Looking at the change journey for individual two (C_2) in figure 5.1 shows a similarly shaped but much more efficient response to the change brought about by the announcement of the same Event A. The period of initial shock and excitement is much shorter, and the valley of despair is not as deep or as long-lived as that of the colleague represented by curve C_1. Also, the time necessary for experimentation, decision-making, and acceptance is much shorter.

Note also that individual two is able to achieve a higher level of morale, confidence, and competence once the change event has been fully integrated into their "new normal" as indicated by the vertical distance between point B_2 and B_1. This is a critical point that's often lost in the shuffle of discussions on the topic of change management: that *learning* and *growth* are key components of the change process!

It's also instructive to review best and worst-case change curves to illustrate the boundaries of a change process. In figure 5.2 on the next page, the best-case scenario is shown in the diagram to the left. In this case, the individual processes change efficiently—moving from a steady state of competence, confidence, and morale prechange to the new steady postchange very quickly. Note that there is a nearly linear increase in competence, confidence, and morale during a relatively short adjustment period. No valley of despair, no loopbacks—only acceptance, learning, and growth.

In contrast, the hypothetical individual shown in the diagram to the right in figure 5.2 moves slowly from initial steady state to their postchange steady state. Note that competence, confidence, and morale all deteriorate over a lengthy adjustment period as the change is consistently resisted as are opportunities for learning and growth. This individual yearns for the past and actively works against the forces of change in their organization, likely becoming actively disengaged in the process. Their active resistance to change *will* negatively impact their colleagues and *will* turn the atmosphere into a toxic wasteland if left unattended and unchecked.

Figure 5.2: Best- and Worst-Case Change Curves

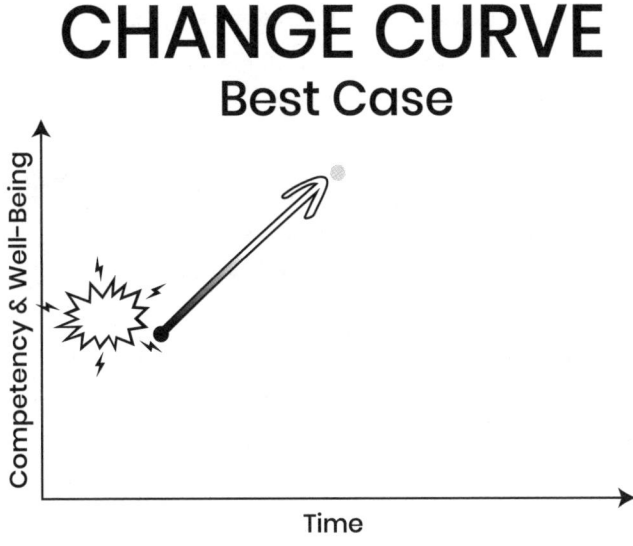

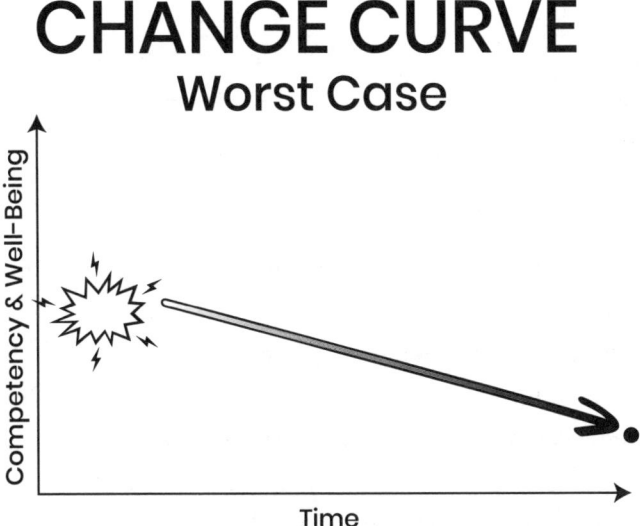

If you're reading this and seeing a close correlation to the five stages of grief—denial, anger, bargaining, depression, acceptance—that's not an accident. The way we process the two greatest inevitabilities in life—death and change (and perhaps to a lesser extent taxes too)—follows the same emotional process.

Change curve models also demonstrate how human beings can interpret and react to the same information in dramatically different ways. That is why I've put chapter 5 on change right after chapters 2, 3, and 4 on purpose, vision, and culture, respectively. This is the whole punchline of the book up until this point—your organization will always have plenty of opportunities to pursue positive change, but if you don't take the time to understand, implement, and manage change, the previous parts become moot.

You can't control change, but you can manage the process. As I've learned firsthand, if you don't try to manage change, it will manage you. In other words, if you delay in your choosing—if you continue to resist change—you will find yourself at the mercy of circumstance. And if you aren't careful in how you bring others along for the ride, you might turn around one day and find that they're no longer behind you.

One final note on change models. The change curves for individuals one and two shown in figure 5.1 on page 77 are stylized versions of the Elisabeth Kübler-Ross Change Curve®, which was adapted from the five stages of grief that were introduced in her book *On Death and Dying* (1969).

Change in Business

Applying the concept to large global enterprises, change has long been a sticky subject. On the one hand, most of the world's biggest companies throughout history achieved their success, or a portion of it, by anticipating and reacting to change *faster* than anyone else. Consider three of the top-ten companies on the Fortune 500 list today: Amazon, Apple, and Alphabet (parent company of Google). Whether it's the merging of technology and logistics, the simplification and proliferation of personal computing devices, or the ubiquity of information in the digital realm, each of these companies was built during, or just prior to, the onset of major change trends. Do you know what else these companies have in common? They're all relatively young. Amazon was created in 1994; Google was founded in 1998; and while Apple had been around since the mid-1970s, the company was in a period of stagnation before one of its founders was welcomed back into the fold.

When Steve Jobs rejoined Apple in 1997, he believed we were on the cusp of a new era in personal computing. And when he got onstage to introduce the iPhone ten years later, among his first words to the audience were "every once in a while a revolutionary product comes along and *changes* everything."[5] Later, in that same speech, Jobs added that the iPhone was "literally five years ahead of any other mobile phone."[6]

One last thing these three companies have in common: they champion innovation and consider their adaptation to change as a competitive advantage.

So what does this tell us about the relationship between change and business? For one thing, in business, success is fleeting. Some of the companies that topped the Fortune 500 list just twenty-five years ago have fallen off it completely, while new companies that hadn't even been conceived of twenty-five years ago have taken their place. The second is that success requires a certain embrace of change. Businesses don't need a crystal ball, though one would be helpful, but they do need to operate under the assumption that change is constant and adapt accordingly. This is, of course, no small feat. As businesses get bigger, change becomes more difficult and complicated. Former president Barack Obama often compared changing the direction of the American government to steering an ocean liner—the bigger the machine, the harder it is to maneuver. But avoiding a change in direction is always riskier than changing course in the face of new obstacles and circumstances. Making change incremental, working closely with your team to blunt the natural tendencies of team members to resist those changes, and working with folks on various points along the change curve are all key in steering that ocean liner through ever-shifting waters.

Recommendations for Managing Change

Now that we've told some stories, talked about why understanding our relationship with change is so critical, and introduced the basics of change modeling, let's get into some specific recommendations for managing change that apply to both leaders and individual contributors.

- *Hone your listening skills.* One of the most important things you can do to manage change is *listen.* Simply making the time and effort to listen carefully to what's being said at the time of a major change announcement will result in fewer unforced errors in understanding the meaning of and any nuance behind a big change announcement.
- *Double down on clarity and consistency.* Frequent communication through multiple channels and modalities is critical. Ensure the message surrounding a change event is clear and that the "why" is as simple and straightforward as possible. Clarity, frequency, and consistency are key. Messages that change or are incongruent will cause loopbacks that send everyone back to square one.
- *Be calm and patient.* Jumping to conclusions leads to misunderstandings that can generate unnecessary emotional waste and lengthen the duration of any change cycle. Getting all worked up only generates excess frustration, which has the nasty effect of shutting the brain off to new information—information that might be helpful in navigating through change.
- *Focus.* During a change event, it can be really easy to get pulled in multiple directions by different narratives as others in your orbit, who are also affected by the change event, attempt to sway your opinion, protect turf, or build an opposition coalition. Instead, focus on you, your needs, and what you can control.
- *Get educated.* I can't stress enough the importance of education to the process of change. Unfortunately, I've seen it far too often in my career, where a change event happens and individuals dig in their heels, refuse to learn about the change, refuse to learn new skills that will help in navigating the change, and ultimately miss a huge opportunity for advancement and personal and professional growth. Fixed mindsets and change are like oil and water. Education is perhaps the most powerful tool for pushing forward on a change curve and minimizing the most neurologically uncomfortable aspects of any given change.

- *It's a journey.* Although most change models are shown graphically as elegant curves with distinct peaks and troughs, real life does not behave that way. As investor and author Ray Dalio shows elegantly in his thirty-minute video based on his 2019 book, *Principles of Success*, life is filled with disappointments, loopbacks, and obstacles that must be overcome.[7]

- *Remember that everyone is different.* Avoid stereotypes and continually remind yourself that even though on the surface it may appear that a group is handling change in the same way or that an individual in the group is "just fine," under the surface the story may be very different. Avoid blanket assumptions and remember that change is hard for everyone. We are all unique. We all have feelings. No one is perfect. We all need time to process change.

7 Recommendations for Managing Change

1. Hone your listening skills
2. Double down on clarity and consistency
3. Be calm and patient
4. Focus
5. Get educated
6. It's a journey
7. Remember that everyone is different

I've seen the story play out time and again—leaders convince themselves that "everyone will get it" and, as a result, convince themselves that investment in understanding and managing change journeys is not necessary.

To put it bluntly, if you don't manage change, change will manage you. If your business does not have a solid approach to managing change, chaos will reign supreme, and projects will fail for seemingly inexplicable reasons. You'll end up scratching your head as I did and wonder, "Where did everyone go?" as you stand alone, exposed to the elements out in front.

6

Learning and Coaching

At this pivotal moment in human history, as we progress through the Fourth Industrial Revolution, learning and development cannot remain an afterthought.

The traditional approach to learning and development operates on an as-needed basis. You set up shop, develop a strategy, start doing the work, and then your business is off to the races generating revenue! Then, as you near the end of that first chaotic year, someone in HR inquires about your future learning needs. The learning and development (L&D) team, who spend much of the year in some back office, puts forward a team-building retreat that squeezes in some broad educational seminars between beanbag tossing sessions. And there you have it—another box checked.

The problem with that approach is that it no longer fits the reality of today's business environment. In fact, it didn't really fit previous business environments either. When faced with an employee who no longer has the skills necessary for the job, management typically has two options: They can take the difficult route of training and upskilling the staff member, getting them ready to manage the changing business landscape. Or they can take the easy route—fire this underskilled staffer and replace them with someone who has the necessary abilities.

While neither approach is ideal, one is most certainly better than the other.

The easy route, that of firing and replacing, might seem like a simple solution on the surface, but it comes with tremendous costs, some of which are impossible to measure. Among the organizations that have tried to pinpoint the more measurable expenditures, Gallup's "conservative" estimate for replacing an employee is between one-half to two times the employee's annual salary.[1] HR analyst and former principal of Bersin by Deloitte, Josh Bersin, suggests those costs actually range from "tens of thousands of dollars to one and a half to two times their annual salary," once you account for the "total costs" of losing an employee. Those calculations include:

- Cost of hiring a new person (interviewing, screening, hiring);
- Cost of onboarding a new person (training, management time);
- Lost productivity (a new person may take one to two years to reach the productivity of an existing person);
- Lost engagement (other employees who see high turnover disengage and lose productivity);
- Customer service and errors (new employees take longer and are often less adept at solving problems);
- Training cost (over two to three years you likely invest 10–20 percent of an employee's salary or more in training); and
- Cultural impact (whenever someone leaves, others take time to ask why).

I would add one more important intangible to this otherwise comprehensive list of turnover costs, and that's employee relationships. According to a 2018 study by Gallup, those who maintain close relationships with their colleagues are twice as likely to be engaged in their work, produce higher quality work, are better at engaging with customers, are more satisfied, and are less likely to get injured on the job.[2]

Letting go of someone's close friend and colleague can significantly impact their productivity, reversing a lot of the positive work that was outlined in previous sections aimed at improving engagement. You can create a great working environment with a clear purpose, vision, and culture, but all that work goes by the wayside the moment you fire someone's favorite coworker, especially if the option to upskill and keep them was overlooked.

Hopefully, by now I've demonstrated why the "easy route" isn't so easy, but the harder route also has flaws. Upskilling and training staff on an as-needed basis can leave organizations understaffed and underskilled, because training will always be reactionary. If you need a new skill or competency two months from now, but the training program requires more than two months to complete, what do you do in the interim?

Instead, organizations need to develop systems for anticipating their skill and talent needs before those needs arise. In other words, organizations need to weave coaching and learning into the fabric of the business itself. In today's rapidly changing business landscape, organizations that want to remain competitive cannot afford to fire and rehire staff as needed, nor can they maintain an as-needed, ad hoc training and development program.

The Reskilling Revolution versus the Clay Layer

In its seminal work, published in January 2019, the World Economic Forum laid out a compelling case for a Reskilling Revolution rooted in the supply-demand realities of future job markets. Its follow-on report, published in January 2020, identifies specific job clusters in which the demand for reskilling will likely be highest.[3] Both reports are recommended reading for academics and learning professionals, business executives, and government officials who are responsible for shaping corporate strategy, institutional planning, and governmental policy related to economic growth fueled by human ingenuity.

For those unfamiliar with these studies, the following are key highlights:

- Sixty percent of corporations surveyed view skill gaps in their local labor market as the primary barrier to adoption of new technologies, such as data analytics, the internet of things, machine learning, wearables, etc. Forty-six percent of respondents indicated that a lack of leadership capability is a barrier to adoption.

- Human skills such as emotional intelligence, leadership and social influence, creativity, and critical thinking rank among the top-ten emerging skills for the next decade.
- The "professional job clusters" identified as areas for the most change over the next ten years are not exclusively technological. Sales, marketing, and content, as well as people and culture, are on the list of the top growth areas for the jobs of the future.

A Reskilling Revolution will depend critically on a mentally agile workforce that is willing and able to change as the demand characteristics for labor change. A Reskilling Revolution will also rely on the adoption of lifelong learning as the baseline condition for labor market participants.

I contend that a broad swath of the global workforce has not practically adopted a lifelong learning approach, nor has it adopted the mental agility to change and grow. My hypothesis is that while a Reskilling Revolution is the right approach to take and a noble goal, its execution will collide with populations that are not prepared for change—what I've previously referred to as the clay layer—nor do they view lifelong learning as the key to their future success.

Recommendations for Leaders

To ensure we're effectively growing our economies in 2030 and beyond, our responsibility as leaders of businesses and communities is to promote the importance and benefits of lifelong learning to our youth. We must also bring the reality of the existence of the clay layer in our organizations from the shadows into the light. We must invest in these individuals with impactful, measurable training, and engagement opportunities.

The unfortunate reality that all business leaders must come to understand is that nobody is going to do this for them; there isn't a knight in shining armor riding in to save the day. Instead, responsibility for upskilling and reskilling falls squarely on their shoulders. Many businesses have and will continue to partner with educational institutions to provide job-specific skills training, and such partnerships are strongly encouraged, but identifying and pursuing those training opportunities is still up to the business.

In the past, it was often considered the responsibility of the individual to go back to school, on their own time and their own dime, to further their education. The training and skills development needs of our current business environment, however, are so great that we can't just send the entire workforce back to school every few years. Organizations should instead take responsibility for mapping out their skills needs at a high level, translate those needs down to a departmental or team level, and work with individuals to implement training programs that can help fill the gaps that were identified at each level. Governments and educational institutions can't take responsibility for managing the business's changing skills needs either. The reality is that when it comes to the Reskilling Revolution, the buck stops with the employer.

Most important, however, is that in this equation middle managers now hold the key to talent identification and talent management within an organization. While not all middle managers are members of the clay layer, a key component of a manager's responsibility is to evaluate performance, identify talent, and recommend that talent for growth opportunities.

This is why I'm such a strong advocate for killing the annual performance review and replacing it with an annual learning and development conversation (see my side note on performance reviews from chapter 1). If you've already engaged in regular conversations about performance throughout the course of the year, you now have the opportunity to put managers and their team members together once or twice a year to translate the business's skills needs to the individual's skill development goals. Those conversations should include an explanation of the business's future plans, the kinds of skills the team will need in order to achieve those goals, and an overview of the employee's current skills profile as it relates to those needs. The end result should be a detailed plan for making up the gap. Doing so will also go a long way in providing staff with a clear understanding of their career trajectory, which countless studies suggest is a key contributor to employee morale and retention.

Unfortunately, the "accidental manager" does not come into the job with honed talent-management skills, and members of the clay layer routinely shirk their duty as professional managers to do the hard work of properly developing and engaging the members of the workforce who directly report to them.

To effectively implement a Reskilling Revolution, we will need middle managers who are willing, able, and have the courage to identify and recommend talent for reskilling. Unless—or until—they are coached accordingly, accidental and clay-layer managers are likely to be unhelpful in that process, because they haven't built the muscle and mindset for growth and development of the individuals for whom they are responsible.

Work-Learn versus Learn-Work and the Reskilling Revolution

I believe that skill portfolios that are validated through stackable credentials and supported through experiential "work-learn" apprenticeships will be commonplace and just as important as the university degree is today in signaling work readiness.

A 2019 Harvard study, which was published in the *Proceedings of the National Academy of Sciences*, sought to determine whether students retained more information from lectures or practice. Researchers ultimately found that while students *felt* like they learned more from attending lectures, they *performed better* on examinations after engaging in the material through firsthand experience.[4]

Once reserved for skilled trades, hands-on learning opportunities are becoming more common in a range of industries, and for good reason. Educational institutions in Canada, the United States, and elsewhere are increasingly partnering with for-profit businesses to help develop job-ready graduates by providing work opportunities alongside classroom education. For example, in 2019, e-commerce giant Shopify partnered with Carleton University, near its headquarters in Ottawa, and York University, in Toronto, to provide a new kind of educational program. The "Dev Degree" allows students to split their time between classroom education and on-the-job training at Shopify. Not only is the four-year program offered tuition-free but students are also paid for their time at Shopify and graduate with an accredited computer science degree. In 2021 Shopify further expanded the program into a remote format for students in both the United States and Canada, thanks to a partnership with the San Francisco-based Make School.[5]

The Dev Degree program is just one of many examples of how educational institutions and the businesses that rely on its graduates are seeking a different, more hands-on approach to higher education. Classroom education is important and will always have a place in education, but overcoming the challenges of the Reskilling Revolution will require employers and educators to place equal value on practical, hands-on learning and remain open to new learning models. As a hiring manager, you'll need to be fluent in the language of competency, as hiring for skills in lieu of and/or alongside degrees gains prevalence.

Need convincing? A quick Google search for "hiring for skills not degrees" will yield a plethora of results from reputable sources on this trend. In fact, according to a 2022 report by Bain and Company, 60 percent of jobs that pay above a living wage and have limited vulnerability to automation require a four-year degree. When they examined similar job postings, however, researchers found that only one in four good jobs should actually necessitate a bachelor's degree as a condition for employment.[6]

Don't misunderstand—degrees will still be important to our future, but we've got to bring down the cost of an education, improve access to good jobs, increase the fidelity of work readiness signals, and make education more agile and timely.

Old "learn-to-work" models, in which a monolithic credential like the bachelor's degree stands as a gateway to a good job, must make way for more flexible "work-to-learn" pathways to employment.

Traditional learn-to-work models, in which humans remove themselves from the workforce and cloister in academic settings for long periods of time to acquire competency for a new job simply won't be able to keep up with demand. Work-to-learn models will be much more agile and efficient in helping the average human reskill as old skills are made redundant due to technological advances.

A Common Language for Skills

To accomplish the above, businesses, governments, and educational institutions will need to adopt a common language for skills. A common language for skills will help solve one of the challenges that has dogged the university degree for decades: comparability. In the current environment, as a hiring manager, how do I know that a degree of the same name from university X is comparable to that of university Y? How do I know Suzie's degree in discipline Z is the same as Billy's from the same university? You don't on both counts. You're primarily relying on the *brand* value of the institution for signals of competency, not what the individual can actually do.

One more quick Google search for the "definition of competency" is in order to punch the point regarding how loosely the word *competency* is defined in popular literature. One article will call *communication* a skill and another will call it a competency. So which one is it? How can we expect laypeople and non-L&D personnel to understand skill portfolios and competency mapping if we can't agree on the underlying definitions?

To help solve the confusion around competencies, the World Economic Forum is launching their SkillsLink Alliance and has published a Skills Taxonomy in an attempt to create a common language for skills and competencies around the world. For simplicity and consistency, I recommend the adoption of that framework as a starting point for skills and competency mapping within your business.

The Definitions

- *Competency.* "A collection of skills, knowledge, attitudes, and abilities that enable an individual to perform a job role." Examples include leadership, teamwork, problem-solving, and people development. Note that competencies are broad topical areas, with numerous knowledge areas and skills necessary to develop fluency or expertise.

- *Skills.* "A capability needed to complete a task." Examples include, goal setting, time management, scheduling, numeracy, troubleshooting, data literacy, and financial acumen. Skills can be cross functional or specialized to a specific role. Cross-functional skills are "shared" across competencies. Note the relative specificity of the examples of skills versus the examples cited for competency above.

- *Knowledge.* "The body of facts, principles, and theories that are related to a field of work or study." Knowledge can be practical and/or theoretical. Knowledge underpins skills and is a necessary condition to understand the "how and why" behind a skill or competency. Note that both skills and knowledge are teachable and learned.

- *Attitudes.* "Learned behaviors; emotional intelligence traits; and beliefs that individuals exhibit that influence their approach to ideas, persons, and situations." Examples include self-management, attention to detail, stress tolerance, mental agility, and civic responsibility. There is significant debate surrounding whether attitudes can be taught and learned. While some attitudinal characteristics are "hard wired" and immutable, I believe that "tigers can indeed change their stripes," or "old dogs can learn new tricks." For example, with the right coaching, mentoring, and environment, mental agility can be improved through time.

- *Abilities.* "Possession of the physical, psychomotor, cognitive, and sensory means to perform a job." This definition is plain. If the job is NFL quarterback, it would be impossible (using today's technology) for someone who is blind to perform the role.

- *Taxonomy.* A taxonomy is a classification or structure. In learning and education, Bloom's Taxonomy is likely the most well known. The foundation for Bloom's Taxonomy Revised is "remembering" (meaning the regurgitation of facts), with "understanding" as the next level up. As an individual progresses up Bloom's taxonomy, depth of knowledge and the ability to apply that knowledge increases.

BLOOM'S TAXONOMY

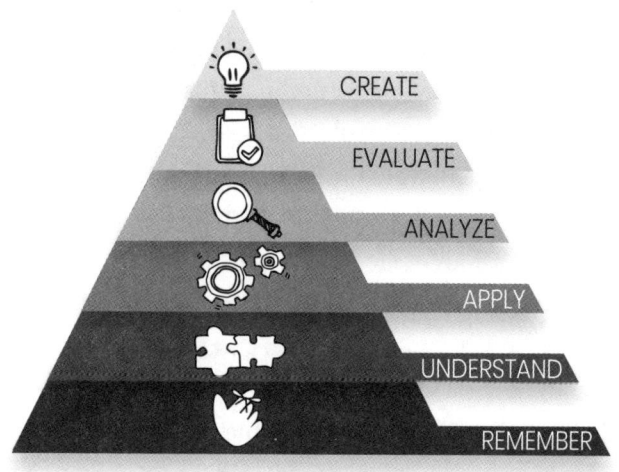

- *Ontology and knowledge graphs.* You'll also hear learning professionals toss around words like ontology and knowledge graphs. You've most likely heard them before and started tuning out of the conversation because of how foreign they sound. What's important for the layperson to understand is that these terms help describe the interrelation between knowledge, skills, abilities, and attitudes (the components of competencies) across competencies, jobs, job classes, and the human talent map of the entire company. For example, the skill of "numeracy" will show up as a baseline skill for many job classes across the organization (it is a cross-functional or shared skill). Likewise, the competency of "problem-solving" is shared across many job roles.

What you end up with is a multidimensional graph that shows how the individual components of competency are shared across competencies and jobs and how "close" one job is to another. This concept of "closeness" is what many vendors and geopolitical organizations use to calculate the "distance" between job A and job B and the amount of upskilling or reskilling that's necessary to close the gap or help an individual acquire the knowledge and skills necessary to move from job A to job B.

As you contemplate the definitions above, note that each item lies on a gradient. Gradients can range from the simplistic to the complex. Most commonly, you see a three-level ranking system like "basic, intermediate, advanced." The Lumina Foundation created an eight-level gradient system in their "Connecting Credentials" framework back in 2015.[7]

Can a skill be a competency? Maybe, depending on how broadly the skill is defined; however, skills are definitely contained in the set of competencies. Can knowledge be a skill? In my opinion, no. Knowledge is the what and the why, whereas skill is the how and depends on acquisition of the what and why?

There's a lot more to this conversation—specifically, how to bring the concept of skill portfolios, skill taxonomies, and knowledge graphs to life in your organization. For now, we've brought you up to speed on the terminology and achieved the goal of outlining a desired future state where the university degree (learn-work) is not the only or primary gateway into a professional career and where skill portfolios, apprenticeships, and stacks of short, sharp, validated credentials (work-learn) provide means for alternative pathways into the world of work. We *must* improve access and equity, reduce cost (both money and time), and improve outcomes.

Finally, to get the conversation started in your organization, pull a few job descriptions out of the filing cabinet, dust them off, and ask, "Why does it say 'bachelor's degree required'?" Ask why as many times as you need to get to the root cause and determine the true underlying set of knowledge, skills, attitudes, and abilities that are necessary to perform the role. Then start work with your HR department and learning business partners on developing alternative pathways into that job.

The Importance of Knowledge and Attitudes in the Competency Equation

As we engage in the Reskilling Revolution to reskill up to a billion people globally over the next decade, developing more cost-effective, direct on-ramps into the world of work and cross-ramps between jobs and careers is imperative.

During those future conversations, however, I don't want you to think that knowledge, attitudes, and abilities should somehow take a back seat to skills. All four components of competency are critical to long-term workplace success.

Above we defined *knowledge* as "the body of facts, principles, and theories that are related to a field of work or study." *Attitudes* are defined as "learned behaviors; emotional intelligence traits; and beliefs that individuals exhibit that influence their approach to ideas, persons, and situations." Many in nonacademic circles rail against the frivolity of theoretical knowledge, the acquisition of facts and principles, and the maturation and expansion of attitudes as "fluff" and recommend instead that the most pragmatic approach to developing competency for a job or career is to focus on demonstrating "what you can do" (a skills focus).

But competency in any setting is the combination of knowledge *and* skills *and* attitudes *and* ability. There is no *or* in the equation for competency and to focus primarily on one element without also nurturing the others will lead to unbalanced outcomes, meaning unbalanced employees and citizens.

Education is both a theoretical *and* a practical-experiential exercise. Any educational journey should continue the process of building skill *and* enhancing an individual's ability to function within teams and society at large. Said differently, the goal of any educational intervention should be to produce work-ready graduates *and* "rounded" citizens.

If I experientially teach you how to do a thing without providing the foundational knowledge about that thing's history or the math that makes it work, there's little chance you'll be able to reach the level of expertise needed to progress to the next level of that thing's use. More importantly, simply knowing how to perform a skill does not mean that you can think critically or creatively about how to use the thing in different ways to innovate and advance a process or system.

Should it take four plus years after high school graduation to acquire a viable set of skills and become "rounded" enough to succeed in the world of work? In my opinion, *no*.

There have to be more cost- and time-efficient ways to build a baseline portfolio of skills needed to perform in a job *and* instill a baseline bank of knowledge and attitudes that support high-functioning individuals and teams in the workplace. Specifically, we need to do a better job as parents, community leaders, and educators to build all components of competency *during* primary and secondary school *and* create alternative work-to-learn pathways that don't require students to remove themselves from the job market until they're "fully formed" upon graduation from college and accumulate mountains of debt.

We must promote the acquisition and pursuit of knowledge and continuous development of attitude as a lifelong endeavor. Not doing so will lead to more fixed mindsets and allow mis- or disinformation to spread even more widely than it does today.

True freedom is a well-balanced education, the continuous pursuit of a growth mindset, and the ability to empathize and communicate with other humans that don't talk or look exactly the same as you.

In our search for more efficient educational pathways, let's not allow the pendulum to swing too far toward a skills-only approach.

Waiting for a Technology Solution to Fill the Gap

Instead of actively addressing the need to participate more fully in the Reskilling Revolution, many organizations are instead pinning their hopes on some sort of AI training solution that can be deployed at scale. While such solutions do show promise, they are by no means sufficient for addressing a gap of this size and scale. The Reskilling Revolution is and will remain a moving target, and while software solutions can help shoulder some of the educational burden, they will not be sufficient.

I recently presented this argument to my dad, himself a lifelong educator, suggesting that there was some promising technology that could help map out long-term skills needs within organizations, identify gaps, offer learning modules, and deliver that training using artificial intelligence. My father, who used to work as an administrator for a local technical college and spent his career trying to bridge the gap between the institution and the skills needs of local employers, just rolled his eyes. He, like many in the field, had been waiting for a holy-grail solution that could do all that since the 1970s, but through his experience he's discovered that such solutions never really work at scale.

The problem is that even the best solution in the world fails without a manager who is activated as a hands-on partner and coach in the learning process. It's sort of like a global logistics network that gets a package from a manufacturing facility in China to the nearest warehouse just outside my hometown in Wisconsin, but never makes it any further. All the technology in the world can't account for that last mile, when someone needs to actually pick up the package and deliver it to my front door. If you don't have the manager who understands that their role is to serve as a coach and mentor driving the last mile, the whole system falls flat, despite all the fancy tech that got it that far.

Learning needs to be woven into the DNA of the organization, with middle managers serving as facilitators en route to the final destination. That is why there is no room for an accidental manager or member of the clay layer; they are responsible for much of that heavy lifting.

Organizations will only succeed in the Fourth Industrial Revolution if their leaders can activate the clay layer and help middle managers understand that serving as coaches and teachers is one of the primary functions of their role. I'd be remiss if I didn't point out the obvious—that leaders must also *make the time* within normal business operations for learning and coaching to take root and flourish. If learning and coaching are relegated to "after-hours" activities, they will never be viewed as an organizational priority.

7

Defining the *"it"* of a Business

Does your company have the "it factor?" You know, that special quality that helps you stand out from the crowd?

During annual strategic planning exercises, devilishly difficult philosophical questions must be answered. Examples of corporate strategy questions include "What's our purpose?" "What's our vision?" "What are our values?" and "How will we behave?" I've spent hours upon hours in dimly lit conference rooms contemplating those questions with senior teams over the years. Gaining clarity on these difficult questions was both rewarding and exhausting.

The list of questions to be answered or validated each year also includes theoretical softballs, like, "What does our company do?" After stretching and straining our gray matter to the limit, the senior team and I looked forward to a softball or two so we could reset and reenergize. On the surface, this question seems easy. "How hard can it be to define what we do?" was the common refrain that echoed around the conference room.

To the great dismay of the senior team, defining what the company did turned out to be another one of those devilishly difficult questions. The more times we posed the questions to different groups of employees in different departments and different parts of the world, the more we discovered how many different answers there were to this seemingly simple question. Our assumption was one that I would suspect many companies that have been around for as long as Kaplan (well over eighty years) would have too. Of course we know what we do—we've been doing it so long, right? As it turns out, entropy had settled in, and our mutual understanding of what we did was far from clear.

If you look at the "About Us" page of many organizations' websites, especially those who are large and long tenured, what you often find is a series of disconnected points with little cohesive narrative. The reason for this is pretty straightforward. Most companies begin with a clear understanding of what they do, but over time they feel the need to include some reference to the flavor of the day. Whether you're browsing the website of a sneaker company, a global financial institution, or a software giant, you'll probably see a section dedicated to environmental sustainability, diversity and inclusion, and some vague reference to having a "unique culture." While each of these might be worthwhile causes, they don't really tell the reader what the company actually does or why their efforts in any of those categories are distinct from its competition.

In fact, a lot of that content is derived from their 10-K annual report, which is required by the federal government for compliance purposes. Every so often the government will require the company to include management statistics on diversity and inclusion or environmental sustainability efforts. Over time, the "About Us" page turns from a cohesive story to a disjointed series of checkboxes of little substance. While this might not seem like a big problem to most, your "About Us" page serves an important purpose to both existing and prospective employees. It's hard for candidates to understand what they're signing up for, or for employees to understand what to tell their friends and family their company is all about, if they need to tell five different stories that check a series of compliance boxes. In other words, they are left without an authentic company identity.

There are, of course, some important exceptions, though often you'll find these stronger examples among smaller businesses who really have a genuine, authentic, inspiring story that their staff rally around. In an ideal scenario, your company's description should include all the elements we've explored thus far, including purpose, vision, values, *be*haviors, and, as we'll discuss further in this chapter, the thing they actually do. Each of these strategy statements should combine to tell a cohesive, genuine, and authentic narrative and provide that identity piece many organizations struggle with. Organizations spend large portions of their budget on marketing initiatives to tell some sort of story to customers and clients about what they do, but equally important—and often forgotten—is the story they tell themselves and their employees about what they do and why.

In the businesses I've led, each year we'd look forward to quickly "checking the box" of validating the previous year's answer to the strategy question "what do we do?" Each year we'd spend *several hours* ensuring we got the answer right.

So how can a seemingly easy question like "what do we do?" turn into a journey down the rabbit hole? In our case, we would let the answer to what we do idle for a year. The faulty logic we'd apply went something like this: "Only a year has passed since we last discussed this topic. How much can change in a year?" As it turns out, *a lot* can change during the course of a single year.

During a typical year, new products were launched; departments X, Y, or Z were reorganized; a small competitor or two were acquired; and/or an externality disrupted product line A. In isolation, each event seemed minor and inconsequential. Taken as a whole, changes like those mentioned above can significantly alter the trajectory of the business and make answering "what we do" challenging at best.

Flow versus a Seasonal Approach

The fact that a softball question—"What do we do?"—can easily turn into a nasty curveball is one of the stronger reasons to work strategic and tactical planning into the *flow* of the business, rather than relying on an episodic "seasonal" approach to planning.

Placing the answers to strategic business-framing questions (like purpose, vision, values, **be**haviors, and the company's "what we do") front and center throughout the year keeps them top of mind and fresh for everyone in the business. Weaving the answers into the flow of business also minimizes the unnecessary extra work (waste) of having to open the desk drawer where they've been resting, dust off our responses, remind ourselves of what we did last year, and reestablish context and meaning *before* getting started on the heavy lifting.

What Is the *it*?

While some authors and leadership consultants focus on the question "What do we do?" I like to go a step further and ask: "What's the organization's *it*?" Why? Because if you ask about the *it*, then *differentiation* is central to the question. Focusing on the *it* forces a simultaneous evaluation of what the company does with what makes the business different from its competitor's value proposition.

THE "IT"

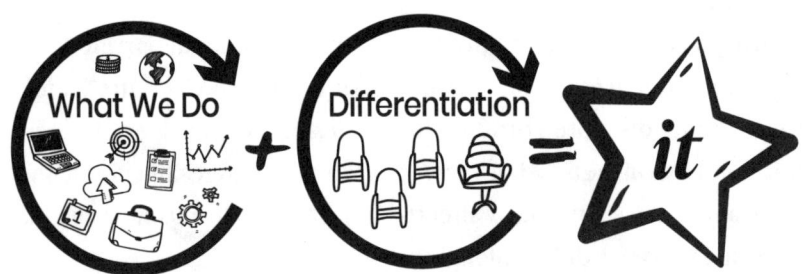

In my book *Balancing Act*, I introduced the concept of *indispensability* and the importance of continually striving to become and remain indispensable to customers and clients; however, a discussion of indispensability is moot without first defining the company's *it*.

The best way to think about the *it* is to scale the conversation *way* back. Back to the beginning, when there was *one* product, and the business was very small. What was the *it* of that singular product? Did you differentiate on service, support, features, or delivery? I still like to use the *it* question when thinking about a new product launch. More than one product owner has been in my office pitching a new idea, only to be sent back to the drawing board by my query: "What's your *it*? What makes the offering different?"

The thought experiment of thinking first about a single product before diving into the *it* of the entire business can be an incredibly useful tool to get the team aligned.

The *it* and Change

That the "*it* statement" combines "What do we do?" with "What makes us different?" bears repeating. This may seem counterintuitive, as I've noted in previous work that combo statements—for example, the mission statement—do too much heavy lifting and are to be avoided. Here creating a combo statement makes sense because avoiding bland, generic, catchall statements that give a business permission to do almost anything within the confines of an industry category is essential.

Why? Because humans abhor unexpected change and hate surprises. If your business is like most, your people—your most valuable asset—are working in an environment of tight deadlines and very little system slack. They're likely so overwhelmed with the volume and cadence of workflow within their department that even *small* changes in organizational direction can send a team into a tailspin that leads to disengagement and job dissatisfaction. Remember: one of our key goals is to build a high-trust, high-accountability culture within the organization.

As a reminder, in chapter 5, we introduced the concept of *change management* as a critical component of your business's management operating system. Being crystal clear about what the company does and what makes it different will make any subsequent change process much easier to ingest and work through. Instead of freaking out and digging their heels in when a merger or new product is contemplated, the team will instead be able to connect the dots between the new offering and the standard work that's currently in place. The questions then become less about "Why are we merging with *Company A?*" and more in line with "Okay, I see the importance of this merger as a way of strengthening our *it*, so let's figure out how we're going to weave the new offering into our existing workflow."

By being clear about what the company does and its differentiator(s), the average individual change management curve gets shorter, and individual morale and competence improves while all else remains the same. Since the average individual curve shortens, and individual outcomes improve, the *organizational change curve* (aggregated curve) gets shorter, and overall outcomes improve.

The Elements of the *it* Statement

Before we introduce a few examples of *it* statements that exist in the wild, let's first define the essential elements of good *it* statements. In addition to being *differentiated*, your "*it* statement" should:

- *Balance specificity with future growth.* Yes, the *it* statement should be as specific as possible to help reduce the inevitable unnecessary waste that accompanies change; however, the human desire for consistency and sameness should not quash the need for continuous improvement and growth. The key to this balance is to ensure that the company's *vision statement* and *it statement* are congruent with one another. Both statements should leave the door open to expansion and business pivots—vision more so than the *it*. There are two mechanisms that help ensure congruence. The first is to use recursive thinking in the initial development and subsequent validation of the company's strategy statements. For example, define the company's purpose, then define vision *and* ensure vision is congruent with purpose. Next, define values *and* ensure that values are congruent with purpose and vision. The second way to ensure congruence is to employ the concept of *catchball* in the creation and validation of strategic statements with the next level down from the senior team (a.k.a. the extended leadership team). Catchball is a wonderful check on the senior team, especially as it relates to the practicality of strategic statements. We'll talk about catchball more in chapter 8 and 11.
- *Be inclusive.* There's not much worse than working on a team that doesn't have a strong fit with company strategy. While the senior leadership team may make excuses and rationalize why this team belongs

in the organization, I guarantee the members of "team odd duck" don't take comfort in those rationalizations and are constantly looking over their shoulders. They're waiting for the other shoe to drop—a reorganization, layoffs, or terminations are surely just around the corner. The members of *every team* should be able to draw a straight line between their goals, their work, and the *it* of the organization. Asking team members to become mental contortionists to continually try to justify the "why" behind their existence is the fast-pass to disengagement.

- *Help define the field of play.* In many industries, the field of play is so broad that using corporate strategy statements to define the boundaries of target markets, customer segments, and product categories is essential to minimize entropy and unintentional product bloat. Some leadership teams may want to spend extra time defining the field of play in a separate statement to enhance organizational clarity, as recommended by Lafley and Martin in their work *Playing to Win* (2013). My advice is to only add to the company's suite of strategy statements if they are *value-adding* to stakeholders. If a strategy statement is redundant, confusing, or a nonvalue-adding word salad, ditch it or start over.

- *Be a communication tool.* Yes, all corporate strategy statements are communication tools to improve organizational clarity across a variety of stakeholders; however, the question your team members will get asked more than any other is "What does your company do?" The last thing you want a team member to do is freeze up and say, "You know what? I'm not really sure." An equally terrible result is that the company is so complicated that the elevator pitch turns into an eye-glazing three-minute response.

A great litmus test is to engage with team members from multiple departments via informal skip-level meetings. Ask them directly how they answer the question "What does your company do?" when approached by a new acquaintance at a cocktail party or by Uncle Bill at the next family reunion. If you get ten different answers from ten different team members, then "Houston, we have a problem."

- *Be easy to find.* All corporate strategy statements should be in one place and be no more than one click from the company's home page on their website.
- *Be concise.* Simplicity is important. Avoid flowery marketing jargon.

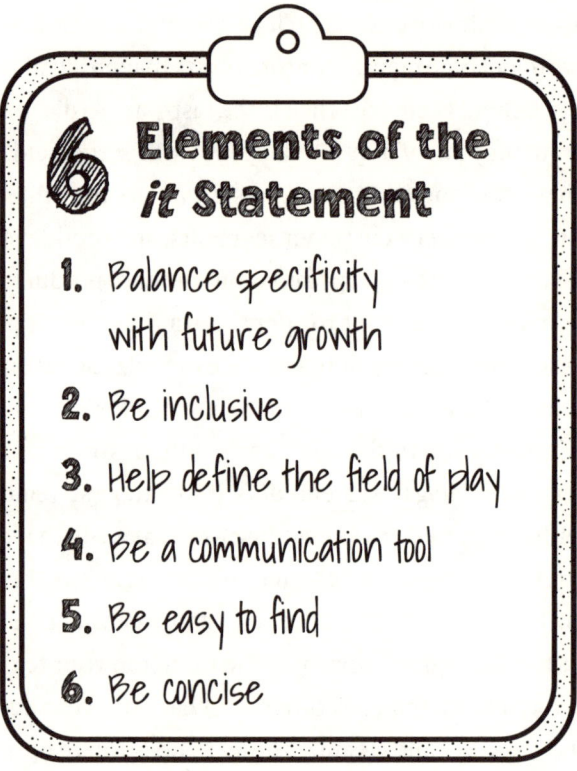

6 Elements of the *it* Statement

1. Balance specificity with future growth
2. Be inclusive
3. Help define the field of play
4. Be a communication tool
5. Be easy to find
6. Be concise

Examples of *it* Statements

The websites of many major corporations are silent on the topic of their *it*. Instead, they make the assumption that such a statement is not necessary or is obvious, based on their history or reputation. This isn't a huge surprise, as most businesses still rely on their mission statements to try to describe why they exist, where they're going, and what they do—way too much information to stuff into a single statement. This is why I indicate above that combo statements are not effective.

Some companies also utilize the headline of their "About Us" web page to explain what they do. In my opinion, hiding "what we do" in a headline on the website is a missed opportunity to provide clarity to stakeholders.

Others rely on their vision statement to explain what they do. I also believe this is a mistake, as vision is designed to be *aspirational*. What the company does *today* and where they *aspire* to go can be two different things.

With that said, here are several examples of "what we do" statements:

Cognizant: "We use expertise that's been proven and tested around the globe to help you get ahead of challenges, sense opportunities sooner, and outpace change."

Unfortunately, neither the company's name, Cognizant, nor its "what we do" statement provide much clarity on exactly what the company does. When the name of a business is contrived, its leadership carries the added burden of clearly explaining to stakeholders what the company does. This statement is overly vague and fails the differentiation and elevator-pitch tests.

Ecolab: "Ecolab is the global leader in water, hygiene, and infection prevention solutions and services. Every day, we help make the world cleaner, safer, and healthier—protecting people and vital resources."

The Ecolab "what we do" is an example of a statement that's embedded in their "About Us" headline on their website. While what they do may be obvious to the designers of the web page, it is not obvious to the casual observer that "About Us" is the same thing as "What We Do." In addition, the "About Us" statement at the top of the page is not the same as the "About Us" statement listed at the bottom of the page, adding to the reader's potential confusion. Since the two statements are not the same, Ecolab fails the elevator-pitch test.

Expedia Group: "We build connections. We leverage our platform and technology capabilities across an extensive portfolio of businesses and brands to orchestrate the movement of people and the delivery of travel experiences on both a local and global basis. We help our travelers and our partners find the right pathways through millions of possibilities to reach the best possible outcome."

I applaud Expedia Group for explicitly indicating what they do. Bravo. The statement checks all the boxes, with the exception of parsimony. Since it is not concise, it will also prove challenging as an elevator pitch.

Owens Corning: "Together, our Mission, Purpose, and Values are the foundation of our unique culture and guide the way we live and work locally and globally. They describe what we do, why we do it, and who we are—it is the essence of our commitment to our customers, shareholders, partners, and each other."

This statement is also the header of the company's "About Us" page. It says that "what we do" is woven into their mission, vision, and values statements, but no such clarity is to be found. Hence, Owens Corning leaves "what we do" up for significant interpretation, and none of the criteria for an effective "what we do" statement are met.

PPG: "PPG is a global supplier of paints, coatings, optical products, and specialty materials. Through leadership in innovation, sustainability and color, PPG helps customers in industrial, transportation, consumer products, and construction markets and aftermarkets to enhance more surfaces in more ways than does any other company."

This was a real struggle to find. All corporate strategy statements should be one click away from the company's home page. In the case of PPG, their "what we do" statement is three clicks from the home page; one of those clicks is to a different website and is not clearly labeled.

P&G: "We make superior quality products and use every ounce of their power to make a difference."

Proctor & Gamble is a gigantic company with a truly global reach. I'm certain that developing an effective "what we do" statement is difficult, but what they've come up with is so broad as to not be meaningful. In my assessment, keeping silent would be better than to produce such a bland, cover-all statement. In fact, this statement is so generic, it could be used by myriad companies across multiple industries.

"it's" Not Fluff

I can't stress enough how important the creation of effective, useful corporate strategy statements are to the creation of high-trust, high-accountability institutional cultures.

Unfortunately, many leaders look upon corporate strategy statements as "fluff" and look forward to working strategy sessions with the same dread that accompanies a trip to the dentist or the family tax specialist.

Remember: clarity is driven from one place—the top of the organization. If you're one of those leaders who thinks that execution and the "doing" is more important than setting and communicating strategy, I implore you to think again. I've been that directive, "Andy said" leader in the past who pooh-poohed the need for clarity and avoided the work that goes into the creation of strategy statements.

In the category of "you reap what you sow," failing to invest in the collaborative creation, routine validation, and frequent communication of corporate strategy statements like the *it* will yield more uncertainty, dissatisfaction, and waste than necessary.

8

Indispensability

Customer loyalty is the most direct path to ongoing business success.

As I've hopefully demonstrated previously, we love a good routine as much as we hate change. Those products and brands that can identify and provide the *it* through extensive competitor, customer persona, and needs analysis provide the foundation for becoming a part of our routines, our habits, and a source of comfort. In other words, they become "indispensable" to us on a deeply personal level.

We all have brands, vendors, and products we keep coming back to time and again for that sense of comfort and predictability. When was the last time you switched shampoo brands or barbers or go-to restaurants?

The average person typically spends some time exploring the market, seeking a solution that checks all the necessary boxes, and if the brand delivers on that promise, it becomes incredibly difficult for a competitor to come along and take their place.

So the big question that every organization needs to consider is "How will we become indispensable to our customers?"

In my experience, there are three key elements of indispensability, which I outlined in my first book, *Balancing Act*. They are people, product, and reliability.

- *People.* People are the ingredient that defines excellence in a service economy. Ask any successful leader what they owe their success to, and they will likely reference their people (at least they should). Even with the best and most reliable products, brands of any kind—and especially those in the services sector—will struggle without passionate and knowledgeable staff. Hiring and retaining the right kind of people is in part an HR practice, but as we've discussed earlier in this book, long-term success often comes down to purpose, vision, and culture. By defining and living the values that make us indispensable to our clients and customers, we can easily align around a "true north" of indispensability, no matter how much the company grows and evolves over time.

- *Product.* Having great staff isn't enough on its own. In order to become truly indispensable, organizations also need to offer a product that their customers love. If people are every organization's most valuable asset, the thing that it offers its customers and clients is likely second. This is where the previous chapter on defining the company's *it* comes into play. Creating a product that people love takes time. Over the long haul, organizations thrive or die based on their products.

- *Reliability.* Reliability refers to both of the previous two points. Just about any organization can come up with a single product people buy once and forget about, but doing so with consistency is more than a happy accident. If you think about brands and products that have become indispensable to you, I imagine a key driver of your loyalty is the fact that they don't let you down. The restaurant I frequent offers a quality meal every time I go, not to mention great service. As human beings, we love the comfort of the familiar, which is why consistency is essential for brands.

Indispensability Examples

Trader Joe's

Trader Joe's is one of the largest grocery chains in the United States, but it started from humble beginnings. Its founder, Joe Coulombe, opened a series of grocery stores in the Los Angeles area in 1958 under the name Pronto Markets in a bid to compete directly against 7-Eleven. By 1967, Coulombe came to realize he probably wasn't going to win that race and instead leaned into the Hawaiian tiki trend that was exploding in popularity at the time. Taking inspiration from a popular tiki restaurant chain Trader Vic's, he rebranded the company in 1967 as Trader Joe's, complete with tiki torches, wood-paneled market-style displays, hand-painted signs, and what can only be described as a "tiki vibe."[1]

The grocery store chain remained confined within the state of California until it came under new management in 1987, former CEO John Shields. He expanded the brand into Arizona in 1993 and then the Pacific Northwest in 1995. The company's first East Coast store only opened in 1996. Under Shields, who retired in 2001, the company quintupled its number of stores and increased profits tenfold.[2] In 2008 *BusinessWeek* reported that the company had the highest sales per square foot of any grocer in the United States—double that of its primary competitor, Whole Foods.[3,4]

By 2019, Trader Joe's had 505 stores in the United States, generating an estimated $13.7 billion in net sales.[5] According to many credible resources and newspaper articles, the brand doesn't have customers; it has fanatics.

What makes Trader Joe's such a success story? It checks all three indispensability boxes boldly and emphatically. For one thing, 80 percent of its products are private label, meaning you cannot get them anywhere else. It also means Trader Joe's can offer certain products at a lower price by cutting out middlemen. According to the company's website, "Our buyers travel the world searching for products we think are exceptional and will find a following among our customers. To earn a spot on our shelves, each product is submitted to a rigorous tasting panel process, in which every aspect of quality is investigated in context of the price we can offer. If a product is assessed as an outstanding value, it becomes an essential part of the Trader Joe's shopping adventure."[6]

The other game-changing attribute of Trader Joe's lies in how it selects, trains, and treats its people. According to Forbes, it was the thirty-fifth-best large employer in the country in 2022 and was third within the retail and wholesale category.[7] In 2019 it ranked number one in all categories.[8]

At that time, its then president of stores, Jon Basalone, revealed what the company looks for when hiring staff in episode fifteen of the company's podcast, *Inside Trader Joe's*. "The instructions we give our crew right when we hire them, it's pretty simple. It's three things: Be yourself. We hired you for a reason. Be genuine. There are no scripts. It's not faked or anything like that. And be nice!"[9] Once onboarded, as of the date of the podcast, the company paid entry-level part-time staff up to $24.75 an hour, provided health insurance, paid time off, a company-funded retirement plan, and shift flexibility.[10] The company even moves its in-store staff around to different roles throughout the day—from cashier to stocking shelves, for example—to combat boredom on the job.

The result is a staff that is willing and able to go above and beyond for customers. According to one employee, "I was empowered to do almost anything for a customer. Spend fifteen minutes in the storeroom looking for a five-dollar item at a customer's request? No problem. If I encountered a customer who seemed to be having a bad day, I could give her a bouquet of flowers on my own initiative. Any time a customer asked, 'What are these like?' I could open a package and give them a free sample."[11] This degree of freedom and autonomy is one of the many reasons why Trader Joe's is considered a top employer in the country. Despite operating in a sector with one of the highest turnover rates in the nation, a full 10 percent of employees have been with the company for a decade or longer.

This well-curated collection of products, highly satisfied and motivated people, coupled with the stores' intentionally quirky and easily recognizable island-themed decor, offer a brand experience unlike any of its competitors. And, most importantly, it offers that experience consistently across its more than five hundred stores, making the brand indispensable to its loyal customers, or "superfans."

You Need a Budget

For many organizations, success doesn't necessarily require owning the greatest market share or even being the most profitable. For many, it's about having a small but loyal group of customers and a small but loyal group of employees. That is the case for You Need a Budget, or YNAB (pronounced *why-nab*) for short. The company was born out of a romance between cofounders Julie and Jesse Mecham, who tied the knot in early 2003 while they were still in school and were worried about their finances.[12]

Together the pair developed a complex spreadsheet system that helped them anticipate and prepare for their future financial needs. After a year and a child, the pair was looking for an extra source of income, as any financially responsible parent would, and floated the idea of selling their budgeting system online. A few years later, in 2006, a video-game developer offered to help turn that fancy spreadsheet into a software program. A year after that, YNAB released its first paid product, YNAB Pro. In 2013 the company began offering YNAB for Business, and in 2015 the company launched a web app. During that time they gained a reputation for taking good care of the finances of both their customers and staff.

YNAB, which has been fully remote since its founding, employs just over one hundred team members spread across thirty-three states, Canada, Switzerland, Argentina, and the UK.[13] Those staff members get access to a range of financial perks, including 401(k) plans, 100 percent health-care coverage for employees and their families, and profit sharing twice a year. They also get personalized birthday and holiday presents; the company literally consults with their friends and family to come up with a surprise that will really blow them away. Employees are also *required* to take three weeks of vacation every year, which doesn't include the two-weeklong company-wide holiday retreat.

"In the same way that we obsess over how customers experience our product, we're every bit as focused on our employees' experience working at YNAB," its COO, Chance Gurr, told *Fortune* magazine in late 2020. "As your team members gain control of their money and improve their financial situation, they miss fewer days at work, they produce more while they're at work, they smile more, and they don't jump to work for your competitor for a dollar more an hour. It's just good business. And I think a great culture builder."[14]

The company has also taken the time to produce its Core Value Manifesto, a brief publicly accessible Google Doc used to describe their ideal candidate, including all its cultural keywords, such as "humbly confident" and "assume good intentions."

YNAB is a great example of a company that has created a great product, amassed a great group of people, and maintained consistency in both, even as it scaled from ten employees in 2012 to over one hundred today. Today the company has a 4.8-star rating in the Apple App Store from over 38,500 customers, and a five-star rating on Glassdoor from its employees. In fact, the company was named the second-best small employer in 2018.[15] It dropped down to the fourth position in 2019, before reaching the top spot as the best small employer in America in both 2020 and 2021, according to *Fortune* magazine and Great Place to Work.[16]

When Reliability Falters: New Coke versus Coca-Cola Classic

As competition escalated between the world's two biggest soft-drink competitors, Pepsi devised an innovative marketing stunt that could have won them the war of fizzy beverages in the 1980s and 1990s. The brand, as many will recall, set up blind taste tests in what it called "The Pepsi Challenge," at malls around the world. The idea was simple: Pepsi was sweeter, and when people were offered a small sample of both products, the one with the slightly sweeter taste profile typically won out.

This made Coca-Cola nervous. It had been a market leader for nearly a century, and now Pepsi was gradually picking away at its market share. So what did the company do? In 1985 it buckled under the pressure and changed the formula to match the sweetness of Pepsi, calling the new product—you guessed it, "New Coke." The response: absolute outrage.

Customers began boycotting the brand, writing angry op-eds about American history and freedom of choice, and sent more than four hundred thousand letters of complaint.[17] "New Coke" was an absolute disaster that nearly toppled one of the most—if not *the most*—iconic brands in the world. A few months later, the Coca-Cola Company backpedaled and decided to bring back "Coca-Cola Classic," essentially pitting its customers against each other, drawing a new-versus-old battle line across America. In 1992 the company changed "New Coke" to "Coca-Cola II," and a decade later, in 2002, the product was taken off the market for good.

What can be learned from the controversy that nearly killed Coca-Cola? Lots of things, but for the purposes of this chapter of the book, I want to focus on the company's failure of reliability. Coca-Cola became the biggest soft-drink company in the world by creating a product people loved and by giving them the exact same beverage in every bottle (and eventually can). Nothing could have stopped this global behemoth had it just stayed the course, but Pepsi almost did, by pushing the brand into breaking its promise of consistency. Yes, innovation and adaptation are important, but if you already have a great product that people know and love, the worst thing you can do is change too much, too quickly.

When Products Lack a Differentiating *it*: The Star-Studded Tidal Disaster

On March 30, 2015, some of the world's biggest and most renowned musicians of the day lined up shoulder to shoulder onstage of Skylight at Moynihan Station in New York City. The star-studded event featured artists ranging from Rhianna to Jack White to Madonna—even the elusive French DJ duo Daft Punk arrived in full robot garb. Standing at center stage was Jay-Z, arguably the biggest hip-hop artist of all-time, to unveil a more artist-friendly competitor to streaming services like Spotify. Jay-Z had acquired Tidal a few months prior for $56 million, and he promised that the new streaming service would pay artists 75 percent of its revenues. The argument they put forward was clear: as artists, they deserved to be in control of the distribution and pricing of their own content.[18]

Unlike its competitors, Tidal didn't offer any of its content for free. In fact, it charged fans twenty dollars a month, well above its rivals at the time. To many fans, who had been accustomed to ad-supported music content since the invention of FM radio, this was seen as something of a betrayal. Artists, from their perspective, were holding their music hostage on a high-priced streaming service, making it less accessible to the average fan.

Furthermore, it was hard for the average music fan to sympathize with the artists who complained of not earning enough revenue, despite their well-publicized lavish lifestyles. Few fans were shedding tears for the pocketbooks of Jay-Z, who was worth about $560 million at the time, or Madonna, with her reported net worth of about $800 million. Just months after its initial celebrity-filled debut, the streaming service dropped off the App Store's top seven hundred downloads list. In 2017 Kanye West (now known as Ye), an initial backer and board member of the project, jumped ship, and in 2018 the company reported a loss of $37 million, after shedding about one hundred thousand subscribers.[19]

There are a lot of reasons why Tidal went from what many believed to be the future of music streaming to a punchline in such a short period of time, but its primary failure was that of not offering customers a clear point of differentiation. While Tidal claimed to offer better audio quality, its primary selling point was that it treated artists fairly, but artist revenues were never a major problem that the average music fan was excited to solve. Instead, consumers were able to get good-enough quality music content for free between a few ads or at a much lower subscription cost through other services.

When People Are Abandoned: The Rise and Fall of Circuit City

If you were a tech enthusiast, or even owned so much as a VCR in the 1980s and 1990s, you've probably been to your fair share of Circuit Citys. The retailer was everywhere. At one time there were more than fifteen hundred Circuit City stores in the United States and Canada, employing a workforce of about forty-six thousand.

The company made a lot of mistakes in the 2000s, including purchasing less than prime real estate for its large retail locations, failing to move aggressively into digital gaming, which proved hugely beneficial to its competitors, and was slow to adopt a strong online presence. But according to most experts, what really did this one-time retail giant in was poor management, specifically with regard to how it treated its staff.

For example, one of the company's most successful investments was in used car superstore CarMax, which it took 80 percent ownership of in February 1997. The company grew rapidly and was eventually spun off from Circuit City in 2002, allowing both organizations to grow independently. As part of the deal, however, CarMax took some of the company's most talented managers and leaders with them. Over time, the leadership of Circuit City became a revolving door.[20]

The final nail in the coffin came in March 2007, when the company suddenly announced plans to lay off thirty-four hundred of its highest-paid hourly workers without any notice—about 9 percent of its workforce—and replace them with lower-cost alternatives.[21] In the same move, the company also transitioned its commissioned sales associates to new hourly "product specialist" positions, without commission or benefits. To throw salt on the wound, that same year CEO Philip Schoonover reportedly earned more than $7 million in compensation, despite the extreme cost-cutting measures. Eight months later, the company closed 155 of its stores and laid off another 17 percent of its remaining workforce. Three days later, it filed for bankruptcy.

Prior to its own undoing, Circuit City was a primary employer of some of the continent's most avid tech enthusiasts. According to reports from former staff members, they weren't always paid well, but they loved working with the latest and greatest technologies, and that enthusiasm trickled down into the customer experience. Leadership proved itself blind to the importance of its people and assumed it could be equally, if not more, successful without them. This should serve as a strong reminder to any organization that thinks they've reached the top without the support of those below them. Hubris will make leaders think they accomplished everything on their own, but Circuit City demonstrates how vital employees are to the success of any business—even the second-largest technology retailer in the country.

How to Achieve Indispensability with People, Product, and Reliability

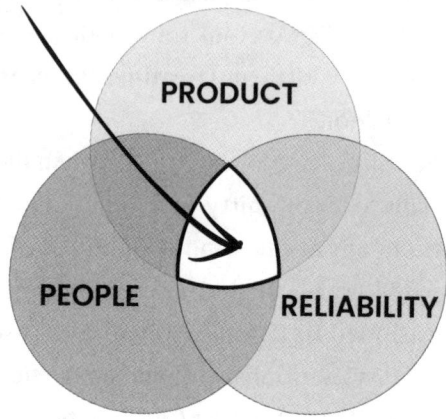

People. There is no shortage of books, studies, and analysis on what makes people tick, what gets them to show up to work every day and give it their all. The results paint what probably should have been a pretty obvious picture. People want financial stability, of course, but that's really a base-level expectation and not enough to inspire them to do their best.

Other studies, which have been noted above, suggest that employees want flexibility, freedom, and autonomy. In other words, they wanted to be treated like adults, with dignity and respect. Again, this shouldn't be dropping any jaws, but what's incredible to me is how many organizations are stunned by how much they're struggling with employee engagement and turnover yet continue to treat their staff like children, especially in this new world of remote and hybrid work, which can be viewed as an extension of dignity and respect. Once employees got a taste for the freedom and autonomy that remote work could provide, without suffering a decline in productivity, forcing them back into the office without a strong reason is akin to treating them like children. "Because I said so" is never a good phrase to use if you want to motivate and encourage staff to be indispensable to your customers.

More importantly, however, people want a sense of belonging and a cause that they can feel excited about waking up and fighting for every day.

In my case, that has always been education. To me, there is no nobler cause than expanding access to and the quality of education. But not everyone is as passionate about education, and not every employer operates in the education space, or even one that has a direct benefit to society as a whole. This is why purpose, vision, and culture are such key tenets of organizational success. The practices and exercises I've outlined thus far are not about self-discovery for the leadership team—they are setting a road map for the organization as a whole.

At a more granular level, employees also want to know that their role matters and that their career is being actively managed. Setting up regular check-ins and one-on-ones to collect employee feedback not only provides useful information to leaders but it helps managers get a sense of the direction that each staff member envisions their career moving. Armed with that information, organizations have two choices: help staff achieve their career goals internally or wait for them to switch organizations in order to realize that vision elsewhere.

Organizations that offer compensation that is consistent with industry norms, autonomy, respect, purpose, flexibility, and career progression will eventually wind up with their industry's best and brightest people and in doing so become indispensable to their customers.

Product. As discussed in the previous chapter, organizations are only as successful as the *it* that sets them apart. As mentioned above as well, bigger isn't always better, and sometimes a small but loyal group of niche users can be more valuable than mass appeal. As with each prerequisite to indispensability, feedback is critical. Understanding your customers at a deep level and working with them to solve their needs is often the best approach to creating a truly indispensable product. Hence, extensive competitor, customer persona, and needs analyses are performed before the first round of discussions regarding how to create indispensability happens. After this part of the process, go back to the *it* and refine as necessary. Repeat until maximum clarity is reached.

Since we've already spent an entire chapter on establishing the *it* of your business—and we'll devote all of chapter 16 to our maniacal focus on the customer—we won't belabor our discussion of product here.

Reliability. Achieving reliability can be more or less challenging, depending on the product and/or service you provide. In some cases, reliability is more a matter of manufacturing consistency; in others, it's about staff training; and in some cases, reliability is primarily achieved through a strong customer service department.

What's important is that organizations understand what makes customers come back to them over and over again and ensure that the core brand promise never wavers. Even as you add new products or update and adapt existing ones, the core value it provides should remain consistent. Coca-Cola betrayed its customers by changing too dramatically and too rapidly. Trader Joe's changes its products regularly, but the customer experience remains consistent. What separates these two examples is that Trader Joe's customers want a consistent experience, whereas Coca-Cola customers expect a consistent product, even if it gets repackaged every few years.

Reliability shouldn't come at the cost of innovation, but it should be a primary consideration in any conversations that center around making changes to existing products and services. So long as the *it* that makes the product or service indispensable remains intact, your customers will appreciate and value continual improvements. Once that core value is diminished, even for the sake of progress, brand loyalty can begin to falter.

The North Star of Indispensability

Indispensability is difficult to achieve, but those organizations that can successfully crack the code get to enjoy a wide range of benefits. Companies like YNAB and Trader Joe's put in a tremendous amount of time and effort, both at the outset and on an ongoing basis, to really understand and follow through on their purpose, vision, culture, and the *it* that keeps customers coming back. They don't just offer products and services people love; they do it with consistency and with a highly engaged staff who is motivated to go the extra mile.

All this effort isn't just for the sake of feeling warm and fuzzy about seeing staff and customers smile and leave positive reviews, although that is a nice feeling. At the end of the day, focusing on people, product, and reliability offers businesses a range of benefits that directly impact their bottom lines. Indispensable companies don't need to spend as much money on advertising or recruiting, since their employees and customers are eager to sing their praises to just about anyone who will listen. They don't need to spend huge sums managing turnover. Instead, they can put their time and resources toward further improving their products, employee experiences, and ensuring brand consistency. While plenty of businesses throughout history have achieved high levels of success without following this model, I can think of no more direct path to sustainable, long-term success than setting a North Star of indispensability and following through by maintaining a laser focus on people, product, and reliability.

9

Setting Master Goals

Creating *flow* within a business is critical to its success.

Flow takes many forms but is best thought of as the minimization of waste in four primary areas: motion, waiting, transportation, and over-processing. You can close your eyes and think of flow as rushing streams of internal handoffs, information, and processes that join together to form a river of finished goods and services that are consumed by clients and customers. These streams and rivers are guided by the strategy statements of purpose, vision, values, **be**haviors, and the company's *it*. Their velocity is determined by clarity of roles and responsibilities, goals cascades, and an unyielding commitment to understanding and satisfying the consumer. We'll explore this metaphor in more detail in chapter 10.

If we've learned anything from the global COVID-19 pandemic, it's that maintaining flow takes continual maintenance and intervention. Externalities that conspire to reduce flow are everywhere. For example, in the years leading up to the pandemic, many industries pivoted toward hyper-efficient, just-in-time production methodologies that proved too fragile to overcome challenges brought on by external realities. In 2019 we could order toilet paper on our phone and have a delivery arrive the next day. In 2020 the world ran out of toilet paper, and in 2022 we were still experiencing supply chain problems that resulted from those hyperefficient and fragile delivery models of the pre-pandemic period.

Instead, we should employ our continuous improvement tools to maximize flow for the things we can directly control. For things that are beyond our full control, we must work to maximize flow *and* develop contingency plans. An area of business design that is *within our control* and is a natural extension of the strategy statements we've discussed thus far is the determination of a company's *master goals*.

Unfortunately, goal setting within a business can be fraught with start-stops, discontinuity, extra processing, and long wait times from ideation to implementation. Most organizations have gotten into the practice of designating a goal-setting season, but the outcomes from episodic goal-setting sessions often aren't nimble enough to evolve alongside external realities. Furthermore, the master goal-setting process can itself be a huge source of waste. Goal setting is hard and time-consuming, especially when it is approached in this episodic manner. Each year leaders step away from their day-to-day work to dust off the master goals set long ago and spend too much effort reinventing the wheel. Worse yet, goals that are set in this start-stop manner are often doomed to fail because they don't align with the organization's stated purpose, vision, culture, and *it*, assuming leadership has even defined what those are.

Poorly designed goals that do not connect up, down, and across an organization can do more harm than good. That harm manifests itself in the form of team mistrust, employee dissatisfaction, failed projects, and poor performance. Moreover, if corporate goals change too frequently, the organizational change management curve *and* many individual contributor change management curves can't keep up, leading to—you guessed it—team mistrust, employee dissatisfaction, failed projects, and poor performance.[1]

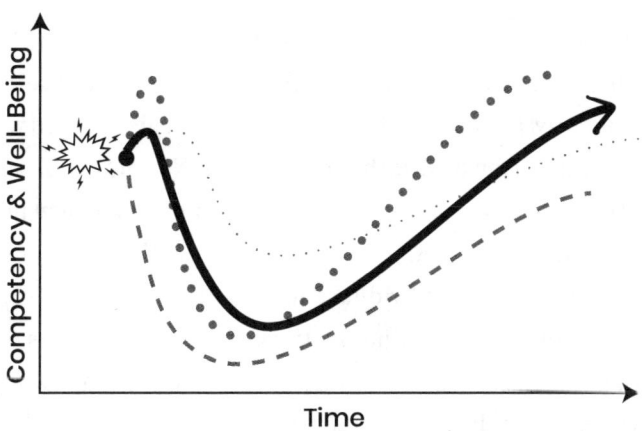

ORGANIZATIONAL
Change Management Curve

My aim is to provide a fresh perspective on organizational goal setting and will be splitting the process into two main parts: (a) goals that are aligned to the corporate vision and (b) those that are specific to the company's annual budget (which come full circle to support the corporate vision). Specifically, we want to help minimize the amount of episodic planning that a team or company engages in, shorten the "seasons" of annual business planning and operational cycles, and place more of this work into the *flow* of normal business operations. As we've discussed, there are many seasons of a business. While these seasons vary across businesses and industries, three "seasons" are common to nearly every business and institution: long-range planning season, budget season, and talent management season. The reality of these distinct planning seasons is that they are often disconnected from each other. Budgets are hard to align with long-range plans, and talent management becomes harder to square with the budget.

Weaving more of this work into the flow of the business will help keep entropy at bay and make goal setting more natural and useful for individuals and teams. Said differently, it will be easier for employees and teams to connect the dots between their day-to-day work and the direction of travel for the business as a whole.

Master Goals and Change Management

As I reflect back on my thirty-plus years in business, one of the biggest "aha" moments I've had is the realization that we altered and tinkered with goals too frequently. Frequently shifting corporate goals collided with the ability of the organization to absorb these changes. No amount of clarity or communication was going to overcome the disconnect between how fast we *thought* the organization could process change and the *actual* pace of change the average team or individual could handle.

During my career, I woefully underestimated the value others derived from checking the box and completing stated goals. The place where this behavior evidenced itself most frequently was in the area of technology. Based on my own experiences, I developed the faulty assumption that technologists embraced change and could work on multiple projects simultaneously with ease. Boy, was I wrong. I would dream up the next shiny ball to add to our tech stack, present it to the technology team, and then receive backdoor feedback along the lines of: "Enough already! Just let us get a few things done before you add more to the list."

Therefore, organizational leaders must think carefully about separating out goals that change slowly from those that need to change more rapidly, such as those established to keep pace with the market or shifting consumer tastes and preferences. Altering corporate goals for the sake of going through the motions of a long-range planning or budgeting exercise should actually be *avoided*. Rather than helping to keep us on track and create clarity, as we had previously assumed, those motions actually served to create waste and sow organizational confusion.

In chapter 11, we'll talk about *quarterly milestone goals* that need to change more frequently and how to design them. Here we're going to build a framework for creating what we'll call the company's master goals.

Master Goals—Where to Start?

The big question is, how can we construct master goals that will endure through time and be resistant to "management shiny ball syndrome" (a.k.a. the flavor of the day)? Where do we start?

The answer is to start with *purpose*, *vision*, and your *it*, three of our five primary corporate strategy statements. To be specific, I'm recommending that these three strategy statements be purposefully included in the goal-setting process and be prominently displayed on all resulting goal communications and documentation (see figure 9.1).

All too often, these statements get constructed and end up buried on the company's "About Us" page, as start-up screens on company computers, or wallpaper in the company break room. They literally become part of the furniture—which is a metaphor for something that slips into the subconscious and only gets analyzed when it's so out of place or out of touch that it's become a problem.

The benefit of starting with purpose and vision is that they become functional, pragmatic statements that are routinely discussed within the normal flow of business, rather than "furniture" that we ignore in our day-to-day, only to trot out on special occasions.

Constructing Master Goals

Our objective with master goals is to promote flow, improve clarity, demonstrate organizational commitment to the path forward, and ultimately improve trust, accountability, and performance. Figure 9.1 represents a highly stylized document that can be used to codify and communicate a company's master goals to internal—and when appropriate, external—stakeholders.

Figure 9.1: Sample Master Goals Template

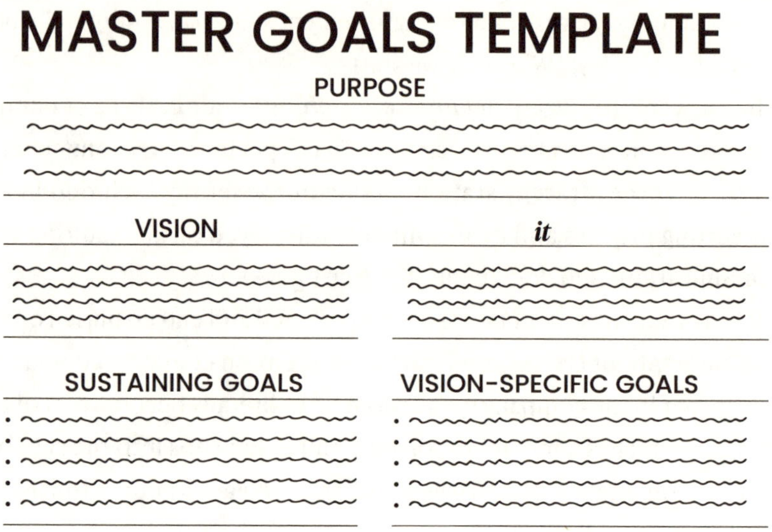

MASTER GOALS TEMPLATE

PURPOSE

VISION	*it*

SUSTAINING GOALS	**VISION–SPECIFIC GOALS**

The components of a company's master goals are as follows:

- *Purpose.* If everything begins and ends with purpose, then the company's purpose statement should be the headline to its master goals statement and be front and center at corporate events, team meetings, and stakeholder communications. Don't hide it away and don't gloss over it. Pun intended, but be purposeful in ensuring that purpose is communicated frequently. Ask team members what the company's purpose means to them and tell those stories in myriad ways—internally and externally. Authenticity should take precedence over glitz and glamor.

- *Vision.* Like the purpose statement, vision typically gets relegated to the company's "About Us" page and doesn't get the sunlight or attention it deserves. If you get *one thing* from this section, I hope it is how to use the company vision statement as *its primary master goal.* Doing so will inextricably link vision to goals and prevent entropy from allowing annual goals to stray from the company's vision or North Star. It makes no sense to create a vision statement for the business and not utilize it in goal setting.

- *The **it***. What the company does and what makes it different from its competitors must stand alongside the vision statement. Stakeholders must be able to draw a straight line from the company's purpose to its vision to the description of what the company does. Avoiding assumptions about what team members, customers, vendors, and investors know about the business is necessary to create clarity. This is an easy trap to fall into, especially when the company has been around a long time or its current leadership is long-tenured. "Why should I have to reiterate something as simple as our purpose, vision, and ***it***?" goes the common refrain. "I've said it a million times—everybody surely gets it." I can assure you memories are faulty, and making assumptions about how stakeholders interpret meaning and nuance leaves the door wide open to misunderstanding and misinterpretation.

- *Sustaining goals*. These are the high-level corporate goals that *change slowly through time*. Year in, year out, the company has a keen focus on these goals. Examples include:

  - Revenue growth. "We strive for revenue growth that exceeds growth in GDP by 2x," or "We expect our rolling five-year revenue CAGR (compound annual growth rate) to exceed X percent."
  - Operating income margins. "We expect our operating income margins to grow to X by 20xx."
  - Governance and compliance. "Our company is built on a foundation of ethical behavior—our words and deeds are one and the same."
  - People engagement. "The Widget Factory is a great place to work—our people are our most valuable asset."
  - Continuous improvement. "We are committed to growth through continuous improvement and learning."
  - Customer insights. "We are maniacally focused on the customer and strive to maintain a minimum NPS (net promoter score) of X."

The examples above are contrived statements but are directional indications of what a sustaining goal statement should look like.

While sustaining goal statements will, by definition, be more generic in nature, not considering how they will be measured and monitored through time is also a huge mistake. *Measurement* is key, and *all* goals must be SMART (specific, measurable, achievable, realistic, and time-bound), which is an essential ingredient of organizational clarity.

- *Vision-specific goals.* Vision-specific goals are what it says on the tin. They are specifically aligned to the achievement of the company vision and do not overlap with sustaining goals. Vision-specific goals are long term in nature and are unlikely to change dramatically year to year but *will* change more frequently than sustaining goals as major milestones toward the company vision are driven to completion or woven securely into the corporate operational fabric.

In chapter 11, we'll be talking about the process of setting annual goals. Both sustaining and vision-specific goals are jumping-off points for the creation of what's most important within a particular year or operational cycle.

The Initial Setup

The process of creating a company's master goal set is at first a difficult, painstaking process. Many hours of executive team effort, several rounds of catchball (tossing draft goals back and forth between the senior team and the extended leadership team to improve clarity and buy-in), and prudent investments in objective, independent third-party consultants—for example, facilitators—are necessary to their completion.

But subsequent rounds of strategic planning become much easier as each strategy statement and element of the master goal set is confirmed for continued relevance and cohesion within the overarching story line. Subsequent rounds are also easier because the master goal set is placed into the *flow* of work and is directly connected to annual, team, and individual goals, as well as *all* major corporate communications events.

Additional Considerations

Here are a few additional considerations—both positive offshoots and words of caution to note:

- An effective set of master goals will improve your team's ability to tell the corporate story. Storytelling is a critical human skill of import to everyone from individual contributors to the chief executive, as I'll explain further in chapter 13. If you want your company's story to be told consistently through time, *make* the time to develop master goals.
- As leaders, we know (or should know) the benefits of improved organizational trust and accountability. When everyone is rowing in the same direction, internal conflict is reduced. When goals are cleanly crafted, there is less wiggle room to allow for finger-pointing and accountability dodging. Alignment is key! To gauge progress and adoption through time, we can employ the brand marketing measurement tool of "internal unaided awareness" by periodically surveying employees and stakeholders for their unaided recall of master goals. If a hundred employees provide a hundred different answers, then the only thing that's clear is that clarity has not been achieved.
- Avoid continual wordsmithing each year. Choose your words and messages carefully during the initial setup exercise and vow to live with them for extended periods of time. Even small changes in wording will generate unnecessary waste and confusion. Constant tinkering and wordsmithing makes storytelling more difficult.
- Beware of the shiny ball syndrome! Adopting the master goal construct will force you to ask more "whys" when shiny balls come across your desk. Don't unduly stress individual and organizational change management curves by flitting between new ideas and strategy angles. Yes, agility is important, but it's a huge evolutionary leap when leaders consciously balance shiny balls with the human need for consistency.
- Make communication of changes to the company's master goals a big deal and utilize multiple channels and methods of communication over extended periods of time to ensure new messages are received and adopted. If you expect to say something once and think everyone

will "get it," like I did fifteen years ago, you'll be disappointed over and over again.

Size Matters

One final note: organizational size and longevity matter.

Generally speaking, long-tenured businesses will be able to "see" further into the future and should therefore be able to create more stable strategy statements and master goal sets. Start-ups and short-tenured businesses live in an environment of much greater uncertainty and will thus only be able to "see" shorter distances into the future. Hence, master goal sets and strategy statements will change more rapidly in comparison. While long-tenured businesses *should* be able to "see" further into the future, however, they also run the risk of becoming complacent and miss opportunities for change and growth. Agility must be balanced with the need for consistency.

Goal setting is not easy, and the work to develop and communicate them is, in some cases, as hard as the execution needed to bring them to fruition. Poorly crafted goals are a sure-fire path to the achievement of poor results. Put in the time and effort up front to reap the rewards downstream.

10

Optimizing Flow

I like to think of a well-functioning business as a series of streams that, when unimpeded, collect to form a powerful river. As you recall, we started this analogy at the beginning of chapter 7.

As the water continues along its path, it intersects with other streams that accelerate and fortify its flow. Over time, with enough inputs contributing to its strength, even a small trickle can turn into a mighty rapid. Each individual contributor represents its own trickle—teams eventually merge together to form streams, and each stream has the opportunity to feed into what can become a smoothly flowing river.

At the same time, there will always be debris and impediments lurking along the shoreline that could stop or slow the river's flow. Too many obstacles, bends, and blockers, and the stream won't reach its full capacity, even if it continues flowing.

ORGANIZATIONAL FLOW

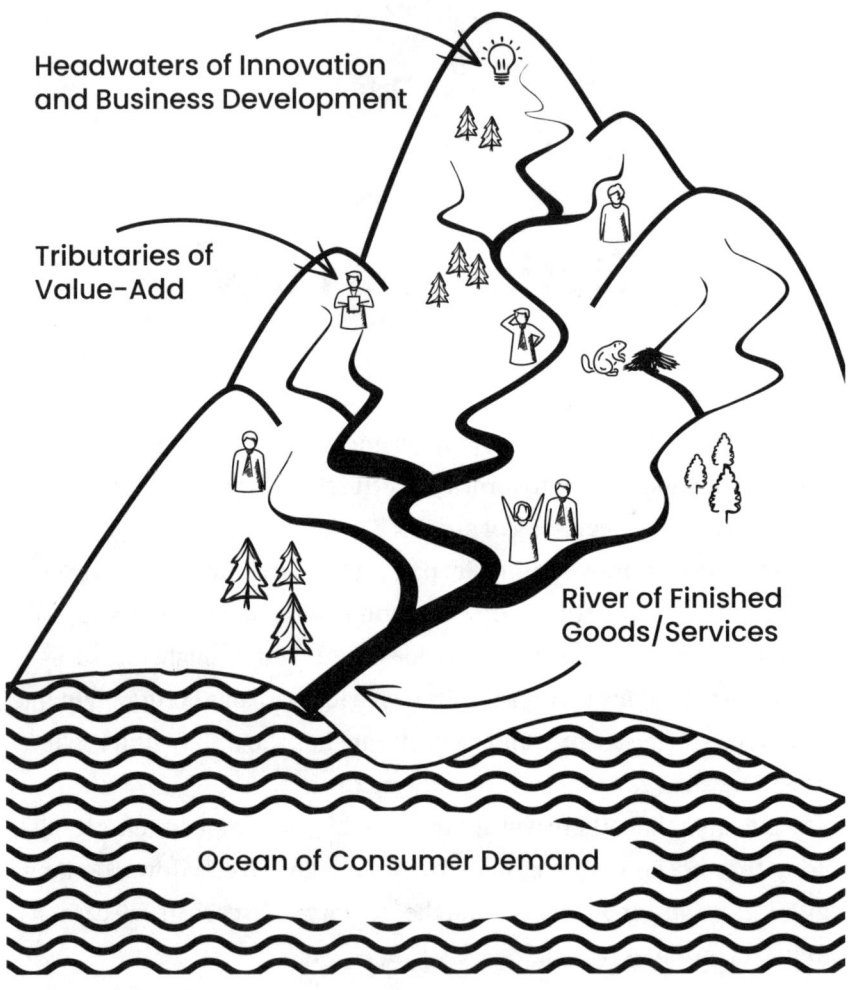

Headwaters of Innovation
and Business Development

Tributaries of
Value-Add

River of Finished
Goods/Services

Ocean of Consumer Demand

In a highly effective organization, each individual and team member is able to feed outputs and work product into the river, unimpeded by obstacles. At the same time, in such a powerful and large system, it's likely that a few obstacles here and there will go unnoticed. The river appears to be flowing smoothly from the ten-thousand-foot vantage point of the C-suite, so nobody questions whether there is an obstacle that needs to be dislodged upstream. Too many obstacles across the river system, however, can cut it off entirely. In business, a dam in one department, which might take the form of an accidental manager resistant to change, could similarly impede the flow of the whole system. If managers prevent their own teams from reaching full capacity, the rest of the river system will move a little slower.

If all this talk of flowing water systems hasn't already caused you to run to the bathroom, bear with me for just one last piece of this metaphor. In my mind, the ocean that all these streams and rivers feed into is the ultimate goal of indispensability. My objective with this book is to help readers break down barriers, improve trust, and ultimately optimize the flow of their business. As with a river, you can't optimize flow when there's a dam forming upstream.

Most businesses, however, are not built to optimize flow. They might break up logjams one by one, but in order to ensure continual flow, organizations need to consider the root causes of delays and detours. One of the primary root causes is an accidental manager, who excelled in their previous role but has little, if any, formal training or experience in leadership. Directly related to the accidental manager is an aversion to change and a preference for "the way things have always been done." This ultimately allows entropy to take hold, causing the business to operate on a foundation of ad hoc rules and unspoken handoffs.

Another potential flow disruptor that often goes unnoticed is the well-intentioned busy beaver. These keeners are typically strong performers with a track record of going the extra mile, but their outsized commitment to their jobs and need to constantly keep busy can have unintended consequences. Busy beavers tend to add a lot of unnecessary waste, not just to their own workloads but to those around them as well. Well intentioned as they might be, busy beavers often build unnecessary dams that disrupt organizational flow.

THE BUSY BEAVER

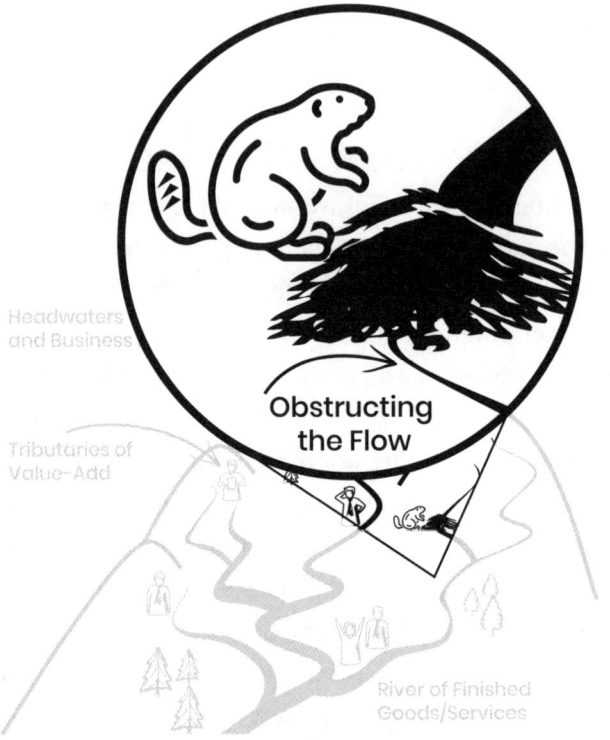

Headwaters
and Business

Tributaries of
Value-Add

Obstructing
the Flow

River of Finished
Goods/Services

This became obvious to my team at Kaplan during our CFA process mapping event, whereupon we discovered that, despite strong performance, there were many instances in which handoffs, work, and wait times were unknown. No one knew, or could codify, how the work actually got done, even though the business appeared to be functioning optimally.

As discussed, businesses are accustomed to operating on a seasonal basis, setting aside a designated time to check a designated box, then stuffing that work into a drawer until the next season rolls around. Following our river metaphor a little further, this stop-and-start methodology is a significant impediment to smooth flow. Instead, the management operating system I propose can keep things moving at all times by imbedding these processes into day-to-day operations. More work might be needed at the outset to build and implement these systems, but once adopted they allow the business to operate more smoothly, more cohesively, and with fewer logjams.

Strategy Statements

Achieving optimal business flow requires everyone in the organization to see the bigger picture and row in the same direction. Doing so, however, is only possible after first defining the destination and charting a clear course. That begins with the four strategy statements outlined in chapters 2, 3, and 4, which are designed to provide a deeper understanding of what your business is all about. The exercise of developing these strategy statements in and of itself can help improve clarity and cohesion among leadership team members, and their dissemination and promotion across the organization will help everyone better understand what they do in the organization every day and, more importantly, why.

As discussed in chapter 2, everything starts with purpose, which I loosely define as the core reason why the company exists. Purpose is distinct from mission statements, and if you're serious about improving your organization's flow, resisting the urge to just call your mission statement a purpose statement is important. They are not the same. Instead, get together with your leadership team and start asking the tough questions: Why do we exist? Who does our company serve? How are we contributing to a better future? Etc.

A strong purpose statement should be transparent; authentic; durable; simple; a conduit for alignment; a way to promote equity, inclusivity, and diversity; connected to societal well-being; specific; and more than a marketing slogan.

Once you have a clear definition of why you exist, the next step is outlining the company's vision. The core question you are trying to answer through your vision statement is "Where do we go from here?" I personally recommend using a Master A3 to outline your current thinking on where you are today, what a better future looks like, and how to best move from the current state to the desired future state. Through this practice, you should arrive at a purpose statement that is forward-looking, realistic, clear, universal, specific, and concise.

After you've worked with your leadership team to develop a clear vision and purpose statement, you can begin to consider your organizational culture, which is codified in two equal and corelated lists of values and **be**haviors. Remember: each is of little value without the other, yet many organizations today mash them together in a nauseatingly long list of feel-good slogans.

Outlining values and **be**haviors that speak to issues your organization and its leadership is passionate about, such as environmental stewardship, diversity, philanthropy, etc., is welcome. But far too many organizations update their website every time a new cause makes its way into the popular discourse by making a new addition to their list of company values. "How can we be in business in 2022 without acknowledging the need for racial justice in America?" First of all, good for you for trying to be part of the solution, but if you think you've "done your part" by listing "diversity and inclusion" as one of your core values, you are doing yourself and your organization a grave disservice.

That is why so many organizations that claim to champion causes ultimately face criticism for betraying their own values. They are driven by public relations, but the values are not internalized or backed up by actions. When crafting your organization's values and **be**havior statements, starting at the top, keeping it short, being authentic, taking your time, being specific, and weaving those values and **be**haviors into everything you do is important. Prominently displaying value and **be**havior statements around the physical—or in some cases, virtual—workspace and demonstrating a true commitment to them is incredibly important.

At Kaplan Professional, we chose to print them on mouse pads and give out company awards based on our values and **be**haviors, but there are plenty of other ways to display and demonstrate a commitment to your values and **be**haviors. Over time, as they become part of your everyday operating cadence, they will eventually become second nature and a deeply ingrained part of your corporate culture. Letting culture build "organically" instead will ultimately leave room for logjams and debris that can build up over time. Remember: what you permit, you promote.

Why Strategy Statements Shouldn't Be Outsourced

Before we go any further I feel that taking a moment to address the elephant in the room is important. A lot of organizational leaders aren't very accustomed to tackling the big philosophical questions because they feel it isn't their job, or they don't have the time to waste on silly thought experiments. That is why so many approach such conversations as a marketing exercise and why they are so often outsourced to an external marketing or consulting firm. There are many such firms who have made handsome profits by helping brands "clean up their image" or "develop their brand story." As someone who has hired one before, I know they aren't cheap. What's worse, getting enough value out of them to justify the expense is extremely rare; yet they still thrive, in large part because most leaders would pay any sum to check this box and move on.

Many of the worst offenders I've come across have been featured in prior chapters, and when a third party has been tasked with cramming a bunch of slogans or brand statements into a company's "About Us" page it is often clear. These firms typically take months to conduct research and interviews to unearth some sort of "brand promise," and the end result is usually ignored by leadership at best and causes confusion among leaders and staff at worst.

A key tenet of your strategy statements is authenticity, and while a third party might be able to work with leadership to draw out their authentic thoughts and feelings on these subjects, the process is completely useless without direct involvement from those at the very top of the organization. The only way you'll get real, lasting value out of the process is by forcing leadership to spend some time in a quiet room bouncing around ideas. There is simply no shortcut. A third-party facilitator might help move the conversation along, but if you hire someone to write your brand story for you, your organization will consistently fail to live up to its promises.

Preparing for the Inevitable

Change is inevitable, but we as humans are programmed to stick with the familiar, even at our own peril. Like our relationship with the two other inevitabilities in life, death and taxes, we tend to avoid thinking about change at all costs. It's a cruel reality that the world is constantly changing, and we must adapt to those changes, even though change goes against our every natural instinct.

Each of us operates on a different set of change curves, and when change is implemented too quickly, someone is ultimately going to feel left behind. Every organization will have plenty of opportunities to pursue positive change, but if you don't make the time to understand, implement, and manage change itself, the previous exercises become moot. For the most part, you can't control change, but you can manage the change process.

It is incumbent on every leader to internalize this inevitability and plan accordingly. Change needs to be methodical. Going back to our river metaphor, putting logs in the river one at a time won't do much to slow its trajectory; putting too many in at one time will create a dam. If you are to implement a management operating system, you will inevitably run into resistance, especially if you change too much too quickly.

Once you've established the more philosophical strategy statements, it's time to put them to use. Specifically, vision, purpose, values, and *be*haviors should serve as the bedrock—or, in this case, riverbed—of a free-flowing organization, but that's just the start. Now you need to fill those streams and put them in motion. Specifically, you need to translate those more philosophical questions into more practical questions, like, "What do we do?" For smaller and more nimble organizations, that *it* of what they do will change frequently through pivots and tweaks, but in larger organizations people often take their *it* for granted. "Of course we know what we do; we've been doing it for decades!"

The problem with that mentality is that, as we just discussed, change is inevitable. Even if your core product has remained consistent for a hundred years, the company's staff members and its broader business context are constantly changing. If you haven't taken the necessary time to define your *it*, you'll become far less insulated from the effects of those changes. Core to defining your *it* is understanding what sets you apart, and the practice of defining your *it* can help you lean into your competitive advantages as you change and grow. If Blockbuster had defined its *it* as being a video content distribution provider rather than a video rental store chain, perhaps it wouldn't have laughed Netflix out of the room when Netflix proposed a $50 million acquisition in September 2000. By the time Blockbuster filed for bankruptcy ten years later, Netflix was worth about $10 billion.[1]

Separating your *it* from a single product or service or feature ultimately makes change more palatable. Instead of panicking at the thought of a merger or new product, team members will be able to connect the dots between the new offering and the standard work that's currently in place. Everything comes back to flow. Establishing your strategy statements will turn what would otherwise be considered sweeping changes into part of your day-to-day processes.

Reaching the Ocean

All rivers eventually feed into the ocean, and in this metaphor the ocean represents indispensability to your customers. Indispensability is incredibly difficult to achieve, even harder to scale, and perhaps hardest to maintain, but it is (or should be) the ultimate goal of any business. Becoming indispensable means you don't need to fight to identify, acquire, and retain customers and clients as hard as your competition. When your product or service is viewed as indispensable, customers will give you a hand in marketing through recommendations, reviews, and positive word of mouth; they will demonstrate loyalty as the business changes and grows; they will be the first adopters of new products and services; they will champion your success in a deeply personal way. Achieving this degree of indispensability requires organizations to use their strategy statements to build an organization with highly motivated people, a product people want, and one that they can rely on. Many successful organizations feature one or two of these three elements, but those that have proven an ability to maintain indispensability over time—like Trader Joe's and YNAB—feature all three. They have optimized the flow of inputs into the business and minimized the four biggest sources of waste: motion, waiting, transportation, and processing.

Externalities that conspire to reduce flow are everywhere, which is why we must work to maximize flow while simultaneously developing contingency plans. Unfortunately, goal setting within a business can be fraught with start-stops, discontinuity, extra-processing, and long wait times from ideation to implementation, all of which impact not just the flow of the business, but employee morale. At the same time, changing corporate goals too quickly can be jarring, especially for team members on different ends of the change management curve. Failing to align on goal setting can therefore lead to team mistrust, employee dissatisfaction, failed projects, and poor performance.

While intentions are usually positive, the practice of goal setting can unintentionally break up the flow of the business and cause undue harm, especially when change is implemented too quickly, or too frequently. That is why resisting the seasonal approach to goal setting and weaving as much of that work into the flow of the business as possible is important. Whenever possible, goal setting should look like one log gently flowing down the river after another, rather than being dumped in all at once. If you put a single log into a river every day, it won't have an impact on the system's overall flow. If you dump a year's worth of logs in what you designate to be "log-dumping season," you'll wind up building a dam.

Fortunately, if you've made the time to fortify your company's metaphorical riverbed by establishing your strategy statements, you're already well on your way to weaving goal setting into the flow of the business. Your master goals should begin with your purpose, using your vision as the primary master goal, your *it* to offer clarity about what the company does and what makes it unique. Then you can begin to break down your master goals into "sustaining goals," and "vision-specific goals." Together they will help keep your organization on track in both a practical, immediate way, and a more philosophical, sustainable way.

Master goals are designed to help leaders map out a path toward achieving indispensability, but there's one more important piece to this puzzle, and that's learning and coaching. Perhaps I'm a bit biased, having spent my life in the skills development world, but all the data suggests we're living in a world of significant skills gaps, and every organization needs to prepare itself accordingly. After all, you can't optimize the flow of your business if your learning and development plan is to replace staff each time a new capability is required. As discussed in chapter 6, what seems like the easy route, or hiring and firing to meet skills needs, is actually more costly to the business over time. Furthermore, an ad hoc, as-needed learning and development plan might help bring staff up to speed, but it also creates waste, impedes flow, and is far too reactive to succeed in the face of today's realities.

Instead, organizations need a plan for weaving learning and coaching into the fabric of their business. Educational institutions, governments, and nongovernment organizations (NGOs) aren't going to fill the skills gap over the next decade; that burden will fall largely on employers. That is why every employer needs to prioritize developing a layer of middle managers that internalizes their responsibility to champion coaching and learning across the organization. As the conduit between leadership and frontline staff, the middle manager is in the best position to identify opportunities for coaching and development and to deliver that mentorship when it's needed. Instead of an annual review about performance, managers should seek to weave feedback into their everyday flow and provide annual or more frequent check-ins to assess coaching and development needs.

Doing so in a culture of accidental managers or in a low-trust environment or with a population that fears and resists change is nearly impossible, which is why establishing all the other strategy statements needs to come first. Getting your team members on board with the company's purpose, vision, values, *behaviors*, and *it* will make clear why they need to continually advance their own skills. There is also no amount of technology, no AI tool, that can stand in for a strong leader, mentor, and coach. In the Fourth Industrial Revolution, organizations will only succeed if they can activate the clay layer and help middle managers understand that serving as coaches and teachers is the primary function of their role.

11

Setting Annual Goals

The first half of this book is designed to challenge leaders to think deeply about the high-level philosophical questions that can help optimize flow. From this point onward, we'll be taking a closer look at some of the systems and practices that will put that work to use with the objective to optimize flow across your business within its annual operating cycle.

Specifically, we'll be moving from big-picture goal setting to more episodic, short-term goal setting and understanding how to streamline handoffs and ensure a clear line of sight toward achieving goals up, down, and through the organization. Next, we'll take a deep dive into establishing clarity and standard work at both the individual and departmental levels to set baseline expectations on which to build trust and accountability. We'll also explore how job descriptions need to become more nimble and less static in the Fourth Industrial Revolution and the vital role that learning and coaching play in the development of the individual and the organization as a whole.

After that, we'll engage in a deeper analysis of communication, its understated role in ensuring optimal flow, and how to establish reliable communication systems and cadence through a practice I've alluded to earlier as "catchball." Following our discussion on communication, we'll explore the ten wastes that threaten to reduce flow—specifically, how to identify obstacles and blockers that lurk just beneath the surface of business operations. Then we'll simplify and demystify the concepts of continuous improvement and introduce the ten essential tools you'll need to begin your organization's continuous improvement journey.

We'll also discuss how to develop and maintain a maniacal focus on the customer, using qualitative data to connect your strategy statements to the end user of your product or service. As we begin to wrap things up, we'll explore the importance of measurement and transparency. We'll explore the concept of accountability and provide guidance on how to determine what should be measured and why visual management systems are necessary to promote transparency within your organizational culture.

Finally, we will engage in a conversation about incentives and why they must align with goals, standard work, key performance indicators (KPIs), and strategy statements, with an emphasis on laying the groundwork for a culture of equity and inclusion.

Here, in the middle of our journey together, it bears repeating that one of my primary objectives is to provide you with the essential tools and applications for your management operating system. You'll note that I'm not providing specific direction on what financial, enterprise resource planning (ERP), customer relationship management (CRM), or marketing content management system (CMS) you should install. The choice of specific tool sets and how they are configured is one of many ways your business becomes one of a kind. Put simply, the first half of this book is populated with the strategic foundations that allow for the discovery of what makes your business special, and the second half contains more tactical tools to promote optimal flow within the annual operating cycle. The entire work is devoted to building a cultural foundation of trust balanced with accountability.

Goal Setting, Continued

Back in chapter 9, we introduced the concept of the master goals template, which is repeated in figure 11.1 on the next page. As a reminder, our aim is to minimize the "seasonality" of business planning and instead focus on flow across the annual operating cycle. We accomplish this by weaving the responses to the strategy statements of purpose, vision, and the *it* directly into the goal-setting process so they become the foundation for all the tactical work and decisions that follow.

The remainder of this chapter of the book is devoted to a step-by-step guide to the annual goal-setting process, beginning with the organization's annual milestone goals, which are broken down by quarter and directly support both sustaining and vision-specific goals. In each subsequent step, we drill down further into the organization until we arrive at goal setting for the individual contributor. Following this process will ensure goals are aligned both horizontally and vertically throughout the organization.

Figure 11.1: Master Goals Template

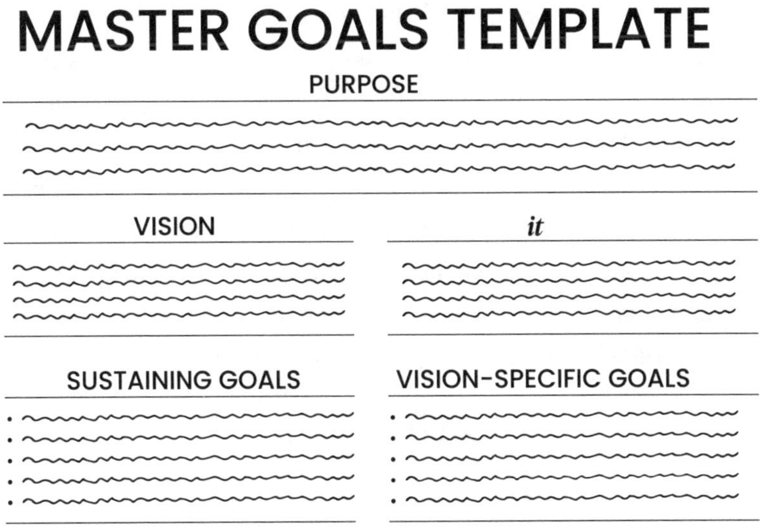

MASTER GOALS TEMPLATE

PURPOSE

VISION

it

SUSTAINING GOALS

VISION–SPECIFIC GOALS

Step 1: Setting Annual Milestone Goals

The good news is that the master goals exercise takes us a long way toward the completion of annual company-wide goals. Purpose, vision, and the *it* are established, as are sustaining goals and the intermediate-term vision-specific goals. The only thing to add are annual milestone goals.

Annual milestone goals represent "what's most important" in the current period to drive forward momentum in either specific sustaining goals or vision-specific goals. Annual milestone goals are:

- *High level, but specific.* In figure 11.2 on the next page, annual milestone goals are broken down by quarter, so the goal must be realistically achievable during that time frame. Depending on the structure of the business, milestone goals could be specific to H1 and H2—first half and second half, respectively—or even broken into thirds or trimesters.
- *Applicable to the entire business.* Although there may be cases where an annual milestone goal is specific to a functional area of the business—for example, technology or sales—they should be crafted in such a way that team members in *every* functional area can see how their work will influence the achievement of the milestone.
- *Established early in the budgetary cycle.* Nothing compacts the clay layer more than having company master goals handed to them late in the budgetary cycle. If master goals show up late or are ill-defined, a tremendous amount of waste is generated through overprocessing and defects created by reworking individual budget components. Playing catchball between the senior executive team and the extended leadership team during the creation of milestone goals will reduce the likelihood of surprises.

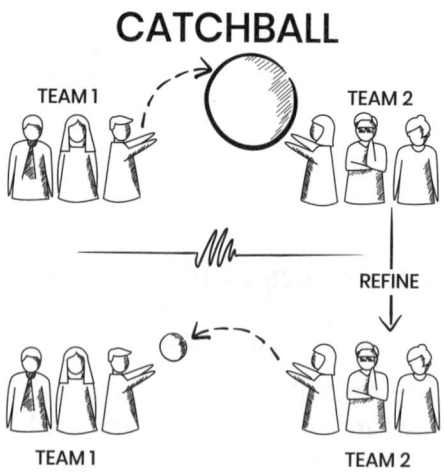

CATCHBALL

TEAM 1   TEAM 2

REFINE

TEAM 1   TEAM 2

- *Achievable.* If I had to pick *one* of the five foundational elements of a well-crafted goal under the specific, measurable, achievable, realistic, and time-bound (SMART) framework, it would be to stress the "A" in the acronym—achievable. Nothing crushes organizational morale more than consistently pushing dates further into the future. Having personally gone through several decades of organizational goal-setting exercises, I am *not* a fan of what are referred to as "stretch" goals. Your teams are already stressed and running at or near capacity. Imagining that a team has 110 percent to give is a false narrative and should be avoided to improve morale. We'll talk more about the SMART goal-setting guidelines in step 4 below.
- *Understandable.* Be deliberate with language throughout the goal-setting process. This is a miss in the SMART framework. So much waste is generated by internal bickering over what a goal is meant to convey. Clarity and parsimony are essential. Avoid flowery or confusing language at all costs.

Figure 11.2: Annual Milestone Goals

ANNUAL MILESTONE GOALS

PURPOSE

| VISION | *it* |

| SUSTAINING GOALS | VISION-SPECIFIC GOALS |

| Q1 MILESTONE | Q2 MILESTONE | Q3 MILESTONE | Q4 MILESTONE |

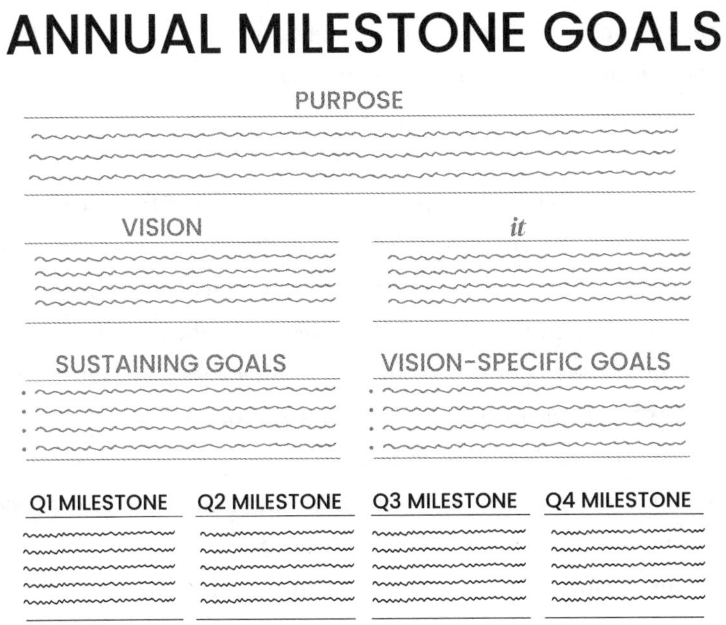

Step 2: Setting Functional Area Goals

In many organizations, none of the "doing" happens at the senior executive level. Instead, each senior executive—with the exception of the CEO and possibly a specialty position—leads a functional area of the business with responsibility for execution of the plan and achievement of strategic objectives. Hence, functional area goals, which are illustrated in figure 11.3, set the tone for the work that will be accomplished to support the master goals and annual milestones. Functional area goals are defined as "what's most important" to a specific part of the organization such as sales, marketing, technology, finance, or legal. Functional area goals are:

- *Supportive of company-wide sustaining, vision, and milestone goals.* This may seem like a no-brainer, but I've seen significant disconnects occur throughout my career between functional area goals and master goals. The underlying symptom of this misalignment is nearly always caused by a functional area leader who nods in agreement to the master goals with their colleagues in the board room but then decides that something else is more important for the success of their department. Dysfunction within the senior leadership team often has disastrous consequences downstream. This dysfunction is primarily driven by weak egos, misaligned incentives (see chapter 18), and ill-defined roles and responsibilities (see discussion on leader standard work in chapter 15).
- *Established before the number-crunching starts.* I've seen tremendous waste generated by overzealous, numbers-focused finance teams and leaders who jump right to building spreadsheets prior to the completion of functional area goals. When this happens, an artificial revenue, expense, or operating margin target becomes the focal point. At that point goal setting moves from an organic exercise based on sound strategy to a futile effort to bend and twist goals to meet an unachievable number that's not grounded in sound logic.
- *Developed using catchball.* Just like the catchball exercise that occurs when setting master goals between the senior leadership team and the extended leadership team, functional area goals should be "tossed" to team leaders within the functional area (or a select group of individual

contributors within the functional area in smaller organizations). This simple feedback exercise ensures buy-in and minimizes unintended surprises—both of which will improve functional area trust.

- *Cross-walked against other functional areas.* This is the place where most organizations fail in their goal-setting activities. Here, functional area leaders play a version of catchball among themselves, sharing and comparing their team's plans to ensure consistency and understanding of handoffs and resource demands. Unfortunately, egos and historical tensions stand in the way of collaboration among senior leadership team members. So much waste gets generated when one hand doesn't know what the other is *really up to.* Sure, high-level goals might be shared, but oftentimes fear of sharing dirty laundry or unearthing skeletons prevents the kind of transparency that's necessary to create true organizational flow.

- *Aligned with incentives.* Speaking of flow, nothing inhibits flow like misaligned incentive plans. If the master goal set says, "Expand product offerings through innovation," but the management incentive plan (MIP) says, "Grow operating profit by 10 percent," which one of these potentially competing statements will win out? It will undoubtedly be the expense control necessary to achieve 10 percent operating profit growth, which will choke off spending necessary for innovation and the launch of new product offerings.

- *SMART(er) than master goals.* While master goals will, by definition, be more high level and aspirational, functional area goals must add an additional level of clarity to bring company master goals to life. This feature of goal setting carries through the process as we move from master goals to individual contributor goals. Goals get SMART(er) as you get closer to where the work actually happens.

Figure 11.3: Functional Area Goals

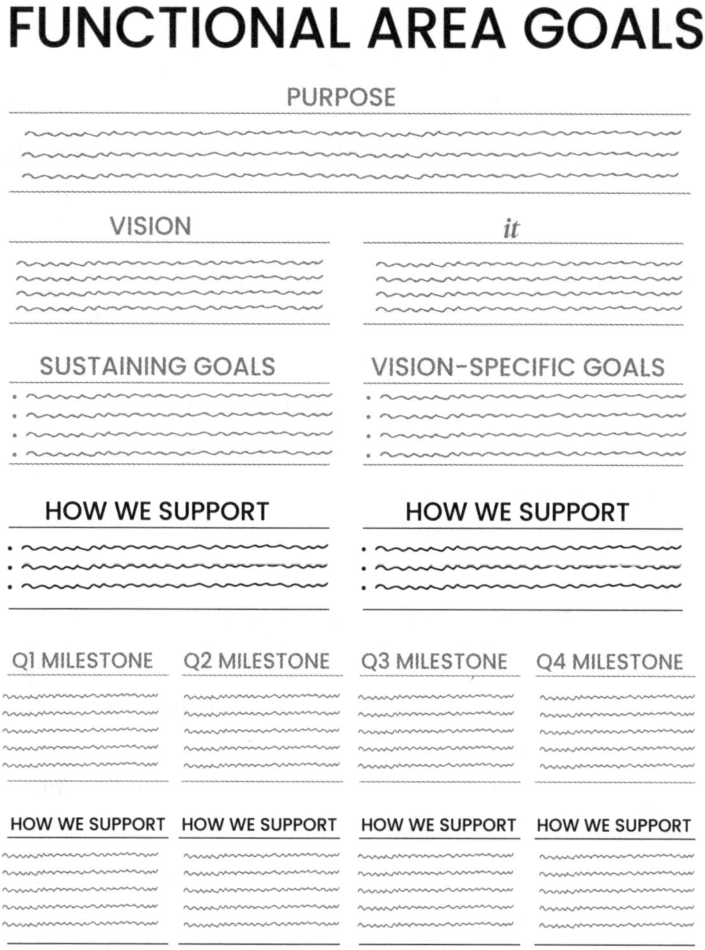

FUNCTIONAL AREA GOALS

PURPOSE

VISION   *it*

SUSTAINING GOALS   VISION-SPECIFIC GOALS

HOW WE SUPPORT   **HOW WE SUPPORT**

Q1 MILESTONE	Q2 MILESTONE	Q3 MILESTONE	Q4 MILESTONE

HOW WE SUPPORT	HOW WE SUPPORT	HOW WE SUPPORT	HOW WE SUPPORT

Step 3: Creating Team Goals

In large organizations, creating team-specific goals may be necessary. This may not be true of all functional areas of the business, but some functional areas may be large enough to warrant their creation. Before automatically assuming that team goals are a necessity, think first about *flattening* the company's organizational structure. Individual team goals may inadvertently create waste and impede flow if their creation is not targeted to the teams that actually need them. Spreading policies like peanut butter can create unnecessary waste in motion and overprocessing.

> **An aside—why individual goal setting is hard:** The creation of individual goals is where the rubber meets the road and where goal setting ultimately succeeds or fails. From my experience, goal setting breaks down at the individual contributor level because the process moves from a strategic planning and budgetary exercise to a human resources or talent management exercise. This is where well-intended human resources information systems (HRIS) and the desire to get goals into the "system" runs headlong into well-crafted goals and organizational flow.
>
> In fact, goal setting at the individual level ends up being combined with the annual performance review process in many organizations, bringing the elegant cascade from master goals to functional area goals to individual goals to a screeching halt. This is because individual goal setting is part of the company's "talent management season" and master and functional area goals are part of the company's "budgetary season."
>
> Hence, at the individual level, goal setting becomes an annual "check the box" talent management exercise that everyone ends up loathing. That is because corporate HRIS systems become bloated over time as one-stop employee and company information shops. They're like air traffic control systems that take so long to build and customize that once they're in place, they're obsolete. Pause for a moment and think about your company's HRIS system. It likely contains compliance, pay, benefits, goals, performance evaluations, competencies, team hierarchies, and a host of other employee and company information.
>
> Moreover, HRIS systems are typically *not* the primary piece of software that individual contributors use day in and day out. Yes, employees will routinely access the software for pay and benefits information, but other parts of the software package may be used

infrequently, forcing the employee to effectively *relearn* how to use it when talent management season rolls around. Goals and goal setting fit squarely into this category. "What are my goals again? Oh wait, let me log into the HRIS system, fumble around to find where my goals are buried, and I'll get right back to you." It's no wonder that there's a divide between the creation of company master goals, functional area goals, and the individual goals that *should* be guiding day-to-day activities.

Step 4: Creating Individual Goals

Our aside on the challenges with HRIS systems—and the clunky handoff of goal setting between budget season and talent management season—illustrates clearly why most goals get hidden away or locked into digital desk drawers, only to see the light of day during annual performance reviews.

In a perfect world, individual goals are part of ongoing performance coaching conversations between managers and individual contributors throughout the year. If goals must be contained within the company's HRIS system, then both employee and manager must be properly trained on its use. While this may come as a surprise to some, many managers, especially accidental managers, are not experts in the operation of the company HRIS system and go through a similar reeducation process each year during talent management season.

Hence, individual goals should be:

- *Visible*. Print your goals on an actual piece of paper and pin them up in your regular workspace. They should be right in front of you as a constant reminder of what's important to help minimize distractions and prevent the inevitable pull toward shiny balls.
- *Tied directly to coaching conversations*. Good managers engage in routine coaching conversations with their direct reports and don't wait to pile all their feedback into an annual performance review. Engaged employees welcome *constructive* coaching and feedback as a gift. At a *minimum*, goals should be discussed on a quarterly basis

between managers and direct reports—preferably monthly. These conversations should focus on progress to date and any midstream changes that need to be made to maximize alignment.

- *Tied to the gemba.* We're going to talk in detail about the gemba walks and gemba boards in chapter 15. For now, all you need to know is that *gemba* is Japanese for "the real place" or "the actual place." In continuous improvement parlance, the gemba is where the work occurs. Personal goals should be tied as closely to the work as possible—this applies to technical goals—for example, get x done by y date—as well as human development goals—for example, acquire new skill z. Gemba walks are typically done at the department level, so tying individual goals to the gemba effectively means that there is a strong linkage between individual and departmental or functional area goals. To maximize flow, tie goals to the gemba.
- *Aligned with incentives.* Keep a keen eye out for misalignment between goals and incentive packages. If individual goals say one thing, but incentives are aligned with something else, a collision will occur— whatever work is most closely related to monetary or nonmonetary incentives almost always wins. We'll take a deeper look into this in chapter 18.
- *SMART(est).* Individual goals are the most granular in the company and the SMART framework should be applied rigorously.
- *Specific.* The language used to craft a goal should be carefully chosen to minimize confusion and the potential for misinterpretation. Since goals are often tied to formal performance evaluations, it is in everyone's best interest to strive for clarity.
- *Measurable.* This is a tricky one. The old saying that's often attributed to Peter Drucker says, "What gets measured gets managed," but this reference has been debunked and strict adherence to this concept can lead to unintended consequences when measurement is forced. Therefore, the manager and individual contributor should think carefully about what "successful completion" means and how success will be measured. Use the "five whys" to explore potential

root causes of measurement challenges and to determine the best way to measure success.

- *Achievable.* As we've discussed before, nothing saps morale more than installing goals that are likely to be unattainable. I've personally awakened on a New Year's Day (or three) with a set of stretch goals that I knew were already under water. Needless to say, those were extremely difficult years. Engagement rises when goals are achievable.

- *Realistic.* This item is closely related to achievability. Are all the resources and support systems in place to ensure the achievement of a goal? Have all dependencies been considered? If team one must deliver *x* before you can even get started working on your goal, and/or team one is known to be unreliable, then don't commit without cross-walking your goal against the goals and resourcing of team one.

- *Time Bound.* Open-ended goals are also morale siphons. Make sure there's agreement on when a project or outcome is to be delivered *and* ensure there's going to be adequate resources available for completion.

Other Benefits of Goal Setting

Effective goal setting can serve to promote organizational flow when there is alignment and consistency of goals up, down, and across the business. Weaving goal setting into the flow of business operations also prevents episodic lurching and waste that's generated when everyone must stop what they're doing to create goals that aren't discussed or reviewed on a regular basis.

Goal setting also has the positive knock-on effect of honing communication and storytelling skills. It's one thing to create a set of goals. To truly get value from the process, it's essential to be able to communicate the story that's encapsulated within a set of goals. Don't make the erroneous assumption that the act of codifying goals represents the end of the process. Continuous communication and reinforcement across myriad stakeholders is essential in order to bring goals to life.

12

Respect for People

Respecting your people isn't just a feel-good concept; it's a vital tenet of a free-flowing organization.

Many of the key concepts explored thus far, including trust, indispensability, wrestling with entropy, goal setting, and change management, are wholly dependent on establishing a culture of respect. There's one more big theme I'd like to add, which we will be dissecting through the parts ahead, and that is *continuous improvement*. We've already touched on the value of continuous improvement, but I'd like to introduce what I've determined to be the key tenets of continuous improvement:

1. Respect for people
2. Identification and minimization of waste (which we'll discuss in chapter 14)
3. Maniacal focus on the customer (which we'll discuss in chapter 16)

PRIMARY TENETS
OF CONTINUOUS IMPROVEMENT

The order here isn't random; there are two primary reasons why continuous improvement relies on respect for people first and foremost. Firstly, tenets two and three require a culture of respect in order to be useful. The second is that FUD (fear, uncertainty, and doubt) often accompanies conversations about continuous improvement and the tools of Lean.

It's important to recognize that while leadership might look at the words *continuous improvement* and see an opportunity to optimize its processes and improve overall business success, most employees look at such terms and start to sweat. That is for two reasons: First, the world of continuous improvement is daunting, filled with complicated concepts, "foreign" language, and what many, especially the accidental manager, read as an indictment of their legacy ways of working. Second, many see terms like *continuous improvement* and think, "This is step one of a long process that results in my job becoming obsolete." They believe that if the organization finds enough efficiency improvements, they won't need as many members on their team to get the work done. Unfortunately, those concerns are not entirely unfounded. Organizations that fail to put respect for people as the primary objective of their continuous improvement journeys often see the process similarly—as a way to "trim the fat." No wonder there is so much excitement at the top—and so much resistance throughout the rest of the organization—when it comes to adopting continuous improvement practices.

As a result, many leaders, especially in service industries, shy away from adopting continuous improvement practices. They believe implementation is too difficult or that the principles only apply in manufacturing or production environments; however, *all* leaders can adopt continuous improvement practices by keeping things simple, focusing on the core tenets, and avoiding a purist "all-in" approach.

Establishing respect for people as the guiding principle of continuous improvement is both a way to ensure buy-in and is also a highly effective lens through which to view the implementation of its tools.

Empathy, Vulnerability, and Change Curves

After a long-standing relegation to the categories of feel-good, unserious, and impractical, the concepts of empathy and vulnerability in business have taken center stage in recent years, in large part thanks to the COVID-19 pandemic. The managers and organizations that ultimately succeeded during a difficult transition to remote work and a general upheaval of everyday life were those that demonstrated high levels of empathy and understanding.

Prior to the pandemic, we all strapped on an emotional suit of armor before walking into work or even get-to-know-you and team-building work functions. Our personal lives were locked up somewhere at home, and that side of ourselves was rarely seen by our colleagues, if ever. Suddenly, within a matter of weeks, teams found themselves peeking into each other's homes and personal lives through cameras and video-conferencing platforms. The mess in the background, the kid screaming for help with their homework, the dog barking at the mail carrier, the way we lived day-to-day became part of our work identities.

Managers and teams that continued to penalize rather than support those who were struggling in those early days of the pandemic likely suffered greatly when the pandemic gave way to the Great Resignation, or Great Reset. Much has been written about the importance of empathy throughout the pandemic, and I won't delve too much deeper into it now, but suffice to say this unprecedented situation finally demonstrated the value of empathy and vulnerability in a professional setting. It's a lesson I implore leaders not to forget as the world returns to one that more closely resembles our pre-pandemic norms.

Empathy and vulnerability are also vital to change management. Managers and leaders who can display empathy and vulnerability, and who understand that all humans are unique, are much better positioned to successfully embark on a mission of continuous improvement. That is because the concept of the change curve, which we explored in chapter 5, implores us to consider others' viewpoints.

Now let's take that concept even further. You and I (and everyone else) have different change curves, but to make matters even more complicated, you and I (and everyone else) also have myriad curves for different situations. How I manage changes to my professional life and my personal life are likely different. How I manage a change to my daily routine, versus the loss of a loved one, versus my favorite restaurant closing down, will also be processed along different curves. Now imagine implementing change among a small group of nine people. Each will manage change at a different pace, depending on both their personal change curves and the specificity of what that change entails. Now imagine a team of twenty thousand. The complexity of even a minor change process in large organizations is astonishing.

Furthermore, we can't leverage the benefits of diverse opinions and viewpoints if we are not empathetic to the intricacies of both individual and organizational change functions. I've seen it many times, and perhaps you have too. An organization announces a major change, such as a merger or acquisition, new innovation, new process, or new product launch. The organization acknowledges there *may* be some friction in making the necessary changes and then proceeds to place a tight deadline on the completion and installation of the major change. These projects often fall way short of the actual time line because leaders forgot to include one key ingredient in their recipe for change: respect for people. They sit around scratching their heads, wondering why a contrived six-month implementation time line actually took two years, but the answer is right in front of them. They grossly underestimated how long implementing the change would take and did nothing to manage it.

Rather than getting their team excited about the change, senior leaders have inadvertently given them reason to resist it. Staff haven't been told what this change means for the business or their team or their careers. They get to work erecting dams to impede flow, to buy themselves more time—all in the hope that "this too shall pass." Anyone who has tried to implement a project that took longer than expected, or was eventually abandoned, can probably trace the problem back to a personnel issue. Unfortunately, however, many will place blame on the individual or team that failed to adapt, rather than the organizational leaders who failed to prepare them for change. The bottom line is this: you can't implement any major changes, much less continuous improvement, without respect for your people, which starts with empathy and showing a modicum of vulnerability.

Empathy encourages us to understand one another's change curves; vulnerability requires that we share our own anxieties and concerns with change; respect for people requires us to work with their change curves in mind. Leaders often like to treat their human capital as just another resource, an input like any other piece of machinery or software, but we are all entirely unique. We can act like robots for a little while, but eventually stress and resentment mold into emotional baggage and reinforce the clay layer.

Really Showing Up to Work

The point of creating a management operating system for your organization is to allow for individuals and teams to display their creativity, to bring their whole selves to work, to celebrate their uniqueness, and to help them manage change effectively. A high-functioning management operating system allows your team members to explore their creativity and employ their ingenuity within its confines.

The concepts of vulnerability and empathy are also vital to strong leadership in the Fourth Industrial Revolution, in which machines do the most robotic work and humans are valued for their most human traits. In order to succeed in this environment, leaders can't pretend to always be the smartest person in the room, nor should they strive to be. A strong leader surrounds themselves with people whose opinions they value, whose feedback they internalize, and whose best ideas are championed. A strong leader works with people who have the potential to surpass them and celebrates the success of others rather than viewing it through the lens of personal competition. Personal competition can make us stronger individually, but as the previously referenced African proverb goes, "If you want to go fast, go alone. If you want to go far, go together."

Leaders and managers have long struggled with the concepts of vulnerability and empathy because of the cultures they've created. Often they are themselves highly ambitious, individualistic, and view their staff and teams as existing in service of their own needs and goals, not those of the organization as a whole. They think if someone is able to thrive—if their direct report is able to eventually surpass their own level—where does that leave them? Instead of promoting and championing their people, they prevent them from reaching their full potential, threatened by how it would reflect on them personally. Good ideas are seen as threats, and those ideas are quickly shot down.

If a leader or manager refuses to show any degree of vulnerability, given their personal success within the organization, a strong signal is sent to those they interact with. It suggests that bringing their whole selves to work, warts and all, is not a path to upper management. This is how businesses operated for much of the last century, but it is not a recipe for success in the modern workplace. In order to thrive, leaders need to create an environment where people are able to demonstrate their creativity, bring forward unique viewpoints, and share their best ideas without fear of judgment or reprisal. That an environment of *psychological safety* is established and nurtured is paramount.

Again, this isn't some sort of feel-good exercise; it is a matter of business success. According to a 2020 study by McKinsey and Company, "For diverse companies, the likelihood of outperforming industry peers on profitability has increased over time, while the penalties are getting steeper for those lacking diversity."[1] In this study, researchers found that:

- Companies in the top quartile of gender diversity on executive teams were 25 percent more likely to experience above-average profitability than peer companies.
- Companies in the top quartile for ethnic and cultural diversity outperformed those in the fourth quartile by 36 percent.
- Companies with more than 30 percent women on their executive teams are significantly more likely to outperform those with between 10 and 30 percent women.
- There is a 48 percent performance differential between the most and least gender-diverse companies, and there is an even greater performance differential between the most and least ethnically and culturally diverse companies.

Organizations have long treated their human capital as cogs in a big wheel. They often got away with it because the workforce relied on their most robotic traits—namely, their ability to follow standard operating procedures repeatedly without error. Today, however, those tedious tasks are increasingly accomplished by software and hardware tools. In order to get the most out of your most valuable asset—your people—you need to create an environment that allows them to bring their whole human selves to work. For more discussion of the "whole self" at work, I've dedicated an entire chapter to the subject in my first book, *Balancing Act*.

Standard Work

A primary element of continuous improvement is establishing and optimizing "standard work." According to the Gemba Academy, "Standard work is the practice of establishing, communicating, maintaining, and improving workplace standards . . . standard work provides a framework for formally facilitating and recording the small changes that drive continuous improvement and, by extension, incrementally raise standards across the board."[2]

Put more plainly, standard work is a process for finding small efficiencies that can add up to big improvements in just about any process. In my opinion, however, the term is a bit of a misnomer. Standard work is anything *but* standard. Sure, the process starts with defining how work is accomplished, but from there everything is called into question to create the next set of best practices. "What if we did it this way?" "How can we do things differently?" "Why is this the way it's always been done?" People see the term *standard work* and believe it's about establishing some sort of unchanging, immutable standard. The whole point of standard work is to break the standard, to understand that processes are not set in stone, and that the way things have always been done isn't necessarily—and usually isn't—the best way to do it. That includes any new processes you add through the practice of standard work itself—even the new and improved process should be questioned!

Of course, this is an oversimplification, and we'll spend time exploring other related concepts for pursuing continuous improvement and to refine standard work in chapter 15. At the end of the day, continuous improvement is all about optimizing business flow, and it all starts with respect for people.

Acknowledging that continuous improvement cuts against the grain of our natural state is important; we abhor change and love leaning on tried-and-true processes. People want to find what they consider "good enough," what is easiest and best for them, and then rinse and repeat, day after day. Any organization that pursues continuous improvement is likely to face challenges, blockers, and active resistance, unless they respect their people enough to engage them in the process. If you give your teams the permission and agency to solve challenges, find incremental improvements, and codify those solutions, they will more readily become trusted emissaries in support of your organization's continuous improvement journey.

If one of your business practices is really broken, team members need social permission to identify it as such. If they know there's a better way to do things, individual contributors need the psychological safety—established through empathy and vulnerability—to speak up. In an ideal world, they should have the ability to raise their hand, point out an inefficiency, suggest an alternative, and see it implemented promptly, without being dragged through a pile of red tape. Remember: Your frontline workers have the greatest insight into how things actually get done; those are insights your managers and leaders don't enjoy themselves. They are often in the best position to identify waste and to suggest small solutions that can add up to significant efficiency gains, but only if they feel respected enough to bring those ideas forward. Again, nurturing an environment of psychological safety is paramount.

Furthermore, this isn't just about one individual's practices and procedures. Standard work also applies to handoffs, information sharing, and other cross-departmental activities. This is where things can get especially contentious. If someone in department A believes they could improve handoffs between their team and department B, it's only natural for department B to take the suggestion as an indictment of their processes. Without an environment of mutual respect, it's impossible for the recommended efficiency gain to be realized; guards go up, and good ideas get shot down.

In Service of the Customer

As I've hopefully demonstrated, respect for people is foremost in the identification and minimization of waste, but it's also vital for the third tenet of continuous improvement: a maniacal focus on the customer. We'll discuss this concept further in chapter 16, but here I'd like to discuss where respect for people intersects with the customer, and it probably isn't what you've assumed. Most people can understand how respect for people creates a stronger working environment, which translates into better customer service, but how does respect for people in noncustomer-facing roles create better outcomes for customers?

When your organization exists in service of its customers, then all the efficiency savings brought by continuous improvement can be invested back into solving their needs. Many organizations approach continuous improvement as a way of trimming the fat, cutting costs, reducing payroll, etc., but I would argue they've approached the process with the wrong aims. Rather than using efficiency gains to reduce head count, an organization that respects its people and maintains a maniacal focus on the customer will use the freed-up resources for the benefit of the customer.

Let's say you embark on a continuous improvement journey, and after some time you've realized a 20 percent efficiency gain. Some organizations would use that opportunity to cut 20 percent of their staff or other resources and keep the savings for themselves and their shareholders, but that's a short-term profit grab, not a long-term solution. Instead, consider how those resources could be used to grow the business or better meet the needs of the consumer. Rather than cutting 20 percent of staff—and in the process sending a clear signal that respect for people is not a top priority—encourage the team to dedicate 20 percent of their time to innovation, creative thinking, and finding solutions that can improve the product, service, and overall customer experience. Alternatively, use the newly discovered time and resources to invest in coaching, learning, and skills development that will improve competency and ensure the relevance, resilience, and engagement of your workforce. Here growth becomes the priority, not short-term profit wins.

Continuous Improvement and the Accidental Manager

The accidental manager often believes they have all the answers and sees their job as one of micromanaging their teams according to their own tried-and-true practices. In an ideal world, however, managers are on the front lines of the war against waste, lead the effort to promote respect for people, and possess a maniacal focus on the customer. They are a key part of the process, but unfortunately many accidental managers aren't up to the task. After all, they were promoted because of their abilities as an individual contributor and likely don't have the emotional or technical tools for the job of being an effective manager.

In order to navigate a successful continuous improvement journey, managers need to demonstrate the opposite talents. They need to learn how to have ongoing performance conversations and conversations about outcomes and goals, with the understanding that learning and development is key to their teams' success. They should also strive to spend large portions of their time thinking about how to fill skills and knowledge gaps, which is where they can provide the most value to the organization. Rather than micromanaging and firefighting, they need to serve as coaches, helping their reports connect the dots on how to make the business more efficient rather than seeking to disenfranchise or reprimand those who speak out.

That is essentially what respect for people looks like in practice for the average manager. At a leadership level, it's about resisting the urge to prove yourself the smartest person in the room and instead surround yourself with good people and empower them to succeed. At the end of the day, the development of standard work and continuous improvement is as much about enriching the employee experience as it is driving better results for customers, as the two often go hand in hand. Establish operational and strategic guardrails and then give people the agency, the respect, and the confidence to thrive. Build the management operating system and then get out of the way.

Writing: A Key Leadership Skill

One of the unpleasant truths of leadership is that the people who populate your organization at all levels are constantly trying to divine your position on myriad topics—everything from purpose and vision to the stack ranking of current period priorities. Like it or not, as a leader, you are a significant topic of conversation, and your position on issues matters.

The less visible you are, the more active the watercooler will be. Infrequent communication from the top provides more oxygen for conspiracy theories and rumors to thrive. Conspiracy theories and rumors breed significant emotional waste that can negatively influence morale, engagement, and productivity.

Although I had help with proofreading and solicited opinions prior to publication, as a leader, the vast majority of my written communication—both internal and external—was produced by my own hand. It's hard work, but I feel strongly that what you choose to put in writing should be carefully considered, and the words should be your own.

So what's the payoff from doing more writing?

1. *Clarity.* Another party can very easily twist your verbal comments to fit their personal narrative, but it's much harder to cherry-pick and bend the written word. Whether it's an annual letter, quarterly update, or weekly muse, you're establishing a level of clarity that's not possible with other forms of communication.

2. *Concision and logic.* The act of writing forces you to carefully construct an efficient argument or thesis. In verbal communication, getting off track and rambling incoherently is easy. Writing makes us slow down and think much harder about the points we're trying to make and whether those points will be clear and understandable to the intended audience.

3. *Creativity.* I find the process of writing sparks new ideas and makes neural connections that add significant value to an idea, position, or recommendation. Yes, bouncing ideas around in a brainstorming session is a highly valuable exercise, but I almost always find new ways of looking at an issue or problem when I commit pen to paper.

4. *Cascade.* I've derived great value by using my writing as a conversation starter with direct reports and their teams. Specifically, I schedule one-on-ones with my direct reports and ask them to come prepared with residual questions they have about company goals, the North Star, or anything else I've written about that needs clarification. I also ask my direct reports to share feedback that they received from their team members on the same issues. To triangulate, I arrange "skip level" listening sessions with my direct reports' teams to field comments and suggestions and answer any questions they might have.

Don't underestimate the power of skip level listening sessions. You'd be surprised how much critical information gets filtered out—usually unintentionally—by your direct reports. Getting as close to the work as possible is key.

5. *The importance of reading and writing.* By routinely putting your thoughts on paper, you're sending a strong signal to your peers and colleagues that reading and writing are important pursuits that should be prioritized. I frequently lament about how little we read on a daily basis and how our skill level as writers has taken a real hit in the age of tweets, emojis, and text messages.

In legacy business cultures, knowledge was power, and team members fought hard to keep information to themselves to ensure their jobs and prove their importance to the business. This behavior led to inefficiency, single points of failure, and a very active watercooler information economy.

Today we live in an age of diversity, inclusion, and accessibility. Knowledge is still power, but obfuscation and information hoarding should not happen within the four walls of your business. As we aspire to flatten organizational structures and tap into the rich vein of ideas and innovation that resides within our people resources, improving the fidelity of communication up, down, and throughout the business is of paramount importance.

13

Communication

Communication, like change, is a natural part of the human experience; and, like change, it too needs to be managed effectively in order to facilitate flow.

Have you ever found yourself in a foreign country, far away from the parts of town that cater to tourists, immersed among a local population with hardly five words of English in their vocabulary? If you have, you know that even when we come face to face with someone whom we don't share a common language with, we can find a way to communicate basic but important messages. It might take some creative hand signals or crude drawings, but eventually you find a way to interact, even if it takes time. This fairly common experience speaks to our natural desire to be understood and our natural urge to understand, even at the most basic level.

People will always find ways to communicate with one another, but our natural modes of communication are often far from efficient. In fact, as alluded to in the previous chapter, miscommunication and overcommunication are both significant drivers of waste and impediments of organizational flow. Rather than letting communication norms develop naturally, organizations need to develop reliable, repeatable communication cadences and methodologies that can help build trust and accountability.

Communication as a business strategy represents an opportunity for tremendous efficiency and value. In fact, I believe communication, trust, and transparency are necessary preconditions for the minimization of waste in any business and are base-level requirements for the creation of flow. So much so that I dedicated an entire chapter of my previous book, *Balancing Act*, to exploring various modes of communication, and still have much more to share on the subject.

Achieving trust through transparency requires equal communication of the good, the bad, and the ugly. Leaders often fall into the trap of being overly optimistic in their internal communications, leaving staff to fill in the blanks when those communications fail to align with the realities they see with their own eyes. In short, you need to show the whole truth—or as much of the whole truth as possible—otherwise, every communication is received with skepticism.

One way to do so is by broadcasting your metrics and key performance indicators for everyone to see. Prominently displaying such data helps everyone keep their oars moving in unison. Instead of hiding problems in the business, or in one department, this form of radical transparency puts challenges and opportunities front and center for the entire organization to see and invites everyone to participate in finding solutions. It is critically important to be honest about how the business is performing to move from emotion to rationality and objectivity, which in turn invites everyone to pitch in on solving challenges and supporting their colleagues.

Transparency is the elixir that shifts a culture of blame to one of shared responsibility, allowing everyone to share in the organization's successes while reducing finger-pointing and other unhelpful emotional reactions when goals are not achieved. Transparency also invites individuals and teams to learn from the mistakes of others and to avoid similar missteps themselves. Most importantly, transparency forces leaders to show constructive vulnerability to their teams. We'll discuss this more in chapter 17.

Establishing transparency begins with an understanding of what gets measured and why. Communicating to your staff what each team and department's key performance indicators are and providing unbiased measurements against those objectives creates a more even playing field. Everyone should have a basic understanding of what's being measured, why those metrics are considered a benchmark of success for the company's goals, purpose, vision, culture, etc., what constitutes a positive outcome, and what are considered poor results.

Building a culture of transparency has gotten more complicated in recent years as a result of flexible, remote, and hybrid work. As you'll recall, Kaplan Professional used a lot of visual cues in and around people's workstations to keep us aligned on our purpose, vision, values, and *be*haviors, and we prominently displayed our KPIs on screens and monitors around the office. Unfortunately, such visual reminders aren't as effective in a remote environment. That is not to say that you should force your staff back into the office for the sake of immersing them in company messaging, but instead that you need to consider how to achieve the same level of transparency across a broader diversity of work settings.

The importance of dedicating thought and energy to leveling the transparency playing field among remote and in-person staff cannot be overstated. If you unintentionally create an environment whereby different messages are reaching different groups at different times, people won't know what to believe, entropy will take over, and trust will evaporate. In order to get this right, there needs to be a degree of consistency, reliability, and persistence in all corporate communications.

> **A side note on duplicity:** For all the talk about the benefits of organizational transparency, leaders, especially the C-suite, live in a world where some things can be said and some things can't. There are times when secrets must be kept from portions of the organization: an upcoming merger, a new strategic direction, or a skunkworks-style product development function are just a few examples. As a general rule, duplicity should be minimized in favor of transparency, and we can use our "five whys" from chapter 15 to frequently assess whether or not we're keeping the right things secret and minimizing internal territorial information wars.

> My advice to leaders is to recognize the tension that duplicity creates within the organization and to be clear with the team as to *why* a secret needs to be kept. Doing this consistently will send a clear message to the organization that secrets are the exception and not the norm. Transparency should be the norm.
>
> Alternatively, my advice for individual contributors and line managers is to avoid getting drawn into the rumor mill and water cooler conspiracy theories. It is the responsibility of both leadership and the general employee population to avoid giving undue oxygen to rumors and conspiracy theories.

Transparency and communication are often two of the greatest challenges for an accidental manager, as well as two of the most important opportunities for learning and development. The accidental manager was tapped for a leadership position because they were a great individual contributor, but the reality is that many don't have the chops to be an effective communicator due to a lack of training in this area. Communication skills should be one of the highest items on the checklist for management and leadership development opportunities, but communication rarely makes the list in lieu of other, "more important" skill development needs.

Communication often falls into the human, or "soft skills" bucket, which has traditionally received less focus and attention than more traditional technical skills. When most of us received our formal education, we studied accounting or economics or biology or engineering, etc., and communication was assumed to be picked up along the way, like other "life skills." Formal communication skills were likely not a part of your curriculum unless you studied a select few disciplines, like psychology, marketing, or public relations.

In recent years, however, there has been a broad awakening to the significant value of human skills across a broad range of disciplines. For example, a seminal 2005 report by the Joint Commission on Accreditation of Healthcare Organizations found that communication failures were responsible for 70 percent of medical errors resulting in death or injury unrelated to the natural course of the patients' illness.[1] In other words, when medical procedures go wrong, the majority of the time a communication error is to blame. As a result, the medical community has taken great strides in improving not only communication training, but also its assessment. In recent years, medical programs have introduced evaluations designed to ensure a base level of communication skills as part of the admissions process. If you are a poor communicator, you probably won't get into medical school, but that's just one example. Countless other industries have also identified the importance of strong communication, making it one of the most important and more transferable skills candidates can offer employers today.

According to LinkedIn, the three most widely cited human skills on job postings in 2020—namely, creativity, persuasion, and collaboration—were related to communication.[2] The Enterprisers Project, a community of CIOs and IT leaders, put communication sixth on their list of the ten most essential skills for IT professionals in 2022.[3] FlexJobs ranked it seventh on their list of fifteen transferable skills that companies want.[4]

Where communication falls on the list doesn't really matter so much as the consistent inclusion of it as a key driver of career success across a broad spectrum of sectors and industries.

The Power and Importance of Repetition

One of the most significant ways of improving communication is also the simplest. Repetition and reinforcement of a consistent message are critical in developing clear communications. The more times you say something, the more important that information is perceived to be. After all, if it was just a fleeting thought uttered in a social setting, it probably doesn't warrant much consideration by others. If that message is repeated in every major work communication, your audience will naturally consider it more intentional, and important.

Unfortunately, however, we need to acknowledge that repetition often goes against our natural instincts and our ego. Everyone—but especially leaders—like to think that their words are taken as gospel; enshrined in stone tablets and revisited and studied by their disciples. The reality is that most of what anyone says is quickly forgotten unless repeated many times over, no matter who they are.

Let's be frank—repetition is uncomfortable. Nobody likes repeating the same old story time and again, especially not to the same audiences, so we tend to spice things up a little bit. As time goes on, we tend to add new details with each telling, thinking it will make the content more engaging for the audience members who have already heard the message. The problem is that diverging from the message opens up room for interpretation, misunderstanding, and misalignment. If you tell one version of the story to department A and a slightly different version to department B, how are they going to square the difference?

Perhaps more importantly, ask yourself whom the change in telling serves. Sure it's more interesting than constant repetition, but to whom is it more interesting? Probably to the one telling the story. You've said the same thing over and over, and giving the same song and dance is starting to get a little frustrating. Changing the message, however, will prove a long-term disservice in exchange for a short-term personal gain. Going back to the concept of the change curve, you probably want to enhance the narrative because you've already reached the end point of the change process—you've accepted the message—but your audience might not be there with you just yet. Your job as a leader is to cater the message to the audience, no matter where they are on the change curve. In most instances, this requires ongoing repetition and reinforcement.

The practices and exercises outlined in the first half of this book should serve as a strong basis for that often repeated corporate message. Establishing and codifying the business's purpose, vision, values, *be*haviors, *it*, and master goals will help keep everyone on message.

Politicians repeat the same stump speech time and again because it's polished and well rehearsed and leaves little room for interpretation. What separates good politicians from the bad—at least by the measure of electoral success—is that they can repeat the same message with the same enthusiasm and conviction each and every time. They know that diverging from that well-worn message is a political risk. The same is also true in business.

The New Year's Letter

Earlier in my career as a leader, I believed I could say something once or twice and my team would "get it." I was bewildered by how twisted messages would become once they were released out in the wild. In an effort to solve this communication gap, I started writing. I wrote annual letters, quarterly updates, posted more frequently to LinkedIn, and wrote articles that appeared in trade magazines and blog sites.

While most organizations issue a flurry of year-end communications, annual, or holiday letters are treated with very different degrees of thought and care. Some leaders see them as a formality and among the least important of their responsibilities. A quick "thank you" for your effort, "happy holidays," and "see you in the New Year," is all that separates them from their vacation plans. I know because I used to be one of them, but over time I started to take a different approach to the annual letter.

Eventually, I started to see the New Year's letter as the first communication in an ongoing dialogue, a device I could refer back to throughout the year as a way of consistently reinforcing key messages—namely, the organization's strategy statements. The annual letter offered a way to tell the stories I thought were necessary for adding context, color, and specificity to the goals that had been established during strategic planning and budgeting sessions. Instead of cramming your New Year's letter with overly positive fluff, your letter to staff is a great opportunity to offer some real substance. Like the organization's strategy statements, the annual letter should be written in collaboration with senior leaders as a way of providing a link from the close of one year and the start of another. Playing catchball with this document prior to its publication yields a better product and improves organizational clarity.

As technology advances, many leaders are electing to switch formats and instead offer a video message, but I would advise against that. Call me old fashioned, but there's something about putting pen to paper (or fingers to keyboard) that engages the brain more directly. The act of creation shouldn't be an afterthought and should be treated with real care and attention. Hence, I would advise against outsourcing the creation of the annual letter to the communications department. Your staff can tell when your "voice" is not present in a document. To be clear, it is beneficial to create a video message as a way to reinforce the message, but I would avoid relying *solely* on video as the primary delivery medium.

Establishing and then repeating annual letters in writing proved effective for me. I recommend treating the annual letter as an entry point to conversations throughout the year that tie back to the goals and aspirations set out at the start. I even made a practice of bringing the annual letter into meetings months later and placing it on the table to show that I haven't forgotten what I wrote, it's still important to me, and that I wasn't going to let it be forgotten.

Communication and Technology

Back in the old days—and by that I mean just a few years ago—we all went to the same place every day, sat at the same desk, saw the same login screen as each and every one of our colleagues, and crisscrossed each other in the halls. In this visual and tactile environment leaders had the ability to communicate key messages in a very direct manner. Remember Kaplan's mouse pads from chapter 4?

Today's reality looks a lot different for most organizations, because technologies and workspaces are more diverse than ever before. In lieu of shared workspaces and communal water coolers, we now have myriad communication and collaboration tools at our disposal. While we may have more platforms, tools, and opportunities to disseminate messages, the flexibility and diversity of tool sets makes consistency and transparency a much greater challenge. Now leaders need to consider ways to keep their message fresh and top of mind for an audience that uses a wide variety of tools and technologies to communicate.

Sure, you have the company-wide email or messaging platform, but different teams and departments are likely to have additional tools they lean on more heavily each day that are specific to their job function. To make matters even more complex, assuming that everyone's utilization of and proficiency with each of these tools is the same is never safe. Some might be accustomed to logging into and communicating on a virtual platform every day; others might ignore their notifications and assume that if the message was really important, someone would bring it up in a meeting. Just as our smartphone's operating system is the same for billions of other users, the way in which we engage with the technology is entirely unique to the individual.

Once again we need to bring up the change curve because, in our increasingly virtual work environment, there will be many members of the organization who are struggling to adopt these technologies, and failing to acknowledge them will only breed greater entropy. I've seen it many times—the organization adopts new tools, provides some resources and assistance to help onboard staff, but there are always those who feel left behind. Any change, but especially one as fundamental as your communication medium, has the unintended consequence of alienating a subset of your employee population. Assuming that the right piece of technology will solve your communication challenges will only strengthen the permafrost and make the clay layer more resilient to change.

If communication is a problem at your organization, addressing root cause rather than adding greater complexity to your technology stack is important. There are a lot of remote communication and collaboration tools out there, more than I can possibly list here, and while most come highly recommended, recognizing that what works for one culture might not be a good fit for another is important. Before adopting any remote or digital collaboration platform, take the necessary time to consider your unique culture and needs. Also ensure that, as with any change, new tools come with the appropriate level of learning, coaching, and development to ensure no one is left behind, something I learned the hard way.

A few years ago, someone from Kaplan's IT department waltzed into my office, installed Slack on my work machine, gave me a username and password, and simply walked out, leaving me scratching my head and feeling like a dinosaur. They told me it was super easy, and that I would get it right away. I never did. In fact, I hated it.

This communication platform simply did not fit my communication style. I was the chief executive, and I wasn't the type to have a conversation buzzing around in the background of my computer screen. I couldn't just punch out a message and send it out to the world without taking some time to really choose my words carefully, something that the platform doesn't encourage with its endless scrolling. We often assume we can institute a change, and everyone will catch on, but recognizing that not everyone is able to just "get it" is important. Worse yet, some might actively refuse to even try without the proper training and coaching.

The other trap many fall into is overengineering their communication tool sets. We now exist in an environment where different teams and departments will have their own preferred platforms, each as necessary to one department as they are foreign to another. For example, your sales team might primarily communicate using Salesforce, while your software developers rely on GitHub, and your marketing team primarily collaborates in HubSpot.

Having these department-specific tools can be a huge resource to each team, but if you're not careful you could end up adopting a lot of expensive software, none of which is being used to its fullest. With too many department-specific platforms you're likely to find yourself in a situation whereby each team is only using a handful of the platform's features, but the organization is still paying full price. Having too many tech platforms also makes life more complicated for leadership, who are both trying to disseminate information to a broad, cross-departmental audience and also trying to gather data and insights from each individual platform.

While giving teams the ability to adopt technologies that are necessary to their productivity is important, adopting all this software can be a minefield for decision-makers. That is why I recommend first taking stock of your communications technology stack and regularly assessing whether or not it's delivering enough value to justify the added complexity and cost. Adding too much choice and diversity in terms of communication tool sets can ultimately introduce significant complexity—and waste—to your organization. In order to optimize flow, don't take these decisions lightly, and avoid adopting the latest shiny new tool without factoring in the measurable and nonmeasurable cost of complexity.

14

The Ten Wastes

As we've discussed, I find it useful to dramatically simplify the concepts of continuous improvement (a.k.a. Lean) into three primary tenets: (1) respect for people, (2) identify and minimize waste, and (3) adopt a laser focus on the customer. It really is that simple.

In chapters 11–13, we explored the concept of "respect for people" through the lens of goal setting, standard work, and communication. Trust, accountability, and flow are maximized when roles and responsibilities are well defined and communicated consistently and effectively. Now we'll turn our attention to the second tenet of continuous improvement: identifying and minimizing waste.

The ability to *see* waste is key to the adoption of a continuous improvement mindset. After all, if we can't see waste and inefficiency, how can we continually improve our standard work?

Before we get started, however, it's important to note that most discussions of waste focus on manufacturing and physical production environments. This is natural, as Lean had its beginnings in Toyota manufacturing facilities during the 1930s and 1940s as Kiichiro Toyoda, Taiichi Ohno, and others in the company sought to refine the pioneering innovation of the assembly line that Henry Ford had established earlier in the twentieth century.

In 1990 Womack, Roos, and Jones codified the Toyota Lean process in their seminal book, *The Machine That Changed the World*, and refined those concepts in the 1996 follow-up work by Womack and Jones entitled *Lean Thinking*. I recommend that readers who want to delve into hardcore Lean principles start with these two books. In addition, organizations like the Lean Enterprise Institute (Lean.org) are excellent resources for all things Lean and continuous improvement and cater to everyone from novices to experts.

My favorite book on Lean, *The People Side of Lean Thinking* by Robert Brown (2013), was handed to me by a colleague in the mid-2010s. Brown's book piqued my interest because it looked at continuous improvement through a different perspective, which led me to connect the dots between the practices of organizational health and continuous improvement. I'll be forever grateful for the courage and tenacity of that former colleague.

The book you're reading right now does not contain an in-depth analysis of traditional Lean practice models for two reasons:

- *Language.* The full-on adoption of Lean within a business requires that *everyone* in the company learns the language of Lean—which can be unapproachable and foreign, especially if the concepts are not used each day. I stress *everyone* because in my experience, for Lean to be effective in a business, it has to be adopted by all departments and be embraced by individual contributors, senior executives, and everyone in between.
- *Simplicity.* As I described at the top of chapter 11, my goal in this book is to provide a guide to the *essential* components of a successful business. I'm saying that a business *must:*

  - Build effective and impactful strategy statements,
  - Have a plan for managing change,
  - Define their *it* and how to drive consumer indispensability,
  - Create clarity through long-term and short-term goal setting,
  - Weave learning and coaching into the fabric of the organization's culture, and
  - Adopt a core set of management tools and practices.

If going all the way with Lean fits into a business model and culture, then great! I'm only introducing the continuous improvement tools I believe are necessary conditions for business success.

A Primer on Value Streams

In chapter 15, we'll get into the details of several continuous improvement tools that meet the definition of *necessary tools for business success,* and you'll see what I mean when I say that the language of Lean is unapproachable; however, before we tackle those concepts and talk about identifying and minimizing waste, we must introduce the concept of a value stream.

Put simply, a value stream is a set of activities that add incremental value to a product or service from its inception to its delivery to the customer. Using our analogy from chapter 10, the river of value derives its strength through inputs and contributions from tributaries that feed into it on the way to the ocean of consumer demand.

To illustrate a simple value stream, close your eyes and think about your favorite sandwich shop. From the moment you walk in the door, the value stream to deliver an awesome sandwich kicks into high gear.

- Step 1 is likely the branding and environment. Is it inviting? Do you feel welcome? Is the end of the line clearly marked?
- Step 2 is the menu board. Is the language clear? Options laid out efficiently?
- Step 3 is the ordering process. Bread, condiments, meat choices, cheeses, and toppings—are they all displayed in an appealing and logical manner?
- Step 4 runs concurrently with step 3 and is the production process. Are sandwich inputs in the right order? Are they fresh? Who's responsible for restocking? Does work in progress flow smoothly down the line?
- Step 5 is packaging and payment. Are payment options clear? Is packaging easy to work with for both sides of the transaction?

- Step 6 is exit from the establishment or in-store consumption. Are tables clean? Is the seating comfortable? Are exits clearly marked? Are the staff knowledgeable, well trained, and engaged?

Yes, this is a very simple example, and I'm sure I've missed some steps in the process (we'd need a value stream mapping event for that); but it clearly illustrates the concept of value-addition. When the customer walks in, there is only an idea of a sandwich in the potential consumer's mind. At the end of the value stream is a (hopefully) satisfied customer with a full tummy.

A great exercise to solidify the concept of a value stream is to think about the products and services that you buy—everything from airline tickets to a trip to the grocery store. There are myriad value streams all around you. The next time you go to an event, interact with your smartphone, walk around the office, or drive down the road, be on the lookout for value streams.

The Eight Wastes

Laying out the eight wastes of Lean as a guide to the identification of waste in business is common for practitioners. You may have noticed this chapter is about ten wastes, and we'll get into those two additional sources of waste a little later on. What follows is a brief discussion of the eight most widely cited sources of waste. Note that the eight wastes can be applied to *any* industry or business model, not just manufacturing or production environments.

- *Defects*. This can be either a product or service failure along a value stream. It's important to note that defects can take many forms. As an author and educator, the most egregious defects are typos and errata that lead students to question themselves first and then question my capability level as a teacher second. Even seemingly inconsequential details can be huge dissatisfiers. Does the binding of my book crack too easily? Are the pages too shiny and slippery to accept ink when a student tries to take notes? Defects are a leading cause of unnecessary customer dissatisfaction.
- *Overproduction*. If supply exceeds demand, waste is created. Bear in mind that there are supply-and-demand equations at nearly *every point along a value stream*. Hence, overproduction doesn't apply solely to the finished product or service. For each input or interaction point along a value stream, the supply of inputs can exceed demand.
- *Waiting*. The handoffs that occur along a value stream should be smooth and timely. To illustrate this, think about your own work. How many times have you been waiting for an input to your part of the value stream, only to find out it's been stuck in a queue or, worse yet, in the middle of a disorganized pile on a coworker's desk? In all the value stream mapping events I've been privy to, the waste of waiting has

been the number-one driver of employee dissatisfaction. "What do you mean you've been sitting on my value stream input for three weeks waiting for a signature from your boss. The customer is furious over the delays in final delivery. What the fork?!"

- *Underutilized talent.* People are a business's most valuable asset. Period. Having people in the wrong place with the wrong skills along a value stream can create unnecessary challenges. This is the primary reason why I placed learning and coaching in the list of non-negotiable strategic underpinnings of any successful business (see chapter 6). With the advent of computers that can "think" at low, but ever-increasing levels of cognition, having a plan for keeping *current* employees' skills fresh is critical. The old mindset of imagining that employees are expendable when their skills become obsolete is dead. The costs of hiring and training new team members far exceeds the cost of upskilling or reskilling existing colleagues whose skills aren't up to date.

- *Transportation.* Are warehouses located near the source of demand, or are products being moved unnecessarily prior to sale to the end user? While the waste of transportation primarily applies to a physical goods environment, take a moment to think about the cost and disruption associated with large team meetings and corporate events. Hopefully the COVID-19 pandemic has taught us to carefully balance the benefits of such events with their hard and soft costs. "Soft" or nonmonetary costs can be the bigger of the two!

- *Inventory.* Holding too much inventory drives up warehousing and spoilage costs, but the opposite—too little inventory—can be even more costly. This is another important lesson from the pandemic. In the two decades prior to the pandemic, many businesses had adopted "just-in-time" (JIT) inventory management methodologies as a way to squeeze profitability out of the middle of the profit and loss statement (P&L). JIT works great when (a) everything that is within the control of management is flowing smoothly and (b) when externalities (those things that are beyond the control of management) are minimal. JIT breaks down when these conditions are violated. The lesson is to strike a more appropriate inventory balance and develop more robust contingency plans—the pandemic proved that our supply chains are more fragile than we had previously imagined.

- *Motion.* Does it take ten steps to move from point A to point B, or can a service or production environment be reconfigured so that it only takes five steps? Reducing both waiting and motion can do wonders for morale and productivity. The primary tool used to reduce both is to engage in value stream mapping to pinpoint excess motion and waiting. Beware! Some colleagues may be using excess waiting and motion as job security blankets. Be sure to ask as many "whys" as necessary when mapping a value stream and show your teams that the resources freed up through reductions in motion and waiting can be put to higher and better uses—for example, more fulfilling and value-adding work—versus staffing cuts. We'll talk more about the five whys in chapter 15.

- *Excess processing.* Is the quality standard for a product or service out of alignment with customer expectations? Does the product really need that extra bell or whistle? To some this may seem counterintuitive, but the job of product management is to ensure there's alignment between consumer expectations and service levels or product quality. I speak from experience when I say that jamming more features into a product offering can backfire on both customer satisfaction and profitability.

We're not going to get into the details of how to minimize each of the eight wastes, as those details are heavily dependent on the specific circumstances of your business and the value stream in question. What's important for you to take away is that, as discussed in chapter 13, communication and transparency are essential ingredients for the minimization of waste in your business. Obfuscation and hiding—whether intentional or not—are surefire ways to create waste. In chapter 15, you'll note that the majority of the continuous improvement tools we introduce are designed to improve communication and increase organizational transparency.

The Ninth Waste—Emotion

Now that we're grounded in the eight wastes of Lean, I'd like to introduce another form of waste—a waste that is more insidious and costly than the primarily physical wastes noted above.

Emotional waste is like dark matter and dark energy in physics—we know it's there, but it's difficult to see and difficult to measure.

Emotional waste in the workplace can take many forms. Just a few examples include:

- *Misalignment of purpose.* Showing up every day to a job that doesn't align with your personal purpose is exhausting. Apathy quickly sets in and the work suffers.
- *Unproductive team dynamics.* We've all been part of a team that doesn't "click." Leaders who don't make the time to help team members understand one another are setting the team up for failure.
- *Bad managers.* Working for a domineering, overly directive, or oppressive boss can be soul crushing. If you walk up the stairs to the office every day with a sense of dread hanging over your head, how productive can you be?
- *FOMO and/or control.* Fear of missing out (FOMO) and control are highly interrelated. We seek to control what we can't and have our fingers in as many pots as possible. FOMO is typically found in personal friend circles but creates tremendous waste at the office as well.
- *Active disengagement.* Leaders who allow the actively disengaged to continue to roam the halls of the business are sending clear signals to the rest of the team that a healthy, engaged workforce isn't valued. Remember: you are what you allow.
- *Poorly defined goals and North Star.* If team members are working at cross-purposes or don't understand where the company is going, they will constantly question the value of their work.
- *Misaligned incentives.* Humans want to be treated fairly. Individuals who believe they're being treated unfairly will put in the minimum amount of effort to just get by. Incentives are devilishly difficult to get right, but the reward of getting incentives right can be invaluable.

The amount of emotional waste in your business is a direct reflection of the culture. Much of this book is devoted to the installation of a management operating system that's designed to promote flow and build organizational trust and accountability. We won't spend too much time here reiterating our thesis, but we can reduce emotional waste by:

- *Making learning and development a priority.* Nothing shows you care more than continually investing in your team's skill profile. I'm not suggesting an open checkbook for learning but instead aligning the learning agenda with the goals of the business. To do so, skills inventories must be established at the corporate level and individual skill portfolio evaluations should routinely occur with team members. This allows individuals to clearly see how the new skills they're acquiring will have a positive impact on the company and how they will personally benefit from learning new skills. Learning must be a two-way street, and learning agendas must be implemented with equity.

- *Improving clarity.* Engaged employees know where the business is heading and how their daily contributions will have a positive impact on customers, culture, and both the top and bottom lines. Clarity is established by continually refining and communicating the company's North Star, long range plan, and annual goals. Individual and team goals must then map directly to master company goals; *and* conflicting goals between teams and individual team members must be minimized. There's nothing more frustrating than showing up every day with the mindset that what you do doesn't matter.

- *Building transparency of metrics and key performance indicators (KPIs).* Not only does everyone need to know *what* everyone else is doing to keep the oars moving in unison but letting everyone know *how* the business is doing is also critically important. To move from emotion to rationality and objectivity, put the good, bad, and ugly on display so teams and team members know where to pitch in to help solve challenges and support their colleagues. Here, our message from chapter 13 bears repeating. Transparency is the elixir that helps shift the culture from blame to joint responsibility for both successes and failures. It's also easier to learn from failures if everyone knows what's being measured and what constitutes a poor result.

Emotion is not necessarily a bad thing in a business environment. As a leader, you want to see passion on display in the form of a keen desire to beat the competition and create exceptional value for customers.

I've stood many times in front of teams and reminded them that the enemy is outside the four walls of the business in the form of competitors who want nothing more than to eat our lunch. When the enemy is within, watch out. That enemy within usually takes the form of emotional waste that's draining the life from your company.

Dare I Say the Tenth Waste? Meetings

If I had a nickel for every time I've heard someone grouse about how many meetings they have to attend, I'd be able to fund a really cool charitable foundation. That foundation would be called "Meetings Anonymous" (tongue firmly in cheek).

All kidding aside, the crush of meetings on our calendars is overwhelming and a consistent contributor to employee dissatisfaction and disengagement. Meetings can also represent a significant source of waste in your business.

Next time you're going to schedule a meeting, do some simple math. Start with the number of attendees, multiply by the average wage *with* benefits, add on a facilities and technology support fee, tack on any transportation costs, and then add an opportunity cost factor. Some of the inputs to the calculation will be educated guesses, but the exercise is useful nonetheless.

For example, let's suppose you're hosting a blended, internal technology update meeting with twenty attendees, and the average wage is forty dollars per hour. Your company's all-in benefits rate likely runs between 15–25 percent to cover the company's direct payments (on your behalf) for things like health insurance, retirement plan contributions, federal and state mandatory withholding, and that gym membership that only gets used in January of every year (snark). For this example, we'll use 20 percent as our estimate.

In a flexible working environment, some individuals will gather in a company conference room and some will be online. Enterprise Zoom licenses are not free and neither is the conference room everyone is sitting in. Conference room costs include per square foot lease rates, utilities, technology support, custodial maintenance, and amortization of fixtures and equipment. To hold a meeting with twenty attendees in a blend of online and live, the facilities cost is low but not zero. We'll use an estimate of fifty dollars per hour for an internal company conference room. If the meeting is off-site, then you'll be paying a hotel or conference facility two to five times that number *and* face the costs of transportation and meals.

The *opportunity cost* is where the educated guess comes in. For those not familiar with the concept, opportunity cost is the forfeiture of a potential gain from engaging in an alternative activity. If your meeting is the *highest and best use* of all its inputs—for example, people, facilities, and time—then its opportunity cost is zero; however, it's highly likely that the alternative use of one or more meeting inputs will add more value to the company—for example, serving customers, developing a new product, or getting an existing product to market more quickly.

Unfortunately, ego and hubris typically blind us from thinking about opportunity cost. "Of course *my* meeting is the most important thing my colleagues have to do!" Don't get caught in this trap. In fact, thinking of a meeting as the *least* value-adding activity you and your colleagues can engage in will force a conscious computation of how your meeting will *add value* and not detract from it.

So how much does our hypothetical meeting cost?

(20 x $40)1.2 + $50 + unknown opportunity cost = at least $1,010

If your meeting will create more value than $1,010, then go for it! If bearing a cost of $1,010 to provide a technology update gives you pause, then consider other communication methodologies.

> **Side note:** In a CBS Sunday Morning interview that aired on April 16, 2023, executives from Canadian e-commerce company Shopify shared that they are including an estimate of the cost of each meeting in the meeting invite description field. Congratulations to Shopify for shining a bright light on meeting costs in an effort to improve business acumen and reduce the waste of meetings!

Tips to reduce the waste of meetings from the perspective of the individual:

- *Work on yourself first.* Some folks I hear complaining about how many meetings they have to attend will also complain about feeling left out (a form of FOMO) and actively work to muscle in on meetings they really don't need to attend. Mistrust is usually a root cause of this intrapersonal conflict. To expose potential FOMO or trust issues, ask yourself "Why do I feel the need to attend this meeting?" A culture of transparency and trust is the most powerful antidote to FOMO-driven meeting attendance.
- *Don't become a meeting spectator.* Ask yourself the following question after each meeting: "Was I a spectator in the last meeting I attended?"

If you were watching from the sidelines and not meaningfully contributing to the conversation (or not learning from it), you were likely a spectator who didn't need to be on the field of play. Shifting analogies, nobody likes to see "tourists" in their meetings unless they're specifically invited with that intent.

Tips to reduce the waste of meetings from the perspective of the team:

- *Assign delegates.* In many cases, assigning a delegate from your department to attend a meeting and report its outcomes back to the broader team can be an effective way to reduce waste and free up time for more value-adding work. Assigning a delegate will also have the positive knock-on effect of forcing the delegate to hone critical-thinking, presentation, and communication skills through a crisp readout of the meeting's key outcomes in a regularly scheduled team gathering.
- *Establish a team charter and a simple RACI diagram (Responsible, Accountable, Consulted, Informed).* With the charter and RACI, who must be in team meetings and who's optional or can be updated via email or other team collaboration tools—for example, Slack—becomes clear(er). Remember that charters and RACIs are not set in stone and should be revisited and adjusted periodically. We'll discuss both of these concepts in greater detail in chapter 15.
- *Require an agenda.* Ensure the meeting agenda and assignments are created well in advance. If there's no agenda or you and your team are constantly scrambling to put agendas together at the last minute, take a step back and ask, "Why?" as many times as necessary to get to the root cause.
- *Talk as a team about the number of meetings that are on the books.* Meetings are typically set in isolation and we seldom look at the meeting cadence of our functional area (or our business) holistically. Your manager or functional area leader is likely unaware of all the meetings that are occurring under their watch and is also likely unaware of the meeting requests that are coming from other functional areas of the business.

Tips to reduce the waste of meetings from the perspective of the company:

- *Make the costs of meetings known.* The CFO or head of facilities should periodically remind team leaders about the hard and soft costs of meetings within the context of the business. Be sure to work the benefits of camaraderie and team building into the opportunity cost calculation. If done well, meetings can be a net positive for the organization by promoting relationship building and encouraging cross-departmental communication and collaboration.
- *Avoid quick fixes to the meeting problem* (for example, "meeting-free Fridays"). These blanket policies are just Band-Aids and do not get at the root cause of the waste of meetings. Search for root cause first and address the issue from there. If meeting-free Fridays are the answer to creating focused work time, then great! But simply proclaiming there shall not be meetings on Friday will only serve to shift a host of unproductive, soul-sapping meetings to other days of the week.
- *Create a master meeting calendar.* This high-level calendar should contain all known meetings that senior management is committed to—board meetings, major conferences, quarterly updates, financial readouts, town halls, budget defense sessions, etc. Publish this calendar as early as possible and to as broad an audience as possible. This will give middle management plenty of time to build their calendars around the master calendar and will help avoid last minute jockeying and rescheduling, which is itself a huge waste generator.
- *Adopt an organizational strategy for meetings.* The popular business literature is filled with advice on how to run an effective meeting and how to establish a cadence for meetings that is value-adding. My advice is to choose a strategy for meetings and propagate that strategy throughout the organization. Allowing each leader or manager to adopt their own strategies just leads to chaos. Start with Patrick Lencioni's *The Advantage* (2012) and go from there.

TIPS TO REDUCE WASTE OF MEETINGS

INDIVIDUAL
- Work on yourself first.
- Don't become a meeting spectator.

TEAM
- Assign delegates.
- Establish a team charter and a simple RACI diagram.
- Require an agenda.
- Talk as a team about the number of meetings that are on the books.

COMPANY
- Make the costs of meetings known.
- Avoid quick fixes to the meeting problem.
- Create a master meeting calendar.
- Adopt an organizational strategy for meetings.

A Note on "Digital Transformations"

Both McKinsey and Boston Consulting Group (BGC) estimate that a whopping 70 percent of digital transformations fail to achieve their stated objectives.[1,2] Digital transformations are large technical and business process change projects that span most, if not all, of a company's existing operations. They can take many forms but often include a fundamental shift in the business model from physical to digital delivery. Posttransformation, the company will interact with its customers in new ways, and employees will need to adopt entirely new ways of working both internally and externally.

Even if these studies overestimate the failure rate by, let's say 50 percent, digital transformations rank among the top waste generators in the business landscape. The underlying reasons for these excessively high failure rates are the usual suspects of talent misalignment, lack of strategic clarity, pushback from the clay layer, leadership overconfidence, and little or no focus on change management.

Flow mechanics and handoffs that were established prior to the digital transformation must be fundamentally reengineered. Digital transformations that are poorly executed leave the business in a kind of "twilight zone" for extended periods in which teams and individuals are required to work using both old and new world tools and processes. Morale and engagement suffer as digital transformations drag on; everyone ends up feeling like they're working in mud.

I want to be careful here. My goal in introducing the eight wastes of Lean and the two additional wastes of emotion and meetings is more about developing the ability to *see* wastes clearly than it is about properly classifying them. Getting into a drawn-out debate as to whether a waste in your business is excess processing or motion is itself waste.

15

The Ten Essential Tools of Continuous Improvement

The path to a high-trust, high-accountability culture is built upon the smooth flow of value addition along your company's value stream(s). In this book, I am advocating for the installation of continuous improvement and organizational health tools to achieve flow, establish accountability, and cultivate trust. In theory, the journey toward establishing this high-trust, high-accountability culture is logical and reasonably straightforward. In practice, the organizational change necessary to install the tools of continuous improvement and organizational health is tricky, at best.

Back in chapter 5, we discussed the importance of managing change, because change—even nominal change—runs against the grain of the human experience. I've personally made the tactical error of assuming that my teams could adapt more quickly than they actually could—I grossly overestimated the shape and duration of their change management curves. Adopting the tenets of continuous improvement and asking individuals and teams to embrace a new way of thinking will represent a change journey that your people will push back against. For example, as we embarked on our own continuous improvement journey at Kaplan Professional, we bit off more than we could chew by adopting the principles of

Lean more quickly than we should have.

Therefore, I'm recommending a minimum viable continuous improvement tool kit for your business. What follows is the set of continuous improvement tools I believe will be the most impactful toward the creation of optimal flow within your organization and those that are the most easily understood. Hence, utility and speed of adoption will be our guide.

Adding Value

If I were pinned down and forced to get *one* point across in this book, it would be the importance of *adding value along the value stream*. If everyone stopped periodically to think critically and carefully about the value they're creating as they interact with the value stream, businesses would be more productive, flow would be enhanced, and trust and accountability would improve. Too often, we go on autopilot in our work and subconsciously *assume* that our work adds value to the organization and its customers.

Looking through the lens of value addition is essential for the following reasons:

- *Improving business acumen.* Determining how an individual or small team adds value along the value stream requires an understanding of how the value stream functions. Doing so makes it impossible to keep one's blinders on and solely think about the work that happens within a single department or team. Understanding how the outputs of your work are consumed as inputs to the work of another team depends on learning more about the goals and outcomes of the downstream team. A "win" for you or your own team is only a win for the organization if your win helps create a win for your colleagues.
- *Staving off entropy.* Maintaining focus on adding value at each step along a value stream keeps the concept of value addition in working memory and avoids the inevitable relegation of how work gets done back into the subconscious. Once we go on autopilot, the door is left wide open for entropy to romp around and wreak havoc.

- *Enhancing transparency.* Once value addition is in the foreground across teams and departments, sharing wins and progress toward further value enhancements becomes easier. Jointly solving challenges becomes easier, because everyone understands how the value stream operates, and their personal contributions to it. Instead of hiding failures and information, it becomes in everyone's best interest to share the good, bad, and ugly to continuously improve the entire value stream—not just individual components of it.

My own lightbulb moment with the concept of value addition came during a cross-divisional collaboration exercise earlier in my career. After a well-intended presentation of how our division would contribute to the project under consideration, a former colleague of mine leaned over and whispered in my ear that, while he enjoyed the presentation, our division's outputs would present unnecessary challenges for his division: "Andy, you're not adding the value you think you are, because some of that value will be destroyed once we receive your work product. We're just not set up to work in the way you think we can." Clearly, my business acumen was not as strong as it should have been. Had I invested more time in understanding his division and their way of working, our proposed solutions would have been much different.

> **A note on nonvalue-adding activities:** It's important to pause for a moment and add a reminder that not all work fits in the category of value addition and that value addition depends on the perspective of the individual or team. Certain compliance and governance functions will be viewed by some as nonvalue-adding activities—like the sixty-page legal contract you think should be two pages or the regulatory training course you've done every year for the last fifteen years. The important thing is to have periodic open conversations between all parties to ensure that (a) everyone understands the "why" behind real or perceived nonvalue-adding activities, and (b) there is routine verification of the ongoing need for

such activities. Unfortunately, many compliance and governance tasks are on "set-it-and-forget-it" status in many companies.

Introducing the Ten Essential Tools of Continuous Improvement

With the concept of value addition top of mind, let's begin exploring the ten essential tools of continuous improvement.

Tool 1: Pull the Andon Cord

Like many of the continuous improvement tools we'll discuss in this chapter, the term *andon* is of Japanese origin and refers to some visual or auditory signal that's used to highlight an anomaly or failure.

In a production environment, andon cords hang above the production line and are there to stop the line in the event of a failure. When the andon cord gets pulled, the entire production line, or a segment of it, comes to a screeching halt. The line restarts when the identified challenge is fixed and the line can be safely restarted.

ANDON CORD

If you've ever pumped gasoline into an automobile, there is a type of andon device at the pump. It's the little red button you push if a fuel spill occurs that shuts the machine down to prevent an even bigger spill. Ever ridden an escalator? There's a type of andon device at both the top and bottom of each run of the escalator. Again, it's a conspicuous red button that you hit if the escalator starts eating a shoe to prevent part of a human being eaten too.

In my opinion, andon cords should not be the sole province of production lines. I believe strongly that they should also be featured in service and professional environments. While you might not need a physical cord or button, there needs to be some mechanism for quickly reporting a service failure or challenge along the value stream.

A key feature of an andon device is that it should be available to everyone on the team. Calling out a challenge along the value stream should not be restricted to certain personnel; however, it's important to note that "pulling the andon" should only be done when a failure reaches a level of severity that warrants the immediate pause of a value stream. Later in this chapter, we'll be introducing the concepts of kaizen and managing for daily improvement (MDI) that can be used for minor challenges to the value stream that don't entail shutting everything down.

The definition of *severity* is completely dependent on the specifics of the work environment, and everyone on the team should be intimately familiar with the definition and case studies that warrant the andon device's use. If a team member pulls the andon for an unwarranted challenge, leadership should use the experience as a coaching opportunity and avoid making a negative example of the "cord puller."

Tool 2: The Five Whys

While we've introduced the concept of the five whys earlier in this book, we must include them here to stress the importance of building critical-thinking skills in your team members.

Unfortunately, critical-thinking skills are in short supply. Blindly following orders from a directive boss or rigidly following an existing process is much easier than questioning it. I'm sure you can think back to a time when you were quickly put in your place for questioning the motivations of a leader, or the efficiency of a hand off within a team. Although smackdowns like this were rare in my own work experience, I've seen them happen with regularity to others and personally recall with great discomfort the sting of my own run-ins with members of the clay layer who have mastered the art of the smackdown.

As a quick reminder, the five whys is a line of inquiry aimed at the discovery of the root cause of a challenge or business failure. While there are times when you can literally ask why over and over again to determine root cause, the more likely scenario is deeper and deeper exploration of a challenge through well-crafted questions that probe an issue from multiple perspectives to "peel back the layers of the onion." Sorry, literalists, the implementation of the five whys rarely means that why is asked five times!

Installing the five whys as a continuous improvement tool within your business has the following benefits:

- *Improved agency.* One of the biggest employment dissatisfiers is the feeling that you're just another cog in a big wheel and lack a "voice" to share concerns and question how work is done. Encouraging questions throughout all levels of the organization can build confidence and enhance organizational trust. Beware that giving individuals a voice requires leaders and managers to commit themselves to improving their listening skills. Without improvements in listening, your people will simply feel like they're shouting into the wind with their newfound voices.

- *Your people ask better questions.* With the exception of joining a debate team, there is no better way to hone the skill of asking good questions than doing so in a live-fire environment that's coupled with strong coaching from a manager who understands the value of asking good questions. The latter part of the previous statement is crucial for success. As an effective leader, you already know the value of a good question. Your responsibility is to cultivate this skill in your organization—to pass on your ability to ask a good question to your people.

- *Enhanced critical-thinking skills.* Most "Top Ten Skills in Business" lists include critical thinking as a key future-facing skill. Unfortunately, bad managers inadvertently quash critical-thinking skills through the aforementioned smackdowns that are pervasive in business. Critical thinking is a higher-order skill and relies heavily on the subskills of observation, analysis, inference, communication, self-reflection, problem-solving, creativity, and curiosity, just to name a few. A commitment to enhancing critical thinking in your most valuable asset is a commitment to enhancing a host of "soft" and hard skills.

Tool 3: Checklists

Although I've *taught* accounting in the past and *intellectually* understand the value of procedure and rigor, detailed checklists and my core personality do not get along. My wife, Linda, on the other hand, is the checklist queen! On family vacations, when the kids were younger, I would scoff at her unyielding affection for her vacation checklist. She would remember everything we needed, and I would inevitably forget something. Sunscreen, check. Distractions for the kids, check.

In one of my other businesses, I'm the front man for a rock band called The Remainders—check us out on your favorite music streaming service or visit www.theremainders.com to listen to our tunes.

Beyond the shameless plug for the band, putting on a live rock show is a complicated endeavor in which a single cable or component can mean the difference between success and maddening frustration.

I used to keep a lot in my head, believing I could remember everything I needed to do in our preshow routine, only to be burned on multiple occasions. Not having a checklist created unnecessary risk and a lot of avoidable waste that came mainly in the form of waiting, transportation, motion, and extra processing.

Years ago, I was turned on to a little book called *The Checklist Manifesto* by Atul Gawande, and it changed my mind about checklists. After this quick but important read, I looked around the midsize education company I was running and was astounded as to how many work processes lived in my team members' heads!

We'll talk about the concepts of standard work, which is in and of itself a great checklist, and value stream mapping in just a bit, but for now, insist on checklists for as many of your business processes as possible. Those checklists will be a crucial part of your team's standard work and will save myriad headaches down the road.

Tool 4: 5S—Shine, Sort, Set in Order, Standardize, Sustain

This continuous improvement tool is exactly what it says on the tin. Put simply, to "5S" is to continually work against the forces of entropy. Do we work in an environment of chaos and disorganization, or is everything clean and in its place (physically and digitally)?

The point of 5S is to bring cleanliness, order, and standardization into working memory. This tool is especially useful for people like me who are in a lifelong struggle to maintain an orderly work environment. Yes, I was—and still am to a lesser degree—that guy whose desk has piles of papers and reports that follow no logical classification system other than my own recollection of where things are.

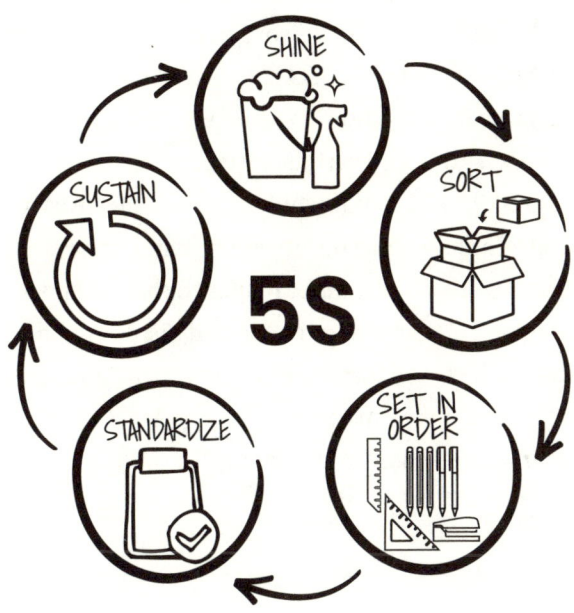

As I've mentioned, I'm the polar opposite of my dear wife Linda in this regard. Through the years, we've expended unnecessary emotional waste navigating through *my* issues with order and standardization. When we worked together during the formative years of the Schweser Study Program for the CFA Exams and later at Kaplan, we drove each other crazy fighting against our distinctly different ways of working.

At the time, I thought I stood on solid ground when I'd ask her and the rest of the team to meet me in the middle. I now recognize that my arguments were faulty, and those who struggle with order have an obligation to move more to the side of standardization and cleanliness than the other way around. Why the imbalance? My way of working would require others to read my mind and anticipate what comes next. The value stream has no hope of being fluid and efficient if my organization mindset were to prevail.

The bottom line is that no one should be expected to read someone else's mind.

It's taken me years of effort to accept the 5S framework in both my personal and professional lives, and I can attest that my relationships with colleagues and my family are stronger as a result. If you're a leader or manager who thrives on chaos and disorder, I recommend that you engage in some self-reflection on the impact your way of working has on your colleagues and organizational culture. You may be, most likely inadvertently, creating unnecessary waste of various varieties.

Am I fully "cured" of what some would consider the disease of disorder? The answer is an emphatic no. I purposefully maintain some spaces where my chaotic way of working prevails to help feed that inner need—that I still don't fully understand—for a bit of chaos and disorder in my life. My personal case study is the space that the boys in the band and I use for practice and recording. It's a grungy "man cave" that's perfect for our weekly gatherings for camaraderie and musical therapy.

Tool 5: Value Stream Mapping

Back in chapter 1 of this book, we told the story of a multiday cross-departmental meeting, where we asked a small but mighty group of individual contributors and managers at Kaplan Professional to map the revision cycle for one of the company's most important product lines from start to finish. The revision cycle for this product line was an example of a value stream, and the detailed description of how the value stream operated is called a value stream map.

After several days and loads of work, no such map was to be found. This team of highly qualified professionals couldn't build a holistic map, because too many pieces of the puzzle lived within human memories or were stuffed away in desk drawers. The inability of the team to generate a map was all the more surprising because this revision cycle had taken place in various forms for more than twenty years!

Figure 15.1: The Value Stream Map

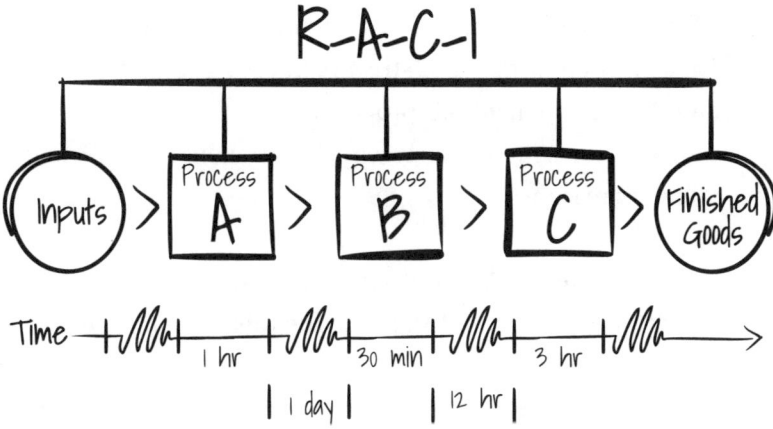

Figure 15.1 above is a crude depiction of a value stream map and consists of three primary rows to illustrate flow. The top row shows work assignments and responsibilities, the middle row conveys the flow of work from start to finish, and the bottom row indicates the timing of each component part of the value stream.

The place to begin in interpreting the value stream map is in the middle row of the diagram. Moving left to right, we start with the inputs to the value stream and then identify the processes and actions that are necessary to form a finished good, product, or service. In figure 15.1, there are three processes that are necessary to compile the finished good.

Next, we focus on the bottom of the chart. This line identifies the time that it takes to move from inputs to finished goods and includes both processing time and wait time (shown as the squiggly lines). Here we insert the average time it takes to complete each step and the average time between steps.

Finally, we work on the top row, which outlines who's responsible for what in the form of a RACI chart. The RACI acronym refers to "responsible, accountable, consulted, and informed." In figure 15.1, we drew in lines that resemble an "org chart" for each component of the value stream. For example, above the vertical line that feeds into the "Process A" box, you would write down who is responsible for Process A, who's accountable, and who needs to be consulted and/or informed.

As we described in chapter 1 of this book, a value stream mapping event is a set of cross-disciplinary meetings in which experts from all departments that contribute to the value stream gather to *physically* map a value stream and all its component sub-processes.

I list value stream mapping as an essential continuous improvement tool for the following reasons:

- *Identification of waste.* Without a map, how can we effectively identify waste within the business? Mapping the value stream specifies the components of a process that are value additive and those that are not.
- *Relationship building.* Value stream mapping is difficult and sometimes painstaking work, but it's a wonderful way to build camaraderie across teams using practical, real-world data. Why run a moderated team-building workshop using hypothetical situations? I find that buy-in and outcomes improve when real work is getting done—value stream mapping is the ultimate two birds, one stone trick.
- *Trust enhancement.* When run with an effective facilitator, all the desk drawers are opened up and the parts of the process that are squirreled away in someone's head are made visible. As the map begins to take shape, clarity is established and all the handoffs that happened as a matter of subconscious routine are codified. These are essential conditions for the growth of organizational trust.
- *Accountability.* How can a manager or leader hold a team or individual contributor accountable if the structure of a process is unknown or unclear? Value stream maps show clearly who's responsible for the outputs that are another team's inputs.

What do you need to run an effective value stream mapping event?

- *Facilitator.* I've found that an effective third-party facilitator is an essential ingredient to a successful value stream mapping event. Yes, you can cut costs by asking someone from within your organization to lead the event, but having someone from the outside who's skilled at getting people to open up and share will lead to better outcomes. Using an insider may not lead to the kind of candor that's necessary to pull information from the clutches of a turf protector.

- *Space.* Value stream mapping should be an in-person event if possible, and the space chosen for the event will also have a marked impact on outcomes. Research on physical space dynamics has shown that certain colors and environmental elements like natural light and live plants contribute to more creative and productive outcomes. Stuffing your team members in a dingy room with terrible coffee will place a gray cloud over the proceedings.

- *Open minds.* Remember how important change management is to your business? A value stream mapping event is no different and will be viewed by some participants as a threat to current ways of working and possibly even a threat to their job. A bit of coaching before the event starts on its rationale and intended outcomes can help soften otherwise calcified mindsets, leading to better results.

- *Management support.* Before embarking on value stream mapping, management from *all* departments need to fully understand and support the effort. Even one manager who's not in agreement can poison the well and hinder progress. Be prepared to provide clear answers to the inevitable questions of "Why are we doing this?" and "What are we going to do with the map once it's created?" If a value stream mapping event is seen as a box to check or an exercise in futility, then it will be resisted from the start.

As a final note of support for value stream mapping, many of our other continuous improvement tools are dependent on value stream maps. Examples include standard work, managing for daily improvement, and kaizen events. We'll discuss each of these items next.

Tool 6: Kaizen and Kaizen Events

A warning before we proceed. The concept of *kaizen* is very straightforward. Its practical application, however, is not, as I'll explain in a moment.

The word *kaizen* is a Japanese term that means "change for the better" and also translates to "continuous improvement." The supposition is that nothing is perfect and everything can be improved incrementally. The trick is to understand the cost-benefit trade-off between the status quo and the next incremental improvement to a process, task, or job. Look for different ways to improve the process if cost outweighs benefit. That's the simple bit.

The complication comes in its implementation, so we're going to significantly constrain kaizen events as a tool in your continuous improvement tool kit. For our purposes, a kaizen event will refer to a short-burst or sprint working session with a small cross-functional team to solve a specific failure or challenge along a value stream.

As an example, let's assume that the value stream has been mapped and a consistent service failure is determined at a specific point along the value stream. As soon as practical, a small working team is established to clearly identify the failure point and determine the best fix to the issue at hand.

What makes a kaizen event special is that the team is empowered to implement the change recommendations that result from the sprint working session *immediately* or with significant haste. Bureaucracy and approvals from "on high" are frowned upon.

My favorite example of an impromptu kaizen event was during the Apollo 13 lunar mission, when the crew had to hide out in the lunar module for most of the return flight home after the catastrophic explosion that crippled the command and service modules (a.k.a. *Odyssey*). The lunar module's (a.k.a. *Aquarius*) air scrubbers were designed to accommodate two crew members—not the three who occupied *Aquarius* during the return trip. Worse yet, the scrubbers on *Odyssey* were a different shape and size compared to those on *Aquarius*!

Back at mission control in Houston, a cross-functional team quickly gathered to determine a fix to the scrubber issue on *Aquarius* and came up with an ingenious solution that ultimately helped get the crew back to Earth safely.

So now let's go back to the complication with kaizen. A quick internet search of kaizen will yield a dizzying array of options. Cube kaizen, point kaizen, and system kaizen to name a few. Some practitioners wield kaizen events as heavy weapons of change which involve multiday events involving dozens of people from across the company. In my experience, those events should be reserved for value stream mapping, and kaizen should be used to continually improve weaknesses and challenges along the value stream. Kaizen should not be used for large process reengineering initiatives. For large process reengineering initiatives, get the project managers involved and follow rigorous project management standards—build a project charter, develop a RACI diagram (responsible, accountable, consulted, informed), and follow other project management best practices.

Tool 7: Plan, Do, Check, Act (PDCA)

Plan, do, check (or study), act (PDCA) is less of a tool and more of a mindset. When combined with kaizen, instilling PDCA as a mindset into the culture of the organization acts as a natural preventative to stagnation. PDCA and kaizen also help hone the skill of critical thinking in your team members because the "check" and "act" portions of the PDCA cycle promotes consideration of alternative courses of action.

The PDCA mindset can be applied to myriad changes within a business or institution—new products, policies, technologies—anything that represents a shift or change in the organization. For each proposed change or step-function improvement along a value stream, apply the following cycle:

- *Plan.* All four elements of PDCA are of equal importance, but bad planning leads to poor results, so spending the right amount of time and effort in the planning stage is critical. Planning tools abound, and we're not going to spend much time introducing specific tools. With that said, essential planning elements include effective forecasting, strengths, weaknesses, opportunities, and threats analysis (SWOT), scenario analysis, benchmarking, and contingency planning. It's at this point that I'll insert a plug for building the capability of financial modeling into your business. Finance is the language of business and having your plan supported by an effective financial model is an essential part of the planning process.

- *Do.* At the culmination of the planning stage, the proposed change is implemented. I like to think of the "do" stage as experimentation. As a general rule, bigger changes require more experimentation, but even small changes need some degree of experimentation before they're fully adopted into the value stream. Too often, the decision to implement a change "comes from on high"—for example, the C-suite—and teams jump into action and move straight to the doing stage of the cycle. In this type of directive management environment, experimentation is neglected because teams make the assumption that the decision to adopt the change is a foregone conclusion and nothing will change leadership's mind. To correct this, PDCA and kaizen must be adopted at all levels of the organization—not just in certain pockets. If your organization is on a continuous improvement journey but the C-suite has opted out, believing that its tenets don't apply to them, beware. In this case, the organization's continuous improvement journey is likely to be more akin to wandering in the desert.

- *Check and/or study*. After implementation of the initial experiment, the change is studied or checked for its efficacy. Here, the benchmarks and key performance indicators (KPIs) that were identified during the planning stage are used as tools to determine the efficacy of the experiment with, or initial installation of the change. Hence, measurement is an essential part of the check/study part of the cycle. In many organizations, skill deficiencies relating to measurement, analysis, and evaluation rear their heads, and this part of the cycle either gets ignored or the short shrift. The organization instead relies on a small group of measurement and evaluation specialists that are so backlogged that by the time they get around to measuring the results of an experiment, the window of opportunity for the check and/or study period has passed. This lack of measurement skills can become a critical chokepoint for any value stream.

- *Act*. You've planned, experimented, and measured outcomes—now it's time to make a decision. Do we go back to the drawing board or make minor adjustments and run a more holistic experiment? Is it time to weave the change firmly into the value stream? What data and statistics support our decision? Are there any blinking red lights or yellow lights of caution? Thorough planning, thoughtful experimentation, and rigorous measurement are the necessary conditions for good decision-making. From my experience, more corporate value is destroyed through poor decision-making than from any other source. Poor decision-making stems from many sources, but the most likely suspects are hubris, weak ego, and a lack of data and/or a rigorous financial model to support objectivity.

PDCA is a *cycle*. The larger the change, the more times around the PDCA cycle the team should go. In my experience, for any given change, PDCA doesn't last forever and over time gives way to kaizen—that is, the normal continuous improvement cycle—once the change becomes integrated into the value stream.

Tool 8: Managing for Daily Improvement (MDI)

Remember the good old suggestion box? There's a reason why you don't see them around much these days. The anonymity of inputs allowed for suggestions that were unhelpful at best and toxic at worst. Also, the suggestion box was rarely opened, and when it was, its contents were quickly discarded and ignored.

MDI is like a transparent suggestion box that actually gets opened and evaluated on a regular basis. It's a tool for crowd-sourcing ideas from your team for small, incremental improvements to specific points along the value stream.

If your team is physically colocated, MDI is as simple as finding a whiteboard, placing it in a conspicuous place, and letting the fun begin! Please note that MDI is most effective in a team or departmental environment. MDI is seldom implemented at the company level because, (a) recommendations for small improvements are best triaged at the departmental level, and (b) the opportunity for anonymity increases at the company level. Transparency is essential for MDI to be both a continuous improvement tool *and* a teaching opportunity.

To illustrate the cadence of MDI, we're going to assume that your team or department holds a weekly or biweekly meeting for communication and KPI monitoring. MDI will be added to the agenda for this meeting. To implement MDI in your department, do the following:

- Place a large whiteboard in a conspicuous place and ask your most talented artist to write "Managing for Daily Improvement" across the top.
- Make ample sticky notes available to all team members.
- Instruct the team to write down ideas for *small, incremental improvements* on a sticky note as they do their work in the normal flow of business.
- Team members then place a note with their idea on the whiteboard and *write their name on it*. Anonymity is not allowed in this exercise.
- During the weekly or biweekly team meeting, the manager or team leader pulls that period's sticky notes from the board and asks the team member whose name is on the note to present their idea to the

group for consideration. Nothing needs to be prepared for this presentation—no shiny PowerPoint™ deck, no handouts, just a simple explanation of the proposed improvement.

- The team leader or manager then leads a short discussion on the proposal, asking for feedback from the rest of the team.
- Finally, the proposal is either accepted, rejected, or tabled for further discussion and/or analysis, if warranted.

MDI ideas should be simple enough to fit on a single sticky note. If the idea is more complex than a sticky note can handle, then the idea is likely too complex for MDI. Also, if an MDI idea is accepted, then it should be implemented as quickly as possible. PDCA still applies, because, depending on the business environment, even small changes to how the value stream operates can have significant consequences downstream. *Always* consider downstream effects.

Why is MDI important?

- It's an easy way to give your people a voice.
- Presentation skills are honed in a low-risk, psychologically safe environment.
- The value of continuous improvement is reinforced by management.
- Small changes can have a big impact on performance.
- MDI review sessions are a wonderful opportunity for real-time team coaching.

Warning: Don't engage in MDI if you're not going to do anything with the suggestions. Remember: actions speak louder than words.

Tool 9: Gemba and Gemba Boards and Gemba Walks

The word *gemba* is Japanese and translates literally to "the real place," or "the actual place." For our purposes, the gemba is where the action happens and where value is created along a value stream. Later in this book, we're going to talk in more detail about the importance of measurement and transparency, so we'll reserve a deeper conversation about the practical application of the gemba for chapter 17. For now, we'll focus on the answer to the following question: "Andy, why do we need to add another Japanese word to our business lexicon?"

My response to this question is that managers and leaders routinely get so lost in budgets, KPIs, planning, governance, and external relations that they neglect the true source of value in their business—the gemba. Putting a name to the place where value is created is a useful tool to remind leadership to routinely pull their heads up out of spreadsheets and shiny decks and go to where the action happens.

In a manufacturing or service environment, finding the gemba is straightforward—there's invariably a production assembly line, storage facility, kitchen, maintenance room, or some other physical location where the value stream is in the open and visible. For other business types—for example, professional services—the gemba can be more difficult to locate, especially in hybrid and/or fully remote working environments. But just because your business is decentralized or utilizes what some would still refer to as "nonstandard" operational models doesn't mean the gemba doesn't exist and certainly doesn't give leadership permission to avoid getting their hands dirty (either literally or figuratively) by going to the gemba.

Before we go further, two definitions are in order:

- A *gemba board* is a physical or digital board that houses a team or department's vision, goals, key wins, blockers, KPIs and metrics, hot topics, and an indicator of overall team health. While we've provided a stylized gemba board for reference, I recommend that the senior leaders of the organization agree on a standardized gemba board format that includes *required* elements for all departments—for example, the aforementioned list—and then allow for individual team or department customization. That way, leaders will have some familiarity with the layout as they move from department to department but also maintain some degree of flexibility to a particular team to make their board as useful to them as possible. This last point is critical. If a gemba board has no real or perceived value to the department that's in charge of maintaining it, then it will get created once and then die on the vine of apathy.

- A *gemba walk* is an intentional visit to a department or team by a member of senior management or other organizational leader to the gemba. In other words, a gemba walk is a visit to where the work happens. In a gemba walk, the leader(s) and select members of the team gather physically around the departmental gemba board and/ or another location in the department that either needs attention or should be showcased. In hybrid or fully remote work environments, the leader(s) and team members gather around the department's virtual gemba board.

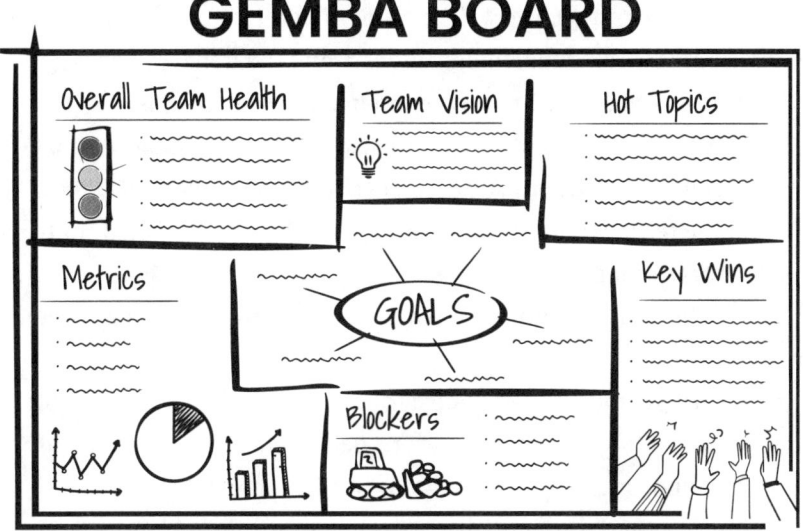

A gemba walk is an opportunity for leadership to *see* how work is accomplished with their own eyes, *listen* carefully to the challenges and opportunities the team faces, and ask questions. The intention is to *understand* challenges and opportunities so they can be an *advocate for* and *supporter of* the team or department. There are no "gotcha" moments in a gemba walk.

Gemba walks are also:

- *Scheduled.* Leadership should avoid being disruptive to departmental flow by scheduling their visit with ample lead time. Avoid surprise gemba walks. Note that I'm not suggesting that stopping by and saying hello to your people is a bad thing. I'm suggesting that a gemba walk is not a social visit.
- *Brief.* A gemba walk should be brief and not disruptive to the team or department. If everyone is colocated in a physical space, team members who are involved should stand during the walk.
- *Focused.* In an ideal scenario, everyone will put their phone on silent and the guests of the walk (leadership) will show the team respect by avoiding multitasking. Give the team your undivided attention.
- *Value-additive.* The walk should bring value to both the leader(s) who are the department's guests *and* the department. A gemba walk is *not* a perfunctory readout of results and KPIs.
- *Inclusive.* Gemba walks are a time for everyone to stand (literally) on equal footing. Egos and deference to titles are checked at the door. The manager of the department should allow individual contributors the opportunity to speak and shine. A gemba walk is the perfect opportunity to show through actions that "we're all in this together."

In my own personal experience, I found gemba walks to be one of the most valuable things I did as a leader. I had to check my ego at the door, quiet my mind, open my ears, keep my phone out of my hand, and really pay attention to what the team was saying. I especially liked to hear the voices of employees who I otherwise would not have gotten a chance to hear from! The feedback I would routinely receive after gemba walks is that team members also enjoyed the experience, because the usual trappings of hierarchy were nonexistent: *I was on their "turf," and I showed a genuine interest in their work.* Gemba walks are your opportunity as a leader to show that you're an authentic, vulnerable human being who cares about their people and the work they do.

The same warning from our MDI discussion applies here and is magnified, because, well, senior leadership is added to the equation. Don't engage in gemba walks if you're not going to do anything with the information you receive. *Actions speak louder than words*.

Tool 10: Standard Work

Our final tool in the essential continuous improvement tool kit is standard work. As we discussed in chapter 12, standard work is the codification of the current best practice for a work process associated with a value stream. You can develop a standard work document for an individual, team, or a segment of a value stream. Note that a value stream map (tool number 5 above) is the ultimate standard work document, and each individual, team, or process standard work document is a subset of, and contributes to, one or more value stream maps.

The development of the organization's *initial set* of standard work documents can be time-consuming and tedious, especially for established businesses who are embarking on a continuous improvement journey. But don't get discouraged, because standard work documents are *living documents*, as they represent the *current* best practice for a job. Since we're on a continuous improvement journey, standard work documentation will change each time an improvement is made.

Here's something that might put a smile on your face. Remember that thing called a job description that nobody ever looks at and that really doesn't describe the work you do anyway? Standard work is the real life, useful version of that. In fact, job descriptions should be living documents that are an extension of standard work documentation and add in all the human resources related details—for example, work experience requirements, etc.

STANDARD WORK

Description of the Work

- ~~~~~~~~~~~~~~~~~
- ~~~~~~~~~~~~~~~~~
- ~~~~~~~~~~~~~~~~~
- ~~~~~~~~~~~~~~~~~
- ~~~~~~~~~~~~~~~~~

Instructions	Time	Input	Dependencies
1. ~~~~~	~~~~	~~~~	• ~~~~
2. ~~~~~	~~~~	~~~~	• ~~~~
3. ~~~~~	~~~~	~~~~	• ~~~~
4. ~~~~~	~~~~	~~~~	• ~~~~

Skill Requirements

- ~~~~~~~~~~~~~~ • ~~~~~~~~~~~~~~
- ~~~~~~~~~~~~~~ • ~~~~~~~~~~~~~~
- ~~~~~~~~~~~~~~ • ~~~~~~~~~~~~~~
- ~~~~~~~~~~~~~~ • ~~~~~~~~~~~~~~
- ~~~~~~~~~~~~~~ • ~~~~~~~~~~~~~~

Essential elements of a standard work document include:

- A brief description of the work, including pictures;
- Clear instructions for each component of the work;
- Expected time spent on each task;
- The sequence of the work;

- Input requirements from other departments—for example, raw materials or work in progress;
- Skill requirements—for example, a list of skills required to do the work effectively; and
- A list of key work partners and/or dependencies from other parts of the company and how handoffs occur to ensure proper flow.

For the sake of clarity standard work is:

- *Dynamic.* I can't stress this point enough. People see the word *standard* and immediately jump to the conclusion that standard work is static. Standard work represents the *current* best practice and routinely changes to accommodate improvements that are made.
- *Transferable.* When codifying work, ensure that documents focus on the work and not the current individuals or teams that are performing said work. When someone leaves the organization, the new incumbent doing that same job should be able to pick up the current standard work document and use it as a guide to get up to speed more quickly.
- *Concise and clear.* Standard work documents should be concise and contribute to departmental and organizational clarity.

We could go on and on about the topic of standard work, but examples of standard work are so idiosyncratic to specific work environments that to do so would be futile. The internet is awash with standard work templates and explanations of standard work for particular industries, so I'll point you to places like the Gemba Academy, iSixSigma, and Lean.org for more information.

We will, however, conclude our brief discussion of standard work with a few words on leader standard work. That's right—leaders and managers are not exempt from establishing their own standard work. In my first book, *Balancing Act: Teach, Coach, Mentor, Inspire,* I included a section on leader standard work and its importance in establishing and reinforcing clarity, as well as bolstering organizational trust and accountability. To many within your organization, the work of leadership can be a complete mystery.

225

Publishing the structure of your work to the rest of the organization can help lift the veil of secrecy that surrounds many executive positions and has the added benefit of keeping you, the leader, focused on what you've determined to be the most important ways you'll add value to your teams on a daily basis. Remember the shiny balls we've talked about on numerous occasions throughout this book? Establishing and conforming to leader standard work will help you avoid the inevitable distractions and shiny balls that flit in and out of view.

The Start of Your Journey

So there you have it! Of course, there is much more to the full adoption of continuous improvement within a business or institution, but in my experience it can take *years* to weave complete adherence to continuous improvement into a company's culture. These ten essential tools will get you started and pretty far down the road. They are also, in my experience, the most impactful tools, and the ones that will add the most value to your organization in the short term. From an employee engagement and change management perspective, they are also the easiest to understand and implement. The second you start throwing around terminology like *takt time*, *kanban*, *poka-yoke*, and *muda*, just to name a few, your people will begin to tune out—unless adding new terminology to your business lexicon adds value.

My advice as you expand on your continuous improvement tool kit is to be judicious and do so in a purposeful, stepwise manner with cost-benefit squarely in the foreground. For each new tool you introduce to the work environment, think carefully about the value it will add to the organization and your teammates. There are definitely diminishing returns to the introduction of additional tools, and it's easy to introduce unnecessary complexity into the organization—the very thing that embarking on a continuous improvement journey is meant to avoid.

As a final aside, you don't need to use the Japanese terminology for any of these tools within your organization. I have deep respect for the Japanese and their contributions to the field of continuous improvement. But if adding Japanese terminology to your business lexicon doesn't fit with your culture, introduce your own terminology. For example, if the culture is right, call your andon devices "the OSB," (the "oh shucks button"). If things are more formal, pick something else. The bottom line is to conform the lexicon of your organization to your unique culture—trying to cram in terminology that's unlikely to resonate won't help anyone.

16

A Maniacal Focus on the Customer

It is shockingly easy to lose sight of your number-one stakeholder.

In my travels through the business world, within the company I ran and beyond—and in conversations with people from all walks of life and all manner of professional expertise—I've seen many who have fallen down the same slippery slope.

In the vast majority of cases, businesses exist to serve their customers first and foremost. It's a concept so basic and so seemingly obvious that it often goes unsaid. That's the problem. When you spend all your time and energy focusing on internal goals—on meeting quarterly targets or pleasing the manager or getting facetime with the CEO—losing sight of who keeps the lights on, and who keeps you employed, can be easy.

The customer is often so far removed from our day-to-day existence, and our managers and colleagues are so intimately involved in our work experience, that it's easy to forget which one we actually serve. Unless you're in a select few customer-facing departments, you will likely see your role as primarily serving your managers, colleagues, CEO, or other customer-facing departments, like sales, customer service, and product development.

That is especially true when you begin to implement changes to the business, such as those I am proposing in this book. It becomes incredibly tempting for staff, who are naturally resistant to change, to see such exercises as existing in service of productivity for its own sake or to appease the leadership team's latest fad management style.

Getting caught in your own echo chamber is so easy–to put the blinders on and push paper around for its own sake–that the customer very often fades out of view. Instead, the focus remains squarely on meeting quarterly targets or implementing some new system or having the budget finished in time.

This is what we call an internal customer, and when it comes to facilitating flow, it can pose a real threat. That is because things like urgency, cadence, commitment, and quality can wane significantly, depending on whom you imagine the intended recipient to be. For example, most folks in the finance department don't work with customers directly every day, but they do have close relationships with their colleagues in sales. If Suzie in accounting is running late on processing a client refund, she knows her buddy Jim in sales will probably let this one slide. After all, they've been working together for years, and Suzie has a pretty solid track record most of the time, so the occasional slipup isn't much to worry about. In this scenario, the customer doesn't even factor in; it's more about the relationship between Suzie and Jim.

Focusing on an internal customer breeds familiarity, and familiarity doesn't often inspire urgency. It can also lead to an "us" versus "them" mentality; some of "us" are more important than "them" because we serve the customer directly, and "they" serve "us." That mentality, however, can be very destructive to morale. It creates artificial but very real boundaries in people's minds and leaves many in the organization to see their roles as secondary. Day after day of focusing on supporting Jim in sales eventually creates the impression that Suzie's role isn't as important; her team is operating in service of the sales department, or other internal stakeholders, not the other way around.

Once you start to identify internal stakeholders, you inevitably–almost by definition–begin to play favorites. If department A only exists in service of department B, who do you think is going to get the most time, attention, and resources? Anyone who has grown up with siblings, or has children of their own, knows the devastating effect that can result when parents pick favorites. Those words and actions cut deep, and the scars can last a lifetime. The one doted upon as the favorite inevitably feels less pressure to excel because they've effectively already won the approval they crave, and the others can be so demoralized they don't even bother trying any more.

The Enemy Within

The biggest problem with having a focus on internal stakeholders, however, is that it creates internal competition. Rather than focusing your time and energy on the customer, your people will instead spend time trying to prove their worth to their colleagues, and the customer ultimately gets forgotten.

This also applies to the internal struggles that inevitably occur within a business. I distinctly remember having conversations with teams where this "us" versus "them" mentality was palpable, and eventually led to internal strife. Over time, what started as small internal struggles morphed into significant problems of trust and accountability between departments and teams. In some cases I would have to call a literal time out just to stop the shouting and complaining. In those instances, the most impactful thing I could share with them is a reminder that the enemy isn't in this room, it's out there somewhere, waiting to eat our lunch.

Enemy might be a strong word, but in those emotionally charged situations, it does the trick. It was meant to rally the team in the same way a high school coach might choose to deal with conflicts among teammates, but remembering which side you're on when you're all wearing the same jersey is a lot easier. The point is that there is someone else out there trying to pull our customers away from us and toward themselves, and if we shift focus from winning that customer to internal bickering, we're ultimately going to lose.

Remember waste number 9 from chapter 14, that of emotion, which often manifests as unproductive team dynamics? This is a perfect example, and it can be a tremendous source of waste. We all have a tendency to compete—certainly some more than others—and that competitive spirit needs to be directed somewhere. If you as a leader don't actively manage that competitive urge and shift the focus away from the internal toward the external, it can begin to eat away at your organization from the inside. Instead of expending emotional energy, pointing fingers, and engaging in conflicts with other team members, shifting focus toward an external goal is important for leaders—one everyone can rally behind. In most cases, that will be your customer.

Businesses as a whole also have a tendency to get caught up in competition between industry rivals. While this form of competition can be healthy in the right doses, it can also serve to pull focus away from the customer. Sometimes two or more entities compete to be the first to market with this new product or that new feature, without really understanding how it will impact end users. The reality is that sometimes your competitor has it all wrong, and if you're too focused on beating them to the punch, you could be getting it wrong too. Again, competition in business can be healthy, as can some competition between team members and departments, but, if you have a maniacal focus on something other than your customer, you will put yourself at risk of missing out on opportunities.

Remember Who Pays the Bills

Competition, like change and communication, will happen naturally, and, like communication and change, it needs to be managed effectively. Internal competition can lead to obfuscation, and the creation of unnecessary emotional waste between people and departments. Too many individuals and organizations get so focused on internal competition that they completely forget who's paying the bills, and who they ultimately work for. Unfortunately, we live in a society that is so focused on the employer-employee dynamic—on pleasing the manager or the boss—that we forget where the money actually comes from. The only way a business remains sustainable is through satisfied customers who come back over and over again and tell their friends and family to do the same.

Remembering that the customer is not the sole responsibility of sales and marketing and product development teams is also important, though we tend to think of them as such. Often people assume that they don't need to get wrapped up in customer satisfaction, because it's not explicitly part of their job. Going back to an example I've used previously, if you ask the custodial technician at Disney World what her job is, she's likely to answer, "To create memorable experiences for our guests," as she empties trash inside Space Mountain. That is because *everyone* plays a part in creating memorable experiences at Disney. The same thing is also true at NASA. If you asked the custodian cleaning the bathrooms what it is they do, they might say, "I put people on the moon." They might not be personally hitting the launch button, but they are in charge of ensuring a clean and sanitary workplace so that their colleagues can be more efficient and focused on the job at hand. Everyone, and I mean *everyone,* is in charge of adding to the value stream that ultimately leads to the customer.

One effective way of instilling this maniacal focus on the customer is through business acumen (a.k.a. commercial acumen) training—an important topic that most of us aren't taught in school. Unless you took some business classes, it isn't always obvious how money flows from the customer's wallet into the individual employee's paycheck, creating a disconnect and misunderstanding of whom each team member ultimately serves. In the context of that flowing river we introduced in chapter 10, understanding how individual and team contributions feed into the value streams that combine to form a river of goods and services that flows into the ocean of consumer demand is important. That is ultimately what continuous improvement is all about. Each department and function needs to see themselves as a vital part of the process, with the customer serving as the ultimate stakeholder.

This is also why every employee should have a basic understanding of the organization's strategy statements and why those strategy statements should in part be focused on how to consistently provide great customer experiences. To beat up on accounting a little bit more, considering yourself part of that value-add process when the vast majority of your efforts won't come into contact with customers is sometimes hard, but there are still instances when accounting can make the difference between a negative and positive customer experience. For example, accounts receivable is very firmly intertwined with customer satisfaction. Unless you operate a cash-only business you will probably have some receivables, and your accounting department will probably have to have some pretty important, albeit difficult customer interactions regarding collections. Constructively navigating conversations with clients whose accounts are past-due can be tricky.

How are those difficult conversations handled? Do your accounts receivable staff have adequate training to effectively manage that interaction? They might not see themselves as part of the customer acquisition and loyalty process, but a negative interaction on their part could ultimately ruin a customer relationship. On the other hand, their handling of those difficult conversations with the appropriate level of deft and care can add significant value to the business by increasing the timeliness of cash receipts, driving additional liquidity, and allowing the company to use that money to pay off debts or put it toward new investments and innovations. Even if 99 percent of their job is not customer facing, it's important they receive explicit training on how to manage the other 1 percent.

The Third Principle of Continuous Improvement

In chapter 12, I introduced the concept of continuous improvement, which comprises three key principles. In that same section, we discussed the first principle, respect for people, and in chapter 14 we explored the second, the identification and minimization of waste. Here we'll discuss why a maniacal focus on the customer is the third essential ingredient.

Let's consider how a maniacal focus on the customer is correlated with respect for people. Your people are your most valuable asset, and they need a certain degree of business acumen—that is, an understanding of the basic operational principles of the business—to understand the value stream that they participate in every day. Rallying teams around the shared goal of creating amazing and unforgettable products or experiences for customers is in its own way a form of respect. If employees understand the customer and they understand the destination of the company's value stream(s), they are also able to understand the value they bring to the organization every day. The result is a virtuous cycle where work becomes more meaningful and rewarding.

This maniacal focus on the customer is also an effective means for not just reducing waste, but understanding what constitutes waste in your organization. For example, a well-intentioned third party might take a look at your business and identify certain processes that they deem to be wasteful. What that independent prudent person might not understand, however, is how a particular process factors into your offering to customers. If they don't understand what makes you indispensable to your customer, or your *it*, they can't effectively determine what processes are wasteful and which are value-adding. Determining the line between a wasteful and necessary product, feature, process, etc., requires a strong understanding of what it is the customer actually wants.

Another way of understanding continuous improvement is through the concept of standard work. Defining and refining one's standard work processes in search of efficiencies big and small is a mindset that, when instilled, can have a huge impact on the flow of your business. Implementing that mindset, however, is only as good as the ultimate goal that those refinements and improvements are designed to achieve. Continuous improvement for its own sake just gets you nowhere faster. The codification of standard work is always at risk of being perceived as busywork that team members will resist unless it is attached to a very specific purpose. One such purpose is creating happy customers.

As mentioned above, you should anticipate some resistance to a continuous improvement journey for a number of reasons. First, people abhor change and will actively undermine those efforts in order to maintain "the way it's always been done." Second, continuous improvement, with all its complicated terminology, can feel like a completely foreign language. Without a maniacal focus on the customer—coupled with respect for people and the identification and minimization of waste—proving the doubters wrong is damn near impossible. You need all three working in concert together; otherwise, it just becomes another human resources exercise that people have to add to their already busy days—one that they won't see value in.

Without putting continuous improvement practices in clear service of the customer, team members will oppose its adoption, and morale will ultimately go in the wrong direction, because you're just trading one waste for another—reducing the traditional "eight wastes" for the waste of emotion. Operating with a maniacal focus on the customer is the best way to ensure your teams understand why you're engaging in continuous improvement practices, and what you hope to achieve.

Understanding the Customer

Maintaining your customer as your organization's North Star—that shared ideal that everyone can focus their competitive energy on—requires a deep understanding of who the customer is and what they actually want. Tools such as persona identification, customer journey mapping, and conjoint analysis are an excellent way for marketing and product management professionals to determine what your customers value about your product set. Here I want to direct your attention to a customer sentiment tool that *everyone* in the organization should have a baseline understanding of: Net Promoter Score (NPS).

NPS is a widely used metric to determine the proportion of customers that are likely to recommend a product or service (or "promote" it)

compared with those who are likely to recommend against it. The score gives organizations a benchmark, allows them to set goals, and is often used to help determine high-level strategy, such as budget allocations, marketing, and product development plans.

I've seen many organizations resist the idea of tracking their NPS because they feel like they already have a strong sense of their customers' sentiment. "We work closely with our customers every day," they'll argue. "If there was a problem, that would be reflected in our sales figures." While sales and direct customer interaction are important metrics, they only tell a part of the story. Sales might be strong, but that doesn't mean customers aren't running into problems with your product or service. In fact, you might be making the same mistake as your competitors—one that will only become apparent when one of them offers a solution to that common problem, and by that time it's likely too late. This method of calculating customer sentiment can shine a light on problems lurking below the surface, even when things appear to be flowing smoothly.

NPS is a fairly common tool, and while many are familiar with it, not everyone understands how it's calculated. In essence, your NPS is measured by calculating the difference in the proportion of promoters and detractors. Anyone who has purchased a product or service in the last decade is likely to have received an email from the provider asking a key question: "On a scale from zero (not at all) to ten (extremely likely), how likely would you be to recommend this product or service to a friend or colleague?"

The question is worded in this specific way because it requires individual customers to consider whether or not they feel strongly enough to risk their personal reputation among friends and colleagues to stand behind the product or service. On a typical NPS scale, customers who provide a score of either nine or ten are considered "promoters," those who respond with a score of seven or eight are considered "passive," and those who provide a score of six or less are considered "detractors."

To compute NPS, we calculate the percentage of promoters and detractors relative to the total sample size and then take the difference between these two numbers. The percentage of passives are discarded. For example, if 15 percent are detractors, 25 percent are passive, and 60 percent are promoters, your NPS score would be 60-15 = 35. NPS, however, isn't always in the positive range. In fact, scores can range from -100 to 100, with 100 achieved through only receiving customer ratings of 9 or 10 from *every single customer*. A score of -100 means all respondents are detractors and gave a ranking between 0 and 6.

In the image above, we have a total sample size of ten customers, six of which are detractors that have provided ratings ranging from one to six. Two individuals offered ratings of seven and eight and have been classified as passives. Finally, our hypothetical company has two promoters who enthusiastically gave ratings of 9 and 10, respectively. As a result, 20 percent of our sample are promoters (2 of 10) and 60 percent are detractors (6 of 10), yielding an NPS of -40.

If you have ever answered an NPS survey, you've probably been asked for some additional information. If you had the time and the patience, you've likely been directed to a longer and more detailed questionnaire. This additional layer of data can be vital to organizations in understanding *why* their NPS is what it is and how to improve it. The layering of one simple question, followed by additional information, is no accident either. Most people have time to click a quick number between zero and ten—few will actually take the time to complete the more detailed survey. The prominence of this carefully worded question that speaks directly to the idea of recommendation demonstrates just how important that single data point is. If you can only ask your customers one question, make it that one. I've seen some organizations take customers through lengthy surveys without asking that all important sentiment question, and I can't help but shake my head, because the importance of all the other data points pale in comparison to this one.

At the same time, it's important not to forget about those other questions either. NPS is a vitally important metric, but it's highly quantitative and doesn't explain the "why" behind the rating. At the end of most surveys, organizations will ask an open-ended question, like "leave us some feedback about your experience," with a text box where customers can provide more detail. Only a small proportion of customers will take the time to fill this out, which suggests that those who do either (a) have way too much time on their hands, or (b) feel really passionately about the business, product, or service, either positively or negatively. These open-ended responses are filled with rich qualitative data, and I implore you not to ignore it. I can't tell you how frustrating it is when I actually take the time to fill in a survey, leave valuable feedback, and never hear anything back.

Open-ended survey questions contain data you can't get anywhere else; data that can unlock new product or service opportunities, ideas to help identify and minimize waste, ideas on how to better treat your people, and a barometer of how the business is viewed by the general public. If you're not going to take the time to actually put this data to use, then please, for me and all the other customers out there, save us some time and don't bother asking. These days we can't buy a donut at a coffee shop without being asked to provide feedback on our experiences—we all have a certain degree of survey fatigue—and when we take the time to provide feedback, we expect some sort of action in response. Customer complaints should be followed up with an apology and perhaps a coupon or other perk, and compliments should be returned with similar promotions and at a minimum, a simple thank-you in a timely manner.

Similarly, it's important to really invest the time, do some research, maybe even take a course, to understand how to put together a survey that actually provides value. Asking questions for the sake of feeling in tune with your customers has no value if the data that results is unusable. Make sure questions are worded appropriately and crafted with a specific purpose in mind. Yes, your NPS score and other metrics are very important, but they only tell a portion of the story. If you want to understand not just *how* your customers feel about you, but *why* they feel that way and, more importantly, how to *change* their attitude in a positive direction, you need to ask the right questions, and study the answers carefully.

Now you might be saying to yourself "sounds great in principle, but we have three million customers, and if 5 percent fill in the survey, then we will have to comb through 150,000 answers, and we just don't have the time or resources to do that!" My response to that would be fine, you don't need to read each and every one if it's not practical or possible to do so, but you can still get insights from the quantitative data you're collecting. Doing keyword analysis and creating word clouds can give you a strong indication of the general themes and recurring compliments or complaints. Once you have a sense of what people are talking about generally, do a random sampling of responses that include those common keywords.

> **A side note on negative feedback:** If a few people made the time to provide constructive but negative feedback about your product or service, it's highly likely that they're not alone in their assessment. Other respondents just didn't make the time to codify their thoughts in writing. Dig deeper—don't fall into the trap of assuming that a few negative responses represent outliers that should be ignored.

My final piece of advice on measuring consumer sentiment is that you need to utilize some critical-thinking skills here. In the survey world, consistency is important, especially if you want to track responses through time. By asking that same NPS question over and over again, you can get a sense of whether customers are responding positively or negatively to changes in the business, and that's absolutely vital. Not falling into the trap of "the way we've always done it," however, is also important. Asking the exact same questions month after month, quarter after quarter, year after year is somewhat lazy, because neither your business nor your customer is static over time. As you introduce new products, features, and services, asking new questions and thinking really clearly about the construction of those questions is important. In short, you need to find a balance between the value of tracking consistent data points over time and seeking new insights, all without overwhelming your respondents with too many questions or too many surveys.

Balance Emotion with Data

Individual contributors viewing their department's role as being somewhat disconnected from the customer can have a significant impact on consumer sentiment in countless measurable and unmeasurable ways. Surveys and NPSs are particularly powerful tools in creating alignment around a shared purpose and bringing people from various departments together by making such data transparent. The data collected from these exercises should serve as a starting point for fostering conversations about how the business is doing in service of the customer and engage in constructive conflict based on objective data, rather than emotions. Using data, leaders can effectively redirect competitive spirit away from internal competition to an external, maniacal focus on the customer.

17

Measurement and Transparency

To promote trust, accountability, and flow, a business or institution *must* have a strategy for how it will measure results *and* how it will make those results transparent to various stakeholder groups. The word *and* in the previous sentence is critical.

Before we proceed, however, let's dig deeper into the relationship between trust, accountability, and flow. Which one comes first? In many cases, trust is the initial condition to a new employment relationship, but most experienced members of the workforce have developed a skin of skepticism based on previous interactions with bad bosses, the clay layer, or the actively disengaged. Depending on the tone and tenor of that accumulated experience, their skin of skepticism can be pretty thick and difficult to penetrate. Therefore, trust is replaced by skepticism as the initial condition for interactions in the workplace.

As we've illustrated on several occasions, trust is *earned* over time. It is difficult to grow and incredibly easy to destroy. Remember the trust ladder? Each step up the ladder is made through consistent, reliable handoffs, and actions that match words. Once flow breaks down without proper rationale, or it becomes obvious that poor performance is not accompanied by proper accountability, the trip back down to the bottom rung of the trust ladder is swift and jarring.

To be clear, trust is a derivative of both accountability and flow. Without flow, measurement is difficult and unreliable. When measurement of performance and results is arduous, accountability is challenging at best. Hence, to specifically answer the question of order, flow begets accountability, and accountability encourages trust. Measurement and transparency are necessary conditions to this equation.

What Is Accountability at Work?

Accountability at work is difficult to define and even more difficult to see. There are a number of reasons for this, with the primary driver being the veil of obfuscation many managers drape over their fiefdom within the business. "Nothing to see here! Everything's fine in my world. Move along …" Secondary factors include the human resources governance process, employee protections, and privacy laws that vary by geography and culture.

Unfortunately, that skin of skepticism we discussed above is born partially from the "blame society" we've cultivated over the last few decades. When things go sideways at the office, folks want someone to point fingers at, but the aforementioned employee protections make "seeing" who to blame difficult. What results are unproductive watercooler convenings to litigate the matter and pass judgment on the accused without due process or all the facts. All of this represents a significant waste of emotion and a huge distraction to the work at hand.

My goal is to change the trajectory of these ad hoc conversations about accountability and reduce the waste they produce. Instead of seeking to blame others for failures, learning from them as a group is best—to work together to support the development of team members. This will ultimately enhance both technical and human skill, minimizing such failures in the future.

Of course, there are bad apples in nearly every company. We've all worked with individuals who have "checked out" and are riding on the coattails of team members who remain engaged and committed to the company's purpose, vision, and customers; however, I believe that these cases are the exception and not the norm—most folks *want* to do good work and don't deserve to be "canceled" because of a mistake, especially if there aren't mechanisms in place to (a) measure what good work is and/or (b) reskill or upskill team members whose skills have atrophied or have been displaced by technology advances.

So how do we move past a culture of blame to a culture of support and development? A key ingredient is measurement and transparency. If goals are properly set, associated with key performance indicators (KPIs), and aligned up, down, and across the organization, flow is continually monitored. Accountability then becomes a function of the company's measurement and transparency strategy, opportunities for finger-pointing and blame are reduced, and people begin to believe "we're all in this together." As a result, the "us versus them" mentality melts away. If information is shared in a timely manner between all relevant stakeholders, then trust will have the best opportunity to flourish.

What Should We Measure?

It's *really easy* to convince yourself that everything should be measured. Digital transformations and enterprise resource planning (ERP) system installations can easily topple under the weight of too many requests for reports and data that seldom, if ever, get used. I've personally witnessed the creation of tremendous waste generated by teams who've convinced themselves that they need report after report, only to disregard them after one or two uses.

To determine what should be measured, we start at the top. Back in chapter 9, we established the company's master goals by defining both sustaining and vision-specific goals. These high-level goals should be our guide to the definition of the KPIs we care about most. For example, if one of the company's sustaining goals is to grow revenue, then one of our key metrics should be related to revenue growth. Each sustaining and vision-specific goal should have *one* KPI associated with it. These are the company's master KPIs.

Why one for each? Master KPIs represent the top of a KPI tree diagram that should be maintained as one of the company's important documents. As we drill down to the department, team, and individual contributor levels of the organization, the KPIs that matter at these levels should "hang" off the master KPIs like branches from the trunk of the tree. That way, everyone has a clear line of sight to how their KPIs roll up to master KPIs in the same manner that goals are aligned up, down, and across the organization. Building the company's KPI tree diagram should be the responsibility of your data engineering team (a.k.a. institutional effectiveness, business analysis, and business intelligence to name just a few alternatives).

In chapter 11, we discussed how quarterly milestones are set each year for the company's sustaining and vision-specific goals. Each quarterly milestone should have clearly defined expected outcomes that are also developed using the specific, measurable, achievable, realistic, and time-bound (SMART) goal-crafting framework. Since expected outcomes are *measurable*, there must be one or more metrics or KPIs associated with each one. These KPIs are added to the KPI Tree.

Also in chapter 11, we illustrated the process for creating functional area (departmental), team, and individual goal sets that cascade from the organization's master goals. These are the supporting goals to sustaining, vision-specific, and quarterly milestones. In a similar fashion to the organization's quarterly milestones, each supporting goal should have one or more metric or KPI associated with it based on the SMART framework.

GOALS & KPIs

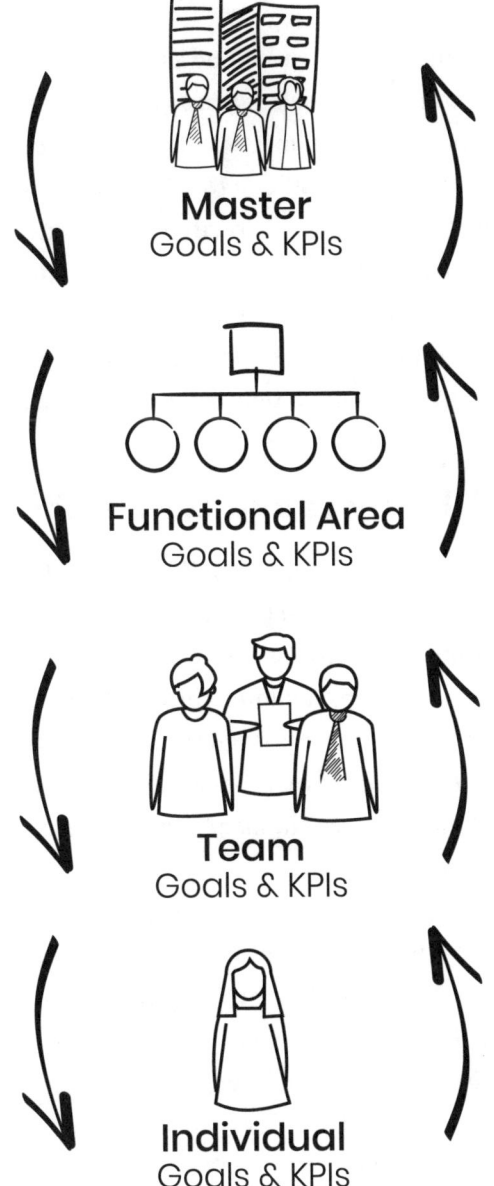

Master
Goals & KPIs

Functional Area
Goals & KPIs

Team
Goals & KPIs

Individual
Goals & KPIs

After reading through all this, you're probably thinking, "Wow, that's a lot of KPIs that need to be tracked!" You are indeed correct, and the KPI tree diagram that accompanies the organization's goal sets should punch the point that KPIs should be:

- *Simple.* KPIs and metrics should be as straightforward as possible. Unnecessary complexity can easily seep into the goal setting and measurement process through metrics that are difficult to compute and whose underlying data is difficult to collect or not readily available.
- *Useful.* KPIs should be directly related to the outcome that's being measured—correlation should be as high as possible.
- *Understandable.* This point is key. If the average person in the organization can't interpret the underlying meaning of the KPI, then even the most earnest transparency intentions will be for naught.

A Note on Objectives and Key Results (OKRs)

In his 2018 book *Measure What Matters: How Google, Bono, and the Gates Foundation Rock the World with OKRs*, John Doerr attributes the planning and measurement philosophy of OKRs to Andrew Grove, the third employee of semiconductor giant Intel. The OKR framework was employed at Intel by Grove before Doerr brought the concept to Google in 1999, where it has been used with great success. Since the release of Doerr's book, the use of OKRs as a measurement framework has increased at companies around the world.

In the practical application of OKRs, the *objective* represents a goal that is to be achieved by the business. In OKR parlance, the objective is a challenging, ambitious goal. The objective's *key results* are the "as measured by" part of an OKR statement. Hence, OKRs are typically written as "we aim to do *objective(s)* as measured by *key result(s)*." Most promoters of the OKR framework recommend using between three and five key results. Key results follow a version of the SMART goal construction philosophy, they are specific (S), time bound (T), **ambitious** yet realistic (A), measurable (M), and **verifiable** (V).

Some authors suggest that the SMART philosophy applies to key results, but the *A* in SMART refers to *achievable*. This, in my opinion, conflicts with the aim of *ambition* that's central to the OKR framework. Unfortunately, STAMV is a terrible acronym, so we won't try to force it on you. The two words in bold above—ambitious and verifiable—are the two things that I want you to remember.

According to Doerr, Grove said this about OKRs: "The key results have to be measurable. But at the end you can look, and without any arguments ask: Did I do that or did I not do it? Yes or No? Simple. No judgments in it." This is why verification is stressed. "Did I do that or did I not do it?"

Let's say your OKR is to increase the company's average deal size by 30 percent in the next fiscal year. The method for calculating deal size is fairly straightforward, as is the benchmark that it's being compared against—that is, last year's deal size. As the year goes on, each new deal is folded into the new average for the year, allowing anyone to easily recognize whether the company is on track or has achieved the desired outcome. There is no ambiguity here, as the numbers speak for themselves.

I mention OKRs here for two reasons. First, based on its adoption and popularity, I would be remiss not to provide you with a reference for engaging in more OKR research of your own. Second, the measurement of supporting goals and quarterly milestones follows an OKR-style approach with two key differences:

- As I've mentioned, I feel very strongly that ambitious goals, sometimes known as stretch goals, can backfire if not used infrequently and with specific purpose. In many organizational cultures, the overuse of stretch goals can kill morale. Therefore, I would urge caution when applying the OKR framework within organizations that don't fit the mold of a fast moving start up.
- Proponents of OKRs recommend between three and five key results per objective. In a complex business environment, this can lead to an explosion of metrics and KPIs that must be tracked. If you just had an "ah ha" moment, that's on purpose. Yes, KPIs and metrics are embedded within key results to support measurement (M) and verification (V).

249

The bottom line is that OKRs can be very useful, but only when applied to the right circumstance. If your culture is agile and entrepreneurial, then the aggressive nature of OKRs may fit very well and produce excellent results as they have at Google and other such organizations. In more mature businesses, however, wholesale adoption of OKRs could pose a challenge. Since OKRs are designed to be ambitious, getting to 80 percent of a target can be considered a win, but many in the organization might view 80 percent achievement as a failure. This can be particularly challenging if incentives are aligned with legacy metrics and have not been adjusted to compensate for the ambition built into an OKR. (We dig deeper into this issue in chapter 18.)

My advice for more mature organizations that want to test OKRs is to do so for a select set of supporting goals within functional areas that exhibit a more *intra*preneurial subculture or for a specific initiative that's being purposefully run as an internal start up.

The Four Key Competencies

In my first book, *Balancing Act*, I outlined four key competencies that will be essential ingredients for the continued success of organizations and the humans that populate them. They are:

- Human skill—for example, emotional intelligence, teamwork, storytelling, communication, etc.;
- Commercial (a.k.a. business) acumen;
- Financial literacy; and
- Data literacy.

All four of these competencies are critical building blocks to an organization's measurement and transparency strategy.

Companies and institutions are awash in data. We now have computing systems that can routinely manage the vast quantities of data that organizations produce on a daily basis; however, the trick is to ensure that data leads to insights. This requires that the data we generate is "clean," meaning it is stored and categorized in a way that makes accessing it as seamless as possible.

To help manage mountains of data, many organizations have built new departments within the functional areas of executive management, finance, operations, and technology. Colleges have the Office of Institutional Effectiveness, and a business might have something called the Department of Business Intelligence, or simply the Department of Data and Analytics. In today's world, these departments serve an incredibly important function. They hire highly skilled data scientists, data analysts, statisticians, and database managers, but their existence also serves as an enabler to others in the organization and can also represent a key barrier to organizational flow.

The specialists in the office of business intelligence can inadvertently become enablers because managers and individual contributors who should otherwise acquire a base level understanding of how data is categorized, manipulated, and interpreted abdicate that responsibility fully to the office of business intelligence. This creates an avalanche of ill-conceived data analysis requests that the specialists have to make sense of, creating a vicious cycle of backlogs and rework that generate waste of various varieties. If your IT department, for example, is already wasting a significant proportion of its time troubleshooting issues that any everyday user of consumer technology should be able to solve for themselves, just imagine what happens when your teams become overly dependent on data specialists.

So how do we maximize the effectiveness of our investments in precious data and analytics resources? We raise the bar across the entire organization by engaging in a continuous experiential learning and training regimen across the four competencies listed at the top of this section. You may be asking why all four are critical and not just data literacy. Here's the rationale:

- Commercial or business acumen represents an understanding of how the business works—how one team's outputs become another's inputs and how value is being created both upstream and downstream from a particular team or individual's activities. Put simply, commercial acumen is the keen understanding of how value is created by the business and how the organization's value stream(s) functions. Well-crafted requests for reports and other business intelligence outputs depend heavily on how data is created and used in other parts of the business.

- Finance is one of the key languages of business. Revenue and expense, assets and liabilities, intangibles, cash flow, and myriad ratios that illustrate the relationship between individual components of the aforementioned categories are essential components of any story-telling exercise. To tell your department or team's story effectively, a base level understanding of finance is required.

- Data literacy is the obvious competency that's a must-have for an effective measurement and transparency strategy. The most important things I'd like to stress for any data literacy training program is the development of the higher order skill of critical thinking and knowledge of data classification systems and terminology. Enhanced critical-thinking skills will yield data requests that are better formed and more thoughtful. Better questions equal better results. Words like taxonomy and ontology need to make their way into our business lexicon to remove some of the language barriers that exist between data specialists and the general population of the organization.

- In just a moment, we're going to talk about the importance of transparency to build trust, accountability, and flow. Transparency is dependent upon the human skills of communication, empathy, vulnerability, and storytelling, just to name a few. I've known many managers who use information as a weapon to make themselves and their teams look better at the expense of their colleagues. Needless to say, trust and flow don't stand a chance in an environment like this. Remember: the competition on which we should focus our energy is outside the walls of the business. Turf wars and internal battles for information are unhelpful at best and create tremendous organizational waste.

Visual Management Systems and Trust

Organizational trust dies in darkness and obfuscation.

When goals are not clear, roles and responsibilities cannot be well defined. When information is not shared, trust cannot flourish. Expecting to establish an environment of trust, accountability, and flow in an organization where information is hoarded and/or protected like state secrets is akin to living a fallacy.

Yes, organizations have trade secrets and competitive intelligence that would be damaging if it were to be leaked (see my side note on duplicity in chapter 13); however, well-crafted employment agreements and effective communication regarding what information is and is not sensitive can provide the necessary guardrails to keep that which is sensitive within the four walls of the organization. There will invariably be a small subset of the organization's data that must be restricted to a subset of the employee population, but those datasets and the individuals or teams that have access to them should be carefully considered and periodically reviewed to prevent more data than necessary being labeled as "classified."

If you've spent time working in a corporate or institutional environment, you've likely run across a domineering boss or two that thrives on internal protectionism and uses obfuscation as a tool to (a) control their employees, and (b) groom their personal reputation with senior management. These boss archetypes are highly selective regarding the data and statistics that make it out of their part of the organization. What these bosses typically can't or aren't willing to see is that when everything appears to be going great all or most of the time, that in itself is a red flag. Also, when viewed through the long lens of time, this behavior is unsustainable for both the boss and the team.

Earlier in my career, I, too, was an information and data protectionist. This, coupled with the "Andy said" culture I cultivated, led to an environment where everyone was looking over their shoulder and waiting for the next shoe to drop. No one but me had the full picture of how the business was doing, and I can attest that running a business that way was more exhausting than it needed to be. I found that more work is needed to obfuscate than to be transparent! Only after I learned to accept that a modicum of vulnerability was the missing ingredient did things start to turn around.

Vulnerability was the key that unlocked hidden potential in both me as a leader and the team as a whole.

You see, if we shed our emotional suit of armor and let others really see what's going on in the part of the business we're leading—the good, the bad, and even the ugly—it turns out that most people want to help make things better. This also places a bright spotlight on the small minority of colleagues who have a deeply fixed mindset and operate by fear and intimidation. Once the majority of leaders begin to sprinkle a bit of vulnerability into their standard work, then the oxygen is removed from those who thrive on obfuscation and mud. Unchangeable fixed-mindset bosses will begin to self-select out of the organization to find other organizations to terrorize. Others will see the benefits of working toward common aims in the spirit of collaboration and discover the joy that comes from winning together.

In chapter 15, we introduced the concepts of the gemba walk and the gemba board. I personally like these transparency and visual management tools because they're so organic and authentic. As discussed, gemba boards should all conform to a certain level of standardization (the required elements) to promote readability and understandability across departments, but then each department can add their own flair to their board. The required elements were very helpful for the gemba walker (me and other senior leaders) to reduce the burden of having to remember myriad formats, but I also loved seeing the individuality that would be put on display, depending on the unique subculture of a particular department. As you might expect, marketing's board looked different than finance's or technology's boards.

To be clear, one of the required elements of every team's gemba board (or other visual management tool) must be the KPIs, metrics, and/or OKRs that apply to that team from the organizational KPI Tree.

The Mud of Obfuscation

You can't help improve that which you cannot see. You can't identify waste that's hidden from view. You can't hold an individual or team accountable for that which is not measured. Visually showing the blinking red or amber lights in your department—in addition to the green ones—lets others in the organization see that your part of the company is not perfect. Adopting and weaving visual management systems into the flow of work is an important tool to show that it is not only acceptable, but expected, that we all work together to improve upon organizational challenges.

Working knee deep in the mud of obfuscation is no fun for anyone, and certainly doesn't promote trust, accountability, and flow.

> **A side note on legal and governance:** In this book, I'm focused on the required elements of any organizational management operating system. One of those required elements is a high-functioning set of legal and governance processes. Therefore, your legal, HR governance, and regulatory compliance teams are essential to your organization's success.
>
> Where I've seen legal, governance, and regulatory teams go wrong is when they do not operate in service of the business and instead act like independent third parties that work as extensions of governmental agencies or oversight bodies. Certainly, there are instances when independence is essential—for example, the office of the ombudsman or similar—to protect the interests of at-risk populations and to provide an open microphone to those who otherwise would not be able to find their voice in a psychologically safe environment. Certainly, these departments act as *conduits* between the business and their respective governance or regulatory bodies and frameworks; however, when legal, HR governance, or regulatory compliance construct *unnecessary* walls or barriers, they quickly become known within the organization as the "department of no," and an "us versus them" subculture ensues.
>
> Instead, the attitude of leaders, managers, and individual contributors in these important departments should be: "I'm saying no to your request as currently written or stated, but how can we work together to achieve a positive outcome for the organization and its customers?" Remember also that the relationship between you, your department, and the functional areas of legal, governance, and compliance is a two-way street. If you come into the legal department with a contract clause that needs to be struck

or reworked for a more positive business outcome, it's important that you approach the conversation with mental agility, curiosity, and creativity. If both parties dig in their heels, watch out! So much waste is generated when legal and their business counterparts take up intractable positions and decide to fight it out.

So instead of defaulting to an adversarial relationship with your organization's legal, HR governance, and compliance teams, I recommend that both parties operate with the word *integrity* top of mind.

I define *integrity* as "compassionately doing the right thing." As you negotiate with your colleagues in legal, governance, or compliance functions, remember that the definition of "do the right thing" may be different, depending upon the perspective of the team or individual. Compassion comes into play because compassion equals empathy plus a willingness to help make things better. Hence, you should do the right thing but should also seek to empathize with other perspectives and be willing to work together as a team to reach mutually beneficial outcomes—outcomes that add value along the value stream and ultimately add value to the customer.

18

Incentives

We've all heard the expression "money talks," and in business there is nothing that speaks louder to employees than monetary incentives. Sure, work flexibility, alignment of purpose, and other nonmonetary perks are becoming increasingly important, but don't fool yourself into thinking that monetary incentives are no longer a primary consideration.

To be even more pointed, the success or failure of everything that's been outlined in this book thus far hinges on incentive planning. An incentive plan that's not aligned with the company's purpose, vision, values, *be*haviors, *it*, master goals, and everything else that's been described in these pages can ultimately serve to undermine all those efforts.

Of course, living in a world where employees enthusiastically take direction from leadership without first seeking to understand how it affects their personal bottom line would be much easier, but that's unrealistic. If incentives aren't aligned with your strategy statements, they're only as valuable as the A3 (or tabloid-sized paper) you've printed them on. I'm adding a discussion about incentives to the list of must-have components of your management operating system because I fear that readers might spend time and energy carefully considering and defining their strategy statements, goals, and new ways of working, only to tell their staff that their annual bonus depends on metrics that aren't in alignment with establishing a high-trust, high-accountability corporate culture.

Incentive planning is complex and requires a lot of difficult decision-making, but the dangers of getting it wrong cannot be overstated. Unfortunately, this complexity often leads organizations to make two major mistakes.

- They make incentive planning the sole province of human resources and finance, often resulting in misalignments and internal struggles.
- They get so intimidated by the complexity of incentive planning that they default to the simplest, most obvious metric we have in our measurement tool kit—namely, revenue – costs = operating income.

Pegging incentives solely to operating income is dangerous, because the equation only gives organizations two methods for enhancing their own compensation. The first is to grow revenue, which can be a healthy and productive pursuit. The second, however, is to cut costs. As it turns out, the former is really difficult for most companies. I've witnessed the difficulty of trying to eke out incremental revenue growth on an ongoing basis, especially in mature businesses. As a result, many place all their incentives eggs in the cost-cutting basket.

I've seen it time and again. An organization starts the year off strong, but by the third quarter or the third month, something happens to threaten revenue—a new competitor, a setback in manufacturing, a product launch delay, a trade war, a global pandemic, shipping delays, inflation, and talent shortages, just to name a few potential culprits. In fact, strong examples from just the last few years alone are too many to list. A sudden panic washes over bonus-eligible staff as their revenue goals suddenly seem unachievable, and they can't help but fixate on the fact that their total compensation will dwindle as a result. The organizational budget that was created during the latter half of the prior year didn't account for this external or internal shock to the system.

To make matters worse, most who receive an annual bonus factor that additional compensation into their personal budgets and spending behavior. To most, the extra cash isn't a "bonus," because it's arrived consistently year after year, often in larger increments with each passing fiscal year. In their minds, or perhaps in a more literal way, the money is already spent, and they cannot afford to lose it.

The next issue is the most obvious and the most damaging to a high-trust, high-accountability culture. The previously established master and annual goals are abandoned as those at the top seek to protect their potential bonuses at all costs.

And there are very real costs to this behavior. Usually vision-specific and growth-oriented goals are the first to go. Unless you're working in a business with some serious venture backing, and thus robust access to capital, you start to fixate on the middle of the profit and loss statement. All the goals that are centered around innovation, or those that offer long-term benefits in exchange for short-term costs, get cut immediately. Growth goals get put on the backburner, or they are abandoned completely. A few years later, leaders may look back at their previously stated long-term goals with regret and realize that the business would have been in much better shape had they just stuck with the plan, but at the time that didn't matter, because their incentives were misaligned. The reason for that misalignment is simple; incentives were likely pegged to one simple short-term KPI, operating income.

This is also where trust and morale start to crater. You spent many hours over the course of weeks or months taking your team through an elaborate planning exercise; you gathered their feedback and opinions and involved them in decisions about where the company should be headed and what matters; you asked your customers for feedback and implored them to fill out lengthy surveys to provide valuable feedback; and then you run into some headwinds, the seas get rough, and the conversation reverts back to cuts. The common refrain in the C-suite during periods of economic stress is "How many staff do we need to cut to protect our bonus?"

This is one reason why continuous improvement and all the other fancy terminology used in prior sections get a bad rap and are often met with resistance. The waters get rough, we fixate on the middle of the profit and loss statement, and we conclude that cuts need to be made to what is most business's biggest expense: payroll.

If your staff has good reason to equate these processes with cost-cutting measures, it's hard to blame them for actively resisting their implementation. Organizations spend time and energy communicating that they're going on a continuous improvement journey to innovate, to grow, to make the company a better place for its employees, and to improve service to its customers, but when push comes to shove, your people—who represent the company's most valuable asset—are typically the first thing to go.

Go All In, or Stay Out

This is why, when it comes to continuous improvement, I implore organizations to either commit to the process, or abstain from it. That is because going halfway in and then peeling out before the process can take full effect causes more damage than maintaining the status quo, no matter how inefficient or wasteful it is. Note that when I use the word *commit*, I'm talking about a commitment to continuous improvement principles as mentioned at the top of chapter 15. It's perfectly acceptable to adopt a small, core set of continuous improvement tools and start slow. The point I'm making here is to avoid whipsawing the organization by chasing flavor-of-the day management philosophies.

A strong example of an organization failing to uphold its values in the face of a difficult financial situation happens to be playing out as I'm writing this, so I'm going to pick on one specific company. If you go to jobs.netflix.com/culture, you will find what appears to be an ideal work environment, one that adheres to many of the practices and features outlined in these pages. Under a pair of images that look like the result of a stock photo search for "young diverse happy professionals" you'll find a list of the company's five core values:

1. Encourage decision-making by employees.
2. Share information openly, broadly, and deliberately.
3. Communicate candidly and directly.
4. Keep only highly effective people.
5. Avoid rules.

Below that you'll find statements like "our core philosophy is people over process," and "with our people-first approach, we can be more flexible, creative and successful in everything we do," followed by a list of "valued behaviors." Those behaviors, each accompanied by a four- or five-point description, include: judgment, selflessness, courage, communication, inclusion, integrity, passion, innovation, and curiosity.

The lengthy "Culture" page also includes a paragraph about how the company values "honest, productive feedback" and its process for addressing controversial topics, which it describes as "disagree then commit." Netflix CEO Reed Hastings even published a book touting the company's culture in 2020 titled *No Rules Rules: Netflix and the Culture of Reinvention*.

To say Netflix had a difficult start to 2022 would be a dramatic understatement. In the first quarter of that year, the company reported a loss of two hundred thousand users, leading to a 38 percent drop in its stock value in late April.[1] To make matters worse, the company projected a loss of two million more subscribers in Q2. In response, the company cut twenty-five staff on April 28 and eliminated another 150 jobs, representing 2 percent of its total workforce, in mid-May.[2] Then came "the memo."

A quick note for context: Netflix's leadership has been at odds with certain members of its organization since October 2021, when controversial stand-up comedian Dave Chappelle released his Netflix special *The Closer*, containing incendiary jokes about the LGBTQ+ community.[3] A few days later, on October 20, staff organized a walkout in protest. In response, Netflix fired the organizers. Then, on May 12, 2022, a memo was leaked by *Variety*—one week before it was set to be distributed to all Netflix employees. The memo is only about four sentences long, but the last two sentences are what grabbed headlines: "Depending on your role, you may need to work on titles you perceive to be harmful. If you'd find it hard to support our content breadth, Netflix may not be the best place for you."[4]

Let's review: Netflix's leadership tells staff that it encourages feedback, that it promotes a people-first approach, that it expects staff to operate with courage, inclusion, and integrity—and its CEO even goes so far as to author a whole book on these principles—but when things get difficult, it resorts to layoffs and a memo discouraging debate and dissent within its ranks.

If you're not entirely surprised by their actions, behaviors, and their focus on shareholder value during difficult times, it's hard to blame you. Netflix is a for-profit business; it exists to generate return for shareholders, not protect its staff from fluctuating market conditions or to champion LGBTQ+ or other causes. It's a business, and this is what businesses do.

That's all fine and dandy for your average organization, but Netflix has taken painstaking efforts over its entire history to establish a reputation as being more than just your average profit-driven business. If you're going to make shareholder value your primary motivator and claim to value transparency, then at least be transparent about your true motivations!

All the effort that's been dedicated to creating and promoting Netflix's culture and values has essentially been diminished during this difficult period, and they may never gain back the credibility, or morale, they have lost in the process. If you're going to claim to live by a different set of principles, that needs to include both the good times and the bad. I can only imagine how much time and money Netflix has committed to defining and codifying its values, to publishing a book on the topic, to the PR and HR efforts dedicated to spreading the gospel of its unique culture. Then the company hits a rough patch, and all those previous efforts are damaged or outright wasted.

I hope the lesson is clear. I'm not saying every organization needs to adopt a continuous improvement mindset and seek to build a culture of trust and transparency, especially if it doesn't fit the reality of their organizational environment. What I am saying is that if you're going to put in the effort, you need to follow through. Either go all-in, or stay out.

In Search of a Better Incentive Structure

Now you might be thinking all this talk about transparency and trust and morale sounds good in principle, but incentives, by definition, need to be tied to operating income and cash flow. After all, the money needs to come from somewhere. That is absolutely true, and I hate to sound like a hypocrite, but acknowledging that money isn't free is important. When it comes to incentive planning, operating income and profitability absolutely need to be part of the equation in some form or another, because at the end of the day, cash flow is king.

The point I am hoping to make here is that consistency counts. As mentioned above, actions speak a much louder than words, and money talks the loudest. In other words, your incentive planning is one of the most important actions you can take to support or undermine your strategy statements, your long-term planning, your continuous improvement journey, etc. So the question then becomes, "how do we design an incentive strategy that is tied to the realities of business performance but also serves to enforce our values? How do we incentivize those people who don't get a cut of the business's profits so they feel like they're working for a company, not an individual who is driven by their own annual bonus?"

This is as important a question to ask as it is a difficult one to answer. While I'd like to prescribe a solution as easy as the default, profit-loss equation, the right answer likely won't be as simple, nor as widely applicable. The best I can do, without knowing the intimate details of your organization, is to provide some direction on how to go about answering this question.

The first step is drawing a stakeholder map. All businesses have one, and they typically list the groups of people that will ultimately define the organization's success, such as customers, employees, shareholders, regulatory agencies, suppliers, etc. Coming up with the list is the easy part. The hard part comes in step two: ranking their order of importance.

In most organizations, the default answer to the rank-order of stakeholders is obvious: shareholders typically take the top spot. What I'm proposing here and throughout this entire book is an order different from the default. I believe number one on that list should be customers, for all the reasons outlined in chapter 16. If you're going to claim to be a "people-first" organization, as Netflix and countless others do, however, you need to reserve a place for them in the number-two position. Again, you don't have to rank them this way, but if you are going to claim to have an unwavering commitment to your employees, codify it in your stakeholder map, and design an incentive structure that reflects it.

Another approach, however, is that of the *triple bottom line*, which puts people, profits and the planet on equal footing. The term was coined in 1994 by John Elkington, who was concerned that capitalism was leaving the world's most important stakeholders—the planet and its human inhabitants—out of the equation. Over the years there have been many companies who have championed this vision, including Patagonia, Ben & Jerry's, and Salesforce, but the concept failed to achieve the widespread adoption Elkington had hoped for. That is why in 2018, on the twenty-fifth anniversary of first introducing the term, he penned an op-ed in the *Harvard Business Review* demanding a recall of this management concept.

"Fundamentally, we have a hard-wired cultural problem in business, finance and markets," he wrote. "Whereas CEOs, CFOs, and other corporate leaders move heaven and earth to ensure that they hit their profit targets, the same is very rarely true of their people and planet targets. Clearly, the triple bottom line has failed to bury the single bottom line paradigm."[5]

There are many companies who have, in Elkington's words, "done well by doing good," including those listed above, but even the creator of the term *triple bottom line* acknowledges that incentive structures are often misaligned with initiatives to support people and the planet.

If your shareholders are your top priority, then your incentive plan should be designed so that operating income, cash flow, stock price, and other derivatives of the bottom line are a top priority. Oh, and be transparent about that reality. If you are a more balanced leader who truly believes in concepts like the triple bottom line, then your stakeholder map—and incentive structure—should reflect that.

One simple practice for considering how to develop this stakeholder map is developing an understanding of why people chose you as an employer. Are they there because you have relatively high levels of compensation? Because they enjoy the culture? Because they feel valued? Because of strong, positive opinions regarding leadership? Considering what inspires people to show up every day can help inform how you prioritize stakeholders. Some organizations just need to fill seats and workstations, and that's fine. Some organizations have attrition built into their business models, and, while not advisable, it can work in some instances.

An in-depth report by the *New York Times* published in June 2021 found that Amazon built its business model around a 150 percent turnover rate for warehouse workers.[6] Many would argue that this is not a great way to run a profitable business, and others would suggest that Amazon's results speak for themselves, but the point remains the same. The company has decided its warehouse workers are not an important stakeholder and operates accordingly. While not an ideal situation, especially for warehouse workers, I would argue that it's better than the Netflix approach—that of preaching one set of values and acting upon another.

> **A side note on the importance of cash flow and fiscal responsibility:** As I outlined in my previous book, *Balancing Act*, during my tenure at Kaplan, I had the distinct privilege of getting to know the chairman of Graham Holdings (Kaplan's parent), Don Graham. In a speech he gave to company executives, Mr. Graham said, "Companies grow with the money they make."
>
> What makes this seemingly obvious and simple statement so profound is that it is a reminder of the importance of fiscal responsibility. Until the Federal Reserve started raising interest rates to fight inflation in mid-2022, we've lived through an extraordinarily long period of time in which it seemed like money was free. Private equity and venture capital-backed companies appeared on the surface to have the luxury of an unending well of capital to fund experiments and expansion plans. Our government—irrespective of which political party was in power—"printed" money like it was going out of style. As a direct reflection of this, the US national debt as a proportion of GDP stands at roughly 120 percent as of Q3 2022.[7] Research by the World Bank suggests that debt-to-GDP ratios above 77 percent lead to a loss of real economic growth.[8]
>
> The point is that in the long run, companies must create economic returns for their shareholders. Yes, debt and leverage can put rocket boosters under a business plan, but there comes a time when a business must "stand on its own two feet" and generate

positive cash flow to fund investments that ensure its future sustainability.

Incentives and Equity

In chapter 16, I explained the potential dangers of viewing internal stake-holders as "customers" and noted that incentive structures often serve to reinforce an "us versus them" mentality. Creating a working environment that claims everybody from the intern to the CEO matters is hard when certain members of that organization are compensated with incentives and others are not.

If you look under the hood of most organizations, you'll find a clear division between those who are bonus-eligible and those who are not. Such divides are not only present in compensation levels but are also present in authority and decision-making power. In many organizations, you either need to be in a particular department, like sales, or at a particular level of seniority, like management, in order to qualify for bonuses. This structure, however, only feeds into the mentality that my job in accounting exists primarily in service of commission-based employees on the sales floor or for my manager, whose compensation is tied to my department's performance. In this way, incentives often serve as ground zero for internal divisions and, as discussed in chapter 14, inadvertently create unnecessary emotional waste.

People below the seniority line or outside the commission roles can't help but feel like their jobs are less vital, less valued, and less necessary than other roles. Initiatives aimed at improving the company's performance are met with resistance by those who don't share in its success. This class system, like all class systems, produces a group of elites who often enjoy the fruits of other people's labor, a group of aspiring elites who have a shot at making it into the club, and a sea of others who have little chance of doing better when the company does well.

There is, however, another way; one that has been proven successful by countless organizations around the world across generations. According to a study conducted by the National Center for Employee Ownership and published in the *Harvard Business Review* in 1987, companies with Employee Stock Ownership Plans (ESOPs) grow their sales and employment at consistently faster rates.[9] Another study conducted by EY found that organizations with ESOPs saw an average growth rate of 11.5 percent between 2002 and 2012, compared with a growth rate of 7.1 percent for the top publicly traded companies.[10] More recently, during the COVID-19 pandemic, companies with ESOPs retained employees better than traditionally owned businesses by a ratio of four to one and maintained standard hours and salaries at "significantly higher rates" than other firms, according to the Employee Ownership Foundation.[11]

Not every company needs to share 100 percent of its profits with its employees; however, those that provide equity in their incentives programs tend to perform better across a variety of metrics. This change in perspective can be considered drastic to a traditional business whose entire structure is focused on the bottom line, but the change doesn't have to be all that extreme.

After all, I've outlined the dangers of changing too drastically too quickly, and if you were to decide one day to change from a company that's maniacally focused on operating income to one that has revised its stakeholder map to put employees higher up on the list, that's a big change. To help mitigate the change, be creative with your language. If focusing on the bottom line is woven into your company's culture, don't try to completely change that culture in one fell swoop; change the definition of what the bottom line is, and what it means slowly and methodically over time. You can still be a bottom line–focused business, but now "bottom line" begins to mean something else in addition to operating profit.

Incentives and Flow

I couldn't in good faith write a book about operational flow without acknowledging the vital role that incentives play in shaping employee behavior, their willingness to embrace change, and their relationship with their employer. Optimizing your incentive structure and tying it to strategy statements and master goals is one of the key enablers of organizational flow. Revising it to be consistent with the organization's vision, values, and **be**haviors helps reduce the possibility of a disconnect between how one's employer or manager says team members should behave and how they are compensated. It creates a greater level of trust and transparency by reducing the unavoidable suspicion that leadership is making decisions in service of their own compensation, not the organization's well-being.

Aligning incentives to broader organizational goals can also reduce the likelihood of incentives-based internal conflict. Often departmental leaders are incentivized based on the performance of their specific corner of the business, which can be an incredible source of conflict and waste. That is because sometimes department A's success requires the cooperation of department B, but department B won't share in that incentive, so why should they go out of their way to support department A? In this environment, collective, organization-wide accomplishments take a back seat to individual and departmental victories, creating internal competition and conflict. If department A and department B's incentives are misaligned, they will ultimately lose focus of the customer, the master goals, etc., in service of those activities that are specifically aligned with their department's incentives.

Worse yet, departmental leaders probably won't be very transparent about their true motivations. Nobody wants to say, "I'm going against the needs of my colleagues in department A because I selfishly want to ensure I get paid my full bonus this year." Instead, teams stealthily act in ways that serve their own needs at the expense of others, tension builds under the surface, and, while they are cordial and polite in person, they actively work to undermine each other's efforts.

A misalignment in incentives, in my opinion, is the single greatest potential inhibitor of flow and a primary driver of organizational mistrust.

19

Putting It All Together

Before we head into the final stretch, I'd like to pause for a moment to ensure I'm not misunderstood. When I talk about the "clay layer," "organizational permafrost," "accidental managers" or refer to a "bad boss," I'm *not* talking about bad people. Yes, a small subset of individuals who populate these categories are indeed bad people with nefarious intentions. This subset wants to control other humans and seek power for its own sake—these people don't belong in business and certainly should not have a seat at the table. They are "net takers" and drain energy from the organization and the humans that surround them.

But most "bad bosses," "accidental managers," and members of the "clay layer" are good people with good intentions. What they lack are agile minds, open ears, a balanced ego, and a continuous learning mindset. Some type of skill gap typically lurks under the surface that explains the calcification of a fixed mindset. Skill deficiencies are likely also coupled with underlying unresolved issues of self-doubt, insecurity, imposter syndrome, and anxieties that manifest themselves in unproductive ways.

Deep down, folks that fit into the latter category *want* to improve skills and make progress against inner feelings of inadequacy and insecurity. If you're reading this book and fit even partially into this category, then thank you and congratulations. The realization that you're not perfect and can develop and improve throughout your lifetime is in and of itself a tremendous accomplishment. Showing even a modest degree of vulnerability is the first step on the journey out of the clay layer.

Who's the first person you should tell about embarking on a personal journey of continuous improvement and learning? Yourself. That's right, before you verbalize the choice to make the shift from adhering to a fixed mindset to that of continuous improvement and learning, ensure that you're aligned internally first. As humans, we have multiple constituents that reside within our own heads, and the mediator between those voices is our ego.

Unfortunately, the word *ego* has gotten a bad rap over the years. "Sheesh, does *he* have a big ego," is viewed primarily as a derogatory statement—meant to imply a blend of narcissism and an overly inflated view of self. In Freudian psychology, the ego is the mediator between the id and the superego. As a quick refresher, the id represents your base, instinctive mind—it lies completely under the surface of the waking mind and evidences itself in the form of irrational impulses and other unconscious biases. When you're operating on mental autopilot, the id can play an outsized role in decision-making. This built-in set of reactions, instincts, and emotions that come prewired into our DNA have been vital to human survival and evolution for millennia and are in many ways still necessary to our survival. At the same time, they can also serve to replace rational thought with emotional responses, which might, for instance, help a prehistoric human survive a bear attack. Those same instincts, however, are often counterproductive in the modern context.

On the other end of the spectrum is your superego, which is an individual's idealized—and often unattainable—self-image. While the id is set very early in our lives, the superego continues to develop over time based upon the acquisition of new role models and other exemplars that we encounter throughout our lives, especially into young adulthood. I like to think of the id as the "devil on my shoulder" and the superego as the "angel." The ego is therefore the "mediator" between the two. A *weak ego* allows the id or superego to have too much agency in our lives, leading to irrational or overly idealistic decision-making. A *strong ego* takes the best of what the id and superego have to say and blends in other data and information to yield better, more well-balanced decisions.

If thinking about the id, superego, and ego is a turnoff for you, another way to frame this discussion in the form of the inner eye. Strong ego or strong inner eye, the choice is yours. There was a time in my life when I, too, thought all this talk about ego, implicit bias, and developing human skill was a load of crap. Just give me the numbers and tell me how we're going to get stuff done. Was I wrong! If I can help you develop a stronger ego or stronger inner eye, we will have made great strides forward.

Cultivating the Inner Eye

Our eyes are incredible pieces of engineering. Light from the visual spectrum moves through the cornea, passes through the lens, and hits photoreceptors in the retina which convert light into electrical signals the brain can interpret.

For those of us fortunate enough to have the gift of sight, we're able to paint rich, colorful images of the world around us. In concert with our other senses, we use our gifts to help formulate opinions, build interpersonal relationships, avoid danger, navigate our surroundings, and make meaningful contributions to family and society.

We use our eyes to look outward and spend the vast majority of our waking moments evaluating what's happening around us. Our central processing system (the brain) is also unbelievably complex and takes in millions upon millions of data points from our sensors. The brain then distills that sea of information into a framework we can interpret and understand. The interpretation framework we cultivate is unique to each of us and is highly dependent on our local environment, upbringing, and the formal—and informal—education we engage in throughout our lives.

As amazing as this system is, it is also fraught with myriad biases. We are not all-powerful, or all-seeing, and continually make conscious and subconscious choices about the information we process at any given moment. The fact is that we all walk the earth with a "one size fits you" set of lenses making it crucial that we cultivate and train our inner eye.

What's the Inner Eye? In my opinion, we spend too little time looking inward. We're inundated with so much information and external stimuli that turning our eyes inward seems unnatural. But I've found that cultivating this hypothetical inner eye can have tremendous benefits, allowing us to strike a more appropriate balance between what's going on outside with what's happening on the inside.

Put simply, the inner eye is intentional self-reflection that challenges our beliefs, biases, and actions, coupled with a willingness and ability to learn, pivot, and change so that we may continually improve as a human.

How Do We Cultivate the Inner Eye?

The first step on the journey to strengthen the fidelity of our inner eye is to recognize our obligation to learn and continuously improve. Without a strong inner eye, we become rigid, fixed and unyielding. Without a strong inner eye, seeing ourselves as part of the solution to challenges is difficult. We easily fall into the trap of a blame mindset—with our ego's survival instincts kicking into gear—and are easily swayed by strong voices that are not our own.

Here are a few recommendations to cultivate the inner eye:

- *Make time for you.* We fill our lives with "busy" and distractions. What little downtime we have is reserved for binging TV and engaging in other forms of entertainment. Instead, be purposeful and set time aside for you. For those who are relentless multitaskers, combining exercise with self-reflection *is* possible in my opinion. Even within a workout, be intentional about your cooldown, and use that time to get quiet and focus your energy inward.
- *Meditate.* Meditation isn't for everyone, but sitting still in a quiet place is something we should all know how to do. Personally, I like to lie on my back with my arms and legs outstretched and allow my body to completely sink into the floor (a yoga position known as savasana). Once I've let go of my body, the focus of my inner eye improves dramatically.

- *Use the mirror.* If you have trouble looking inward like I did as a younger man, use the mirror. It may feel silly at first, but I've had some very serious and productive discussions with myself by standing in front of the mirror and looking directly into my own eyes. I've been pleasantly surprised by how disarming it can be to challenge myself in this way.
- *Bring the concept of bias into working memory.* Half the battle is to recognize that bias is all around you. It lives deep inside all of us; however, many of us have developed a belief system that doesn't account for bias, and it's difficult to accept that we might be biased in one way or another. The time you spend educating yourself on various forms of cognitive bias is time well spent.[1]
- *Use the power of why.* One of the most powerful words in the English language is "why?" As we've mentioned throughout this book, in the parlance of continuous improvement, they're called the "Five Whys." Take an issue, challenge, or position and ask yourself "why do I feel this way?" or "why did I react the way I did?" The trick is to keep asking "why" until you approach the root cause of the issue. Be prepared to accept that sometimes the root cause lies with you.
- *Be intentional.* Sometimes engaging in meditation and just letting your mind wander to see where it takes you is fun, but you don't want to cultivate an inner eye that's random and without purpose. Instead, pick an issue that's particularly thorny or troublesome and focus your attention on that. Then start asking "why."
- *Be willing to ask for help.* There are many resources you can tap into to help cultivate your inner eye. Don't be afraid to engage with a therapist—I'm sure glad I did. Reach out to one of your mentors. Talk. Engage. You're not alone.

One of our most important balancing acts we have as humans is to strike an appropriate equilibrium between the world within and the outside world. Too much attention on one or the other can lead to challenges.

I've found that I am much more mentally agile, accepting of change, and can tap into my full potential by keeping this balancing act in working memory.

The Flywheel

Up to this point, we've used a set of hydrological metaphors to illustrate the concept of flow within an organization. As we come to the book's conclusion, please indulge me with one additional metaphor that is based on mechanical principles and is widely used in business—the flywheel.

Scottish engineer James Watt is most widely known for inventing the steam engine in the eighteenth century, which ultimately democratized mobility and ushered in the industrial revolution. Key to this marvel of engineering, however, was reinventing the wheel, literally.

One of Watt's innovations, and one that enabled the development of the steam-powered locomotive, was the flywheel, which provided a way to efficiently capture, store and release energy using angular momentum. This key development allowed the locomotive to reach and sustain high speeds, while towing heavy payloads, using significantly less energy relative to other available forms of transportation.

Steam engine locomotives, as you may well know from studying engineering or simply watching television and movies set in the Old West, move incredibly slowly at first, requiring huge inputs of energy to get those big, heavy wheels turning. The first full rotation of those wheels is by far the slowest, followed by an ever so slightly faster second rotation, then a third, and so on. Each rotation requires a little less energy. Once the train picks up steam (which is where that expression originates) it can reach and maintain incredible speeds with minimal additional force. That is because the train's heavy wheels, difficult as they are to set in motion, continue to build momentum.

The flywheel was, until recently, long forgotten outside engineering circles, but it has recently made a comeback in the form of the *flywheel effect*. The term was introduced by American author Jim Collins in his 2001 book *Good to Great: Why Some Companies Make the Leap ... and Others Don't*. In it, Collins explored what made certain companies succeed while others faltered. As Collins explains in the book, he expected to find a single moment in which a key decision was made that propelled an organization from "good to great."

"We kept thinking that we'd find 'the one big thing,' the miracle moment that defined breakthrough. We even pushed for it in our interviews. But the good-to-great executives simply could not pinpoint a single key event or moment in time that exemplified the transition," he wrote. "From the outside, they look like dramatic, almost revolutionary break-throughs. But from the inside, they feel completely different, more like an organic development process."[2]

Collins went on to explain that, in contrast to his expectations, companies that were constantly pushing for that one big breakthrough product or solution were constantly losing momentum as they stopped and started. What made the "great" organizations successful was an ongoing commitment to incremental improvement, gradually building on their own momentum, until that big wheel they've been pushing with minimal initial results was moving full speed with relatively little additional effort. These days you'll hear a lot of talk about the "flywheel effect" among those in the start-up community, in the tech industry, and within the marketing discipline, but here I'd like to apply the concept of the flywheel to organizational flow.

FLYWHEEL EFFECT

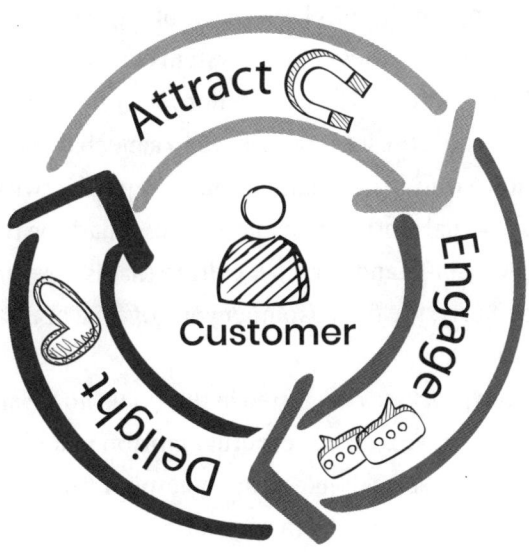

In this metaphor, the virtuous cycle that picks up steam as it chugs along is the force of flow, which helps improve accountability, thus building trust, and so on. It takes a lot to push this locomotive forward, but as the gears start turning it gets harder and harder to slow its momentum. As with a physical flywheel, however, momentum can only be built and sustained when friction is minimized. In this case, friction (or impediments to flow) can take the form of the permafrost or clay layer, accidental managers, aversion to change, poor management of competition and communication, a preference for "the way it's always been done," and all the other challenges outlined in this book. Once impediments to flow are minimized (remember the busy beaver from chapter 10?), and force is concentrated in a single direction, the flywheel effect takes over, propelling the business forward with so much force that it easily plows through external obstacles. Competition, market conditions, and myriad externalities that try to knock the organization off course hardly register.

Mechanically speaking, a flywheel doesn't float alone in space; we live in a physical world bound by the rules of physics. Your flywheel needs to be mounted on an axle of some sort and powered by an engine. In this metaphor, I like to think of your strategy statements as the industrial grade mounting bolts that lock the engine and axle into place. The flywheel is in constant motion, but these bolts keep the whole system anchored in place.

Perpetual motion machines—closed systems that are forever in motion without requiring additional force—are not yet a physical reality, and the flywheel remains the closest thing we have to a mechanical system that is forever in motion. From an internal, cultural, and productivity perspective, this idea of a perpetual motion machine would similarly be the wholly grail of business flow; a set-it-and-forget-it culture that is forever operating at peak efficiency. Sorry, the fidget spinner you got for a holiday gift back in 2019 won't do the trick.

The systems and processes suggested in this book, however, are similarly intended to get as close to that perpetual motion machine as possible, which is why the flywheel feels like an apt metaphor. There will always be a need for reducing friction and furthering momentum, even after reaching top speed. Difficult as it may be to put in motion, once it picks up speed, the management operating system is designed to create a set of conditions that allow the organization to continue improving over time without the stops and starts that, according to Collins, hinder its ability to achieve its full potential. Sustaining momentum requires ongoing learning, coaching, and continuous improvement. Getting everyone to row in the same direction might take some time, but once alignment is achieved and is sustained through flow, accountability, and trust, momentum becomes all the easier to maintain, and all the more difficult to degrade.

Booting Up Your Management Operating System

At the start of this book, I introduced the concept of a management operating system, and I want to finish with a reminder that what I hope to offer are the essential elements for creating the underlying operating system of your business. I also want to point out that I have avoided going into detail about specific enterprise resource planning (ERP) systems and installations, technologies and marketing plans or sales strategies. Their omission is intentional. All these tools and services, while vital to success for a vast majority of businesses, are highly specific to the individual organization. You can think of them as the apps on a smartphone's operating system.

Every smartphone of a specific make and model comes out of the box precisely the same, but by the time you complete the setup process it's already begun to become customized to your way of working. By the time you've downloaded any number of the millions of available apps, your mass-produced product becomes wholly specific to your needs as an individual consumer. The same is true with a management operating system. The strategies and processes outlined in this book should be thought of as the underlying operating system of your organization that is then customized to create your unique business model.

My intention is to provide the "why," and in some cases the "how," but the "what" remains yours to decide. Based on my more than thirty years of experience in business and institutions, this book contains what I believe are the must-have components of your management operating system which then allows for myriad apps to coexist and remain compatible within the confines of your business structure.

Here's the bottom line: The balanced business is one in which there is a rich, rewarding organizational culture where trust is able to take root and flourish. Simultaneously, the balanced business is one that gets things done, leaves its competition in the dust, and proves its indispensability by creating a sea of raving promoters. The creation of organizational flow improves accountability and unlocks trust.

I wish you great success in your business endeavors.

Grace. Dignity. Compassion.

Endnotes

Chapter 1

1 Jim Harter, "Employee Engagement on the Rise in the U.S.," Gallup, August 26, 2018, https://news.gallup.com/poll/241649/employee-engagement-rise.aspx#.

2 "Work Trend Index Special Report," Microsoft, September 22, 2022, https://www.microsoft.com/en-us/worklab/work-trend-index/.

Chapter 2

1 "Ford's assembly line starts rolling," History, November 13, 2009, https://www.history.com/this-day-in-history/fords-assembly-line-starts-rolling.

Chapter 3

1 "Great Expectations: Making Hybrid Work Work," Microsoft, March 16, 2022, https://www.microsoft.com/en-us/worklab/work-trend-index/great-expectations-making-hybrid-work-work.

2 Isao Yoshino, "How the A3 Came to Be Toyota's Go-To Management Process for Knowledge Work (intro by John Shook)," Lean Enterprise Institute, August 2, 2016, https://www.lean.org/the-lean-post/articles/how-the-a3-came-to-be-toyotas-go-to-management-process-for-knowledge-work-intro-by-john-shook/.

3   John Shook, *Managing to Learn: Using the A3 Management Process to Solve Problems, Gain Agreement, Mentor and Lead* (Boston: Lean Enterprise Institute, 2008). John Shook's bio: https://www.lean.org/about-lei/senior-advisors-staff/john-shook/.

4   Anand Udapudi, "Experiential Learning Vs. Traditional Learning, Find out which is more effective?," *Medium*, May 29, 2019, https://medium.com/knolskape/experiential-learning-vs-traditional-learning-find-out-which-is-more-effective-3a8500d78330.

5   Shook, *Managing to Learn*, 1.

6   "Number of McDonald's employees worldwide from 2012 to 2021," Statista, February 2022, https://www.statista.com/statistics/819966/mcdonald-s-number-of-employees/.

Chapter 4

1   Lauren Vesty, "Millennials want purpose over paychecks. So why can't we find it at work?," *Guardian*, September 14, 2016, https://www.theguardian.com/sustainable-business/2016/sep/14/millennials-work-purpose-linkedin-survey.

2   "Theranos," Wikipedia, https://en.wikipedia.org/wiki/Theranos.

3   "About Us," Theranos, http://web.archive.org/web/20180526075822/https://theranos.com/careers.

4   Matthew J. Belvedere, "'Moral compass' was off at Uber under co-founder Kalanick, says new CEO Dara Khosrowshahi," CNBC, January 23, 2018, https://www.cnbc.com/2018/01/23/uber-moral-compass-under-co-founder-kalanick-was-off-new-ceo-says.html.

5   Jim Finkle and Heather Somerville, "Governments around the world launch investigations into Uber following data breach and cover-up," Insider, November 22, 2017, https://www.businessinsider.com/multiple-governments-launch-investigations-into-uber-following-data-breach-cover-up-2017-11.

6   "Ten things we know to be true," Google, accessed December 14, 2022, https://about.google/philosophy/.

7   "Core Values," Coca-Cola, accessed December 14, 2022, https://www.coca-colacompany.com/social-impact/people-values.

8   "Coca-Cola Company Purpose Summary," Coca-Cola, accessed December 14, 2022, https://www.coca-colacompany.com/content/dam/journey/us/en/our-company/purpose-and-vision/coca-cola-company-purpose-summary.pdf.

9   "Our Shared Purpose," Allstate, accessed April 21, 2023, https://www.allstatecorporation.com/about/our-shared-purpose.aspx.

10   "Diversity wins: How inclusion matters," McKinsey, accessed December 14, 2022, https://www.mckinsey.com/featured-insights/diversity-and-inclusion/diversity-wins-how-inclusion-matters.

Chapter 5

1   Ethan Chazin, "Why We Resist Change? Blame Our Brains," LinkedIn, May 30, 2015, linkedin.com/pulse/why-we-resist-change-blame-our-brains-ethan-chazin-mba/.

2   Chris Pennington, "We Are Hardwired to Resist Change," Emerson Human Capital, April 03, 2018, https://www.emersonhc.com/change-management/people-hard-wired-resist-change.

3   Susan McQuillan, "Why Do Humans Resist Change?," *Psychology Today*, October 21, 2019, https://www.psychologytoday.com/ca/blog/cravings/201910/why-do-humans-resist-change.

4   Hunter S. Thompson, Douglas Brinkley (Editor), *The Proud Highway: Saga of a Desperate Southern Gentleman, 1955–1967* (New York: Random House, 1997).

5   Steve Jobs, "Steve Jobs Introducing the iPhone At MacWorld 2007," uploaded December 2, 2010, video, 14:00, https://www.youtube.com/watch?v=x7qPAY9JqE4&t=22s.

6   Patrick Holland, "The iPhone at 15: Steve Jobs Revealed His Greatest Product in 2007," CNET, June 29, 2022, https://www.cnet.com/tech/mobile/the-iphone-at-15-steve-jobs-revealed-his-great-product-15-years-ago/.

7   Ray Dalio, "Principles For Success," May 21, 2018, video, 28:46, https://www.youtube.com/watch?v=B9XGUpQZY38.

Chapter 6

1   Shane McFeely and Ben Wigert, "This Fixable Problem Costs U.S. Businesses $1 Trillion," Gallup, March 13, 2019, https://www.gallup.com/workplace/247391/fixable-problem-costs-businesses-trillion.aspx.

2   Annamarie Mann, "Why We Need Best Friends at Work," Gallup, January 15, 2018, https://www.gallup.com/workplace/236213/why-need-best-friends-work.aspx.

3   "Jobs of Tomorrow Mapping Opportunity in the New Economy," World Economic Forum, January 2020, https://www.reskillingrevolution2030.org/reskillingrevolution/wp-content/uploads/2020/05/WEF_Jobs_of_Tomorrow_2020.pdf.

4   Louis Deslauriers, Logan S. McCarty, Kelly Miller, and Greg Kestin, "Measuring actual learning versus feeling of learning in response to being actively engaged

in the classroom," Proceedings of the National Academy of Sciences 116, no. 39 (September 4, 2019): 1,9251–57, https://www.pnas.org/doi/10.1073/pnas.1821936116.

5   Jared Lindzon, "Shopify is sponsoring free computer-science educations—at $110K a pop," *Fast Company*, April 9, 2020, https://www.fastcompany.com/90482623/shopify-is-sponsoring-computer-science-students-100k-educations.

6   Chris Bierly and Abigail Smith, "Taking Flight: How to Maximize the Potential of Career-Connected Learning," Bain & Company, January 25, 2022, https://www.bain.com/insights/taking-flight-how-to-maximize-the-potential-of-career-connected-learning/.

7   "Connecting Credentials: A Beta Credentials Framework," Lumina Foundation, June 11, 2015, https://www.luminafoundation.org/resource/connecting-credentials/.

Chapter 8

1   Perri Ormont Blumberg, "How Trader Joe's Got Its Name," *Southern Living*, August 6, 2018, https://www.southernliving.com/news/trader-joes-history-of-name.

2   "Trader Joe's: The Trendy American Cousin," *Bloomberg Businessweek*, April 26, 2004, https://www.bloomberg.com/news/articles/2004-04-25/trader-joes-the-trendy-american-cousin.

3   Christopher Palmeri, "Trader Joe's Recipe for Success," *Bloomberg Businessweek*, February 21, 2008, https://www.bloomberg.com/news/articles/2008-02-20/trader-joes-recipe-for-success?leadSource=uverify%20wall.

4   Ashley Lutz, "How Trader Joe's Sells Twice As Much As Whole Foods," Business Insider, October 7, 2014, https://www.businessinsider.com/trader-joes-sales-strategy-2014-10.

5   Catherine Clifford, "From chatty employees to $5 wine: How Trader Joe's turns customers into fanatics," CNBC Make It, March 9, 2020, https://www.cnbc.com/2020/03/09/psychology-behind-how-trader-joes-became-a-favorite-grocery-store.html.

6   "About Us," Trader Joe's, accessed December 15, 2022, https://www.traderjoes.com/home/about-us.

7   "Forbes Profile: Trader Joe's," Forbes, accessed December 15, 2022, https://www.forbes.com/companies/trader-joes/?list=best-large-employers&sh=1879369a1c55.

8   "America's 10 Best Employers 2019," *Forbes*, accessed December 15, 2022, https://www.forbes.com/pictures/5ca4f77ca7ea436c70f19f9b/trader-joes-store-in-nort/?sh=4d4b2cd35899.

9   "You Asked. We Answered," episode fifteen, *Inside Trader Joe's*, June 2019, https://open.spotify.com/episode/6ECOyOzaCFFg1dizaezVjw?si=JgfCiI1mQdib3c9XuJ5S2w&nd=1.

10   Vicky Valet, "America's Best Employers 2019," Forbes, April 17, 2019, https://www.forbes.com/sites/vickyvalet/2019/04/17/americas-best-employers-2019/?sh=337244737c23.

11   Mark Gardiner, "What can Trader Joe's teach the ad industry? A lot.," Drum, February 22, 2019, https://www.thedrum.com/opinion/2019/02/22/what-can-trader-joe-s-teach-the-ad-industry-lot.

12   "We Needed A Budget…" YNAB, accessed December 15, 2022, https://www.youneedabudget.com/about-us/.

13   "Work That Matters," YNAB, accessed December 15, 2022, https://www.youneedabudget.com/careers/.

14   Claire Hastwell, "How 2020 Best Small Workplace YNAB recruits and retains great people," *Fortune*, October 16, 2020, https://fortune.com/2020/10/16/you-need-a-budget-ynab-recruitment-retention-best-small-medium-workplaces/.

15   "You Need A Budget," Great Place to Work, accessed December 15, 2022, https://www.greatplacetowork.com/certified-company/1367344.

16   You Need A Budget," Great Place to Work, accessed December 15, 2022, https://www.greatplacetowork.com/certified-company/1367344.

17   Matthew Yglesias, "Sweet Sorrow: Coke won the cola wars because great taste takes more than a single sip," *Slate*, August 9, 2013, https://slate.com/business/2013/08/pepsi-paradox-why-people-prefer-coke-even-though-pepsi-wins-in-taste-tests.html.

18   Ryan Pinkard, "#TIDALforALL," Tidal, March 30, 2015, https://tidal.com/magazine/article/tidalforall/1-11708.

19   Marsha Silva, "Jay-Z's Tidal Lost $37 Million In 2018—More Than 100,000 Subscribers Jumped Ship," Digital Music News, February 10, 2020, https://www.digitalmusicnews.com/2020/02/10/tidal-jay-z-lost-100-thousand-2018/.

20   Peter Galuszka, "Eight Reasons Why Circuit City Went Bankrupt," CBS News, November 13, 2008, https://www.cbsnews.com/news/eight-reasons-why-circuit-city-went-bankrupt/.

21   Naomi Spencer, "US: Circuit City fires 3,400 better-paid store workers," World Socialist Web Site, March 30, 2007, https://www.wsws.org/en/articles/2007/03/circ-m30.html.

Chapter 9

1   Andrew Temte, "Death, Taxes, and Change," Andrew Temte, accessed December 16, 2022, https://www.andrewtemte.com/saturday-morning-muse/death-taxes-and-change.

Chapter 10

1   "Market capitalization of Netflix (NFLX)," CompaniesMarketCap.com, accessed December 16, 2022, https://companiesmarketcap.com/netflix/marketcap/.

Chapter 12

1   "Diversity Wins: How Inclusion Matters," McKinsey & Company, May 2020, https://www.mckinsey.com/~/media/mckinsey/featured%20insights/diversity%20and%20inclusion/diversity%20wins%20how%20inclusion%20matters/diversity-wins-how-inclusion-matters-vf.pdf.

2   "Standard Work," Gemba Academy, accessed December 16, 2022, https://www.gembaacademy.com/resources/gemba-glossary/standard-work.

Chapter 13

1   "National Patient Safety Goals Fact Sheet," Joint Commission, accessed December 16, 2022, https://www.jointcommission.org/resources/news-and-multimedia/fact-sheets/facts-about-national-patient-safety-goals/.

2   Amanda Van Nuys, "New LinkedIn Research: Upskill Your Employees with the Skills Companies Need Most in 2020," LinkedIn, December 28, 2019, https://www.linkedin.com/business/learning/blog/learning-and-development/most-in-demand-skills-2020.

3   Veronica Rose, "IT careers: 10 essential skills for 2022," The Enterprisers Project, December 16, 2021, https://enterprisersproject.com/article/2021/12/it-careers-10-essential-skills-2022.

4   Rachel Pelta, "15 Transferable Skills That Companies Want: Examples and Definitions," FlexJobs, accessed December 16, 2022, https://www.flexjobs.com/blog/post/transferable-skills/.

Chapter 14

1   "Unlocking success in digital transformations," McKinsey & Company, October 29, 2018, https://www.mckinsey.com/capabilities/people-and-organizational-performance/our-insights/unlocking-success-in-digital-transformations.

2   "Flipping the Odds of Digital Transformation Success," BCG, October 29, 2020, https://www.bcg.com/publications/2020/increasing-odds-of-success-in-digital-transformation.

Chapter 18

1   Chloe Berger, "New Netflix layoffs open old wounds for jilted employees," *Fortune*, April 29, 2022, https://fortune.com/2022/04/29/netflix-layoffs-digital-media-employees/.

2   J. Clara Chan, "Netflix Lays Off Estimated 150 Staffers in New Round of Cuts," *Hollywood Reporter*, May 17, 2022, https://www.hollywoodreporter.com/business/digital/netflix-layoffs-1235148614/.

3   Zoe Schiffer, "Netflix suspends trans employee who tweeted about Dave Chappelle special," Verge, October 11, 2021, https://www.theverge.com/2021/10/11/22720724/netflix-suspends-trans-employee-tweeted-dave-chappelle-the-closer.

4   Todd Spangler, "Netflix Updates Corporate Culture Memo, Adding Anti-Censorship Section and a Vow to 'Spend Our Members' Money Wisely,'" *Variety*, May 12, 2022, https://variety.com/2022/digital/news/netflix-culture-memo-update-censorship-spending-1235264904/.

5   John Elkington, "25 Years Ago I Coined the Phrase "Triple Bottom Line." Here's Why It's Time to Rethink It," *Harvard Business Review*, June 25, 2018, https://hbr.org/2018/06/25-years-ago-i-coined-the-phrase-triple-bottom-line-heres-why-im-giving-up-on-it.

6   Jodi Kantor, Karen Weise, and Grace Ashford, "The Amazon That Customers Don't See," *New York Times*, June 15, 2021, https://www.nytimes.com/interactive/2021/06/15/us/amazon-workers.html.

7   "Federal Debt: Total Public Debt as Percent of Gross Domestic Product," Economic Research, updated December 2, 2022, https://fred.stlouisfed.org/series/GFDEGDQ188S.

8   Thomas Grennes, Mehmet Caner, and Fritzi Koehler-Geib, "Finding The Tipping Point—When Sovereign Debt Turns Bad," Policy Research Working Papers, June 22, 2013, https://elibrary.worldbank.org/doi/abs/10.1596/1813-9450-5391.

9   Corey Rosen and Michael Quarrey, "How Well Is Employee Ownership Working?," *Harvard Business Review*, September 1987, https://hbr.org/1987/09/how-well-is-employee-ownership-working.

10   Darren Dahl, "Are Employee-Owned Companies The Best Investment Around?," *Forbes*, July 19, 2016, https://www.forbes.com/sites/darrendahl/2016/07/19/are-employee-owned-companies-the-best-investment-around/?sh=68bdd6fd50be.

11   "Employee-Owned Firms in the COVID-19 Pandemic: How Majority-Owned ESOP & Other Companies Have Responded to the Covid-19 Health and Economic Crises," The Employee Ownership Foundation, accessed December 16, 2022, https://assets-eof. s3.us-east-2.amazonaws.com/assets/public/2020-10/EOF_COVID_2020.pdf.

Chapter 19

1   "Biases," the Decision Lab, accessed January 18, 2023, https://thedecisionlab.com/biases-index.

2   Jim Collins, *Good to Great: Why Some Companies Make the Leap ... and Others Don't* (New York: HarperCollins, 2001).

About the Author

DR. ANDREW TEMTE, CFA, is the former CEO of Kaplan Professional, author of *Balancing Act: Teach, Coach, Mentor, Inspire*, and host of *The Balancing Act* podcast.

A thought leader on issues related to organizational health, continuous improvement, and workforce reskilling, his articles have appeared in a number of media outlets.

Dr. Temte has also served in the following professional positions at Kaplan: president and global head of corporate learning, interim president of Mount Washington College, and president of the Kaplan University (now Purdue Global) College of Business and Technology. This blend of higher education and professional education experience gives Dr. Temte a unique perspective over the issues surrounding the future of employment and workplace relevance.

Dr. Temte earned his doctorate in finance from the University of Iowa, with a concentration in international finance and investment theory. He holds the CFA designation and has over fourteen years of university teaching experience.

MORE FROM ANDREW TEMTE

Website

AndrewTemte.com

The Balancing Act Podcast

AndrewTemte.com/Podcasts

and on all major streaming services

Books

Balancing Act: Teach, Coach, Mentor, Inspire (2021)

Resources

The Saturday Morning Muse

and

A Personal Planning Guidebook

are available at AndrewTemte.com

Social Media

LinkedIn.com/in/atemte

@AndrewTemte

@AndrewTemte1

@AndrewTemte